Ninja Foodi

Ultimate Cookbook

1000-Day Easy & Delicious Air Fry, Broil, Pressure Cook, Slow Cook, Dehydrate, and More Recipes for Beginners and Advanced Users

Kathleen Butts

TABLE OF CONTENTS

The Ninja Foodi Deluxe—the deluxe pressure cooker that crisps. 9 functions: Pressure Cook, Air Fry/Air Crisp, Steam, Slow Cook, Yogurt, Sear/Sauté, Bake/Roast, Broil, Dehydrate. Deluxe cooking capacity - XL 8-quart pot, XL 5-quart Cook & Crisp Basket and Deluxe Reversible Rack let you cook for a small group. TENDER-CRISP Technology lets you quickly pressure cook ingredients to lock in juices, then give them a crispy, golden air-fryer finish. Deluxe Reversible Rack lets you steam and broil, as well as TEN-DERCRISP up to 8 chicken breasts at once or add servings to layered 360 meals. XL 8-quart ceramic-coated pot: Nonstick, PTFE/PFOA free, and easy to hand-wash. XL 5-quart Cook & Crisp Basket: Large-capacity, ceramic-coated, PTFE/PFOA-free nonstick basket is dishwasher safe and holds up to a 7-lb. chicken to feed your whole family.

You will change your whole life by using a Ninja Foodi, which is really the most multi-functional kitchen appliance in this world now! Everyone should have one!

Ninja Foodi Ultimate Cookbook will help you save your precious time and money regarding cooking your favorite dishes! You are going to have your nutritional and delicious recipes in a short time! This book is the perfect companion of your Ninja Foodi cooking!

This Ninja Foodi can accomplish this feat, thanks to the crisping lid that comes attached with the Foodi itself. When needed, this particular lid alongside the Air Crisp Function and Crisping Basket allows the users to seamless air fry their dishes and give them a satisfying crispy finish!

Welcome to the world of amazing Ninja Foodi cooking!

What is Ninja Foodi Pressure Cooker and Air Fryer?

The Ninja Foodi Pressure Cooker and Air Fryer has nine useful cooking functions: Air Crisp, Broil, Bake/Roast, Dehydrate, Pressure Cook, Steam, Slow Cook, Yogurt, Sear/Sauté etc. It has two lids: a crisping lid and a pressure lid. The crisping lid is used for Air Crisp, Broil, Bake/Roast, and Dehydrate cooking functions. The pressure lid is used for Pressure Cook, Steam, Slow Cook, Yogurt, and Sear/Sauté cooking functions. The

Ninja Foodi Pressure Cooker and Air Fryer comes with a crisping lid, pressure lid, reversible rack, cook and crisp basket, cooking pot, detachable diffuser, heat shield, control panel, cooker base, pressure release valve, float valve, silicone ring, anti-clog cap, air outlet vent, and condensation collector etc. You can prepare food with your favorite cooking option—Bake cakes for your kids on any occasion.

Functions of Ninja Foodi

With the TENDERCRISP technology out of the way, let me talk a little bit about the different buttons and features found in the Ninja Foodi. The following guide should help you understand what each of the buttons does and how you can use them to their fullest extent.

Pressure

The Pressure Button will allow you to simply Pressure Cook your foods using the Ninja Foodi. This will allow you to cook meals almost 70% faster than other traditional methods. Releasing the pressure naturally is often recommended for tough meats while the quick release is often suited for tender cuts like fish or even vegetables.

Air Crisp

This is possibly the most unique feature of the Ninja Foodi. Using the Air Crisp feature, you will be able to use your Ninja Foodi as an air fryer, that allows you to add a nice crispy and crunchy texture with little to almost no oil. This particular setting cooks the food at extremely high temperatures of 300 degrees F to 400 degrees F.

Bake/Roast

This particular function is for those who like to bake! The Bake/Roast function is an awesome mode that allows users to seamlessly use their Foodi as a regular oven (thanks to crisping lid) that allows them to create inspiring baked goods.

Steam

This particular button allows you to use the "Steam" function of the Ninja Foodi. Using steam, you will be able to cook very delicate food at high temperatures. Just make sure to use at least a cup of liquid when steaming your food. While using this feature, make sure to use the Pressure Lid.

Broil

The Broil feature is used in conjunction with the Crisping Lid in order to slightly brown or caramelizes the surface of your food. It cooks food at a higher temperature to create the required brown surface.

Slow Cook

This particular button will allow you to utilize the Slow Cook mode that allows you to use the Ninja Foodi as a traditional Slow Cook. Through this method, your cooks will be cooked at a very low temperature over a prolonged period of time. The time can be adjusted from 12-4 hours, and

once the cooking is done, the appliance will automatically switch to "KEEP WARM" function where the meal stays hot until you open it up.

Sear/Sauté

This particular button allows you to use your Ninja Foodi to brown meat. This feature is excellent when you need searing or browning meat/ Sautéing spices. This same function can also be used to simmer sauces. Similar to Broil mode, this does not come with a temperature setting, rather, once you are done browning, you simply need to press the "START/STOP" button to initiate or stop the process.

Dehydrate

The Dehydrate function allows you to dehydrate food between 105 degrees F and 195 degrees F, and this feature will allow you to make healthy dried snacks out of meat, vegetables, and fruits. However, if you want to use this device, it is advised that you purchase a dehydrating rack for maximum efficiency.

User Guide of Ninja Foodi

The operating buttons on the control panel are pretty simple to understand. You can choose your favorite cooking function and then adjust temperature, pressure, and cooking time according to the recipe's instructions.

FUNCTION

Press "FUNCTION" and then the start/stop button to select cooking functions: Air Crisp, Broil, Bake/Roast, Dehydrate, Pressure Cook, Steam, Slow Cook, Yogurt, Sear/Sauté etc.

TEMP

Press "TEMP" and then turn the Start/Stop button to adjust the cooking temperature or pressure level according to the recipe's instructions.

TIME

Press "TIME" and then turn the Start/Stop button to adjust the cooking time according to the recipe's instructions.

START/STOP Button

Press the Start/Stop button to adjust the cooking time, cooking temperature, cooking pressure and press to Start/Stop the cooking.

Keep Warm

After slowing cooking, steaming, or pressure cooking, the unit will automatically switch to keep warm mode and start counting up. This cooking mode will keep your food warm until you serve it.

POWER

When you press the power button, the unit will shut down and stop all cooking modes.

Tips for Ninja Foodi Users

As time goes on, you will learn how to utilize the power of your Ninja Foodi to its full extent. However, the following tips will help you during the early days of your life with the Ninja Foodi and ensure that your experience is as pleasant and smooth as possible.

• It is crucial that you don't just press the function buttons randomly! Try to read through the function of each button and use them according to the requirement of your recipe.
• It is important that you place the lid properly while closing the appliance as it greatly affects the cooking. Therefore, make sure that your lid is tightly close by ensuring that the silicone ring inside the lid is placed all the way around the groove.
• This is something that many people don't know, once the cooking timer of your appliance hits '0', the pot will automatically go into "Natural Pressure Release" mode where it will start to release the pressure on its own. You can use a quick release anytime to release all the steam at once, or you can wait for 10-15 minutes until the steam vents off.
• If you are in a rush and want to release the pressure quickly, turn the pressure valve to "Open Position," which will quick release all the pressure. But this can be a little risky as a lot of steam comes out at once, so be sure to stay careful.

• If you are dealing with a recipe that calls for unfrounceen meat, make sure to use the same amount of cooking time and liquid that you would use if you were to use frounceen meat of the same type.
• Once you start using the appliance for cooking, make sure to check if the Pressure Valve is in the "Locked Position." If it is not, your appliance won't be able to build up pressure inside for cooking.
• Make sure to keep in mind that the "Timer" button isn't a button to set time! Rather it acts as a Delay Timer. Using this button, you will be able to set a specific time, after which the Ninja Foodi will automatically wake up and start cooking the food.
• The unit should be entirely cleaned after every use.
• Always unplug the unit before cleaning it. Remove all accessories from the unit.
• To clean the main unit, use moist cloth only.
• Remove the cooking pot, cook and crisp basket, reversible rack, silicone ring, detachable diffuser and wash it with soapy water.
• The pressure lid and pressure release valve can be cleaned with water or dish detergent but not put into the dishwasher.
• Clean the crisping lid with a damp cloth or paper towel.
• If food is stuck inside the basket or cooking pot, fill it with warm soapy water and soak it. But, do not use a hard scrubber or cleaning pads.
• When all parts get dried, return to the unit.

Chapter 1-Breakfast Recipes

Authentic Western Omelet

Prep time: 5 minutes
Cook time: 34 minutes
Serving: 2
Ingredients:
- 3 eggs, whisked
- 3 ounces chorizos, chopped
- 1 ounce Feta cheese, crumbled
- 5 tablespoons almond milk
- ¾ teaspoon chili flakes
- ¼ teaspoon salt
- 1 green pepper, chopped

Preparation:
1. Add all the ingredients and mix them well. Stir it gently.
2. Take an omelet pan and pour the mixture into it.
3. Preheat your Ninja Foodi at "Roast/Bake" mode at 320 degrees F.
4. Cook for 4 minutes. After that, transfer the pan with an omelet in Ninja Foodi.
5. Cook for 30 minutes more at the same mode. Serve hot and enjoy!
Nutrition Values Per Serving: Calories: 426, Fat: 38.2g, Carbs: 6.8g, Protein: 21.7g

Soft Eggs

Prep time: 4 minutes
Cook time: 4 minutes
Servings: 3
Ingredients:
- 3 eggs
- 6 ounces ham
- 1 teaspoon salt
- ½ teaspoon ground white pepper
- 1 teaspoon paprika
- ¼ teaspoon ground ginger
- 2 tablespoons chives

Preparation:
1. Take three small ramekins and coat them with vegetable oil spray.
2. Beat the eggs and add an equal amount to each ramekin.
3. Sprinkle the eggs with the salt, ground black pepper, and paprika. Transfer the ramekins to the pressure cooker and set the mode to "Steam".
4. Close the lid, and cook for 4 minutes. Meanwhile, chop the ham and chives and combine them.
5. Add ground ginger and stir into the ham mixture well.
6. Transfer the mixture to the serving plates.
7. When the cooking time ends, remove the eggs from the pressure cooker and put them atop the ham mixture.
Nutrition Values Per Serving: Calories 205, Fat 11.1, Carbs 6.47, Protein 19

Bacon Egg Scramble

Prep Time: 10 minutes

Cook time: 5 minutes
Servings: 2
Ingredients:
- 4 strips bacon
- 2 eggs
- 1 tablespoon milk
- Salt and black pepper, to taste

Preparation:
1. Place the bacon inside the Ninja Foodi. Select Air Crisp mode.
2. Cover the crisping lid. Cook at 390 degrees F for almost 3 minutes.
3. Flip and cook for another 2 minutes. Remove the bacon and set it aside.
4. Whisk the eggs and milk in a suitable bowl. For seasoning, add salt and black pepper.
5. Set the Ninja Foodi to Sauté. Add the eggs and cook until firm.
6. Serve warm.
Nutrition Values Per Serving: Calories: 272, Fat: 20.4g, Carbs: 1.3g, Protein: 20g

Roasted Potatoes

Prep Time: 30 minutes
Cook time: 20 minutes
Servings: 6
Ingredients:
- 2 ounces baby potatoes, sliced into wedges
- 2 tablespoons olive oil
- 2 teaspoons garlic salt

Preparation:
1. Toss the potatoes in olive oil and garlic salt.
2. Add the potatoes to the Ninja Foodi's insert.
3. Seal the crisping lid. Select Air Crisp mode.
4. Cook at 390 degrees F for almost 20 minutes.
5. Serve warm.
Nutrition Values Per Serving: Calories: 131, Fat: 4.8g, Carbs: 20 G, Protein: 4.1g

Avocado Egg Cups

Prep Time: 30 minutes
Cook time: 15 minutes
Servings: 2
Ingredients:
- 1 avocado, sliced in half and pitted
- 2 eggs
- Salt and black pepper, to taste
- ¼ cup cheddar, shredded

Preparation:
1. Crack the egg into the avocado slice.
2. For seasoning, add salt and black pepper.
3. Put it on the Ninja Foodi's insert. Seal the crisping lid.
4. Select Air Crisp mode. Cook at 400 degrees F for almost 15 minutes.
5. Sprinkle with the cheese 3 minutes before it is cooked.
6. Serve warm.
Nutrition Values Per Serving: Calories: 281, Fat: 23g, Carbs: 9g, Protein: 11g

Chicken Breakfast Burrito

Prep time: 10 minutes
Cook time: 45 minutes
Servings: 6
Ingredients:
- 6 large almond flour tortillas (keto tortillas)
- 1 pound chicken
- ½ cup chicken stock
- 1 tablespoon tomato paste
- 1 teaspoon sour cream
- 1 teaspoon ground black pepper
- ½ teaspoon paprika
- 1 teaspoon cilantro
- ½ teaspoon turmeric
- 1 white onion
- 2 sweet bell peppers
- ½ cup cauliflower rice
- 1 cup water

Preparation:
1. Chop the chicken roughly and transfer it to the pressure cooker.
2. Add chicken stock, tomato paste, sour cream, and water. Sprinkle the mixture with the ground black pepper, paprika, cilantro, and turmeric. Peel the onion, and remove the seeds from the bell peppers.
3. Dice onion and peppers and set aside. Sprinkle the pressure cooker mixture with the cauliflower rice and close the lid.
4. Set the pressure cooker mode to "Steam", and cook for 30 minutes. Add the chopped onion and peppers and cook for 15 minutes.
5. When the cooking time ends, shred the chicken and transfer the mixture to the tortillas. Wrap the tortillas and serve the dish immediately.
Nutrition Values Per Serving: Calories 295, Fat 10.8, Carbs 14.3, Protein 35.1

Hash Brown Casserole

Prep Time: 10 minutes
Cook time: 20 minutes
Servings: 4
Ingredients:
- Cooking spray
- 1 lb. hash browns
- 1 lb. breakfast sausage, cooked and crumbled
- 1 red bell pepper, diced
- 1 green bell pepper, diced
- 1 onion, diced
- 4 eggs
- Salt and black pepper, to taste

Preparation:
1. Coat a small baking pan with oil. Place the hash browns on the bottom part.
2. Add the sausage and then the onion and bell peppers.
3. Place the pan on top of the Ninja Foodi basket. Put the basket inside the pot.
4. Close the crisping lid. Select Air Crisp mode. Cook at 350 degrees F for almost 10 minutes.
5. Open the lid. Crack the eggs on top. Cook for another 10 minutes on Sauté mode.
6. For seasoning, add salt and black pepper.
7. Serve warm.

Nutrition Values Per Serving: Calories: 513, Fat: 34g, Carbs: 30g, Protein: 21.1g

Rise and Shine Casserole

Prep time: 10 minutes
Cook time: 10 minutes
Serving: 6
Ingredients:
- 4 whole eggs
- 1 tablespoon milk
- 1 cup ham, cooked and chopped
- ½ cup cheddar cheese, shredded
- ¼ teaspoon salt
- ¼ teaspoon ground black pepper

Preparation:
1. Take a baking pan (small enough to fit into your Ninja Foodi) bowl, and grease it well with butter.
2. Take a medium bowl and whisk in eggs, milk, salt, pepper and add ham, cheese, and stir.
3. Pour mixture into baking pan and lower the pan into your Ninja Foodi.
4. Set your Ninja Foodi Air Crisp mode and Air Crisp at 325 degrees F for 7 minutes.
5. Remove pan from eggs and enjoy!
Nutrition Values Per Serving: Calories: 169, Fat: 13g, Carbs: 1g, Protein: 12g

Chorizo Frittatas

Prep time: 10 minutes
Cook time: 20 minutes
Servings: 6
Ingredients:
- 5 eggs, whisked
- 1 ounce fresh parsley, chopped
- 3 ounces chorizo, chopped
- 1 teaspoon salt
- ¼ green pepper, chopped
- 1 teaspoon butter
- ¼ cup heavy cream
- 1 ounce broccoli, chopped
- 1 ounce Cheddar cheese, grated
- 1 teaspoon cream cheese
- 1 teaspoon paprika
- 1 cup of water (for cooking on High pressure)

Preparation:
1. Grease the springform pan with the butter.
2. Then place the layer of green pepper and broccoli.
3. After this, whisk together eggs, parsley, salt, heavy cream, cream cheese, and paprika.
4. Add chorizo and cheese. Stir gently and transfer the mixture in the pan. Flatten it gently.
5. Pour water in the pan and place the springform cake on the rack.
6. Close the lid and seal it.
7. Cook the meal on High (Pressure mode) for 20 minutes. Then use the quick pressure release method for 5 minutes.
8. Serve it!
Nutrition Values Per Serving: Calories 166, Fat 13.4, Carbs 1.8, Protein 9.7

Crispy Chicken Sandwiches

Prep time: 10 minutes
Cook time: 15 minutes
Servings: 4
Ingredients:
- 1 pound chicken thighs, boneless, skinless
- 1 cup lettuce
- 1 teaspoon apple cider vinegar
- ½ teaspoon chili flakes
- 1 teaspoon red hot pepper
- ½ teaspoon turmeric
- 1 teaspoon white pepper
- ½ cup water
- 1 tablespoon low-sodium soy sauce
- 1 tablespoon butter
- 1-ounce Cheddar cheese, shredded

Preparation:
1. Preheat Ninja Foodi at Sear/Sauté mode for 5 minutes.
2. Toss the butter inside the basket.
3. Then rub the chicken thighs with the chili flakes, red hot pepper, turmeric, white pepper, and sprinkle with the soy sauce and apple cider vinegar.
4. Place the chicken in the basket and cook it for 5 minutes.
5. After this, close the lid and seal it.
6. Cook the chicken on High pressure for 5 minutes – quick pressure release.
7. After this, shred the chicken and remove ½ part of all the liquid from the form.
8. Lower the crisping lid and cook the chicken at 400 degrees F for 5 minutes more.
9. Transfer the cooked chicken on the lettuce leaves and sprinkle with cheese.
10. Taste it!
Nutrition Values Per Serving: Calories 276, Fat 13.7, Carbs 1.4, Protein 35

Air Crisp Cheese Casserole

Prep time: 5 minutes
Cook time: 22 minutes
Servings: 2
Ingredients:
- 1 ounce bacon, chopped
- 2 eggs, whisked
- ¼ cup almond milk
- ½ teaspoon dried basil
- 3 ounces Cheddar cheese

Preparation:
1. Mix up together the whisked eggs, almond milk and dried basil.
2. Add bacon and transfer the mixture into the springform pan.
3. Grate cheese and sprinkle it over the egg mixture.
4. Place the casserole into the Ninja Foodi and set "Air Crisp" mode at 365 degrees F.
5. Cook the casserole for 15 minutes.
6. Check the casserole and cook it for 5-7 minutes more.
7. Serve it!
Nutrition Values Per Serving: Calories 380, Fat 31.5, Carbs 2.8, Protein 22.1

Scrambled Eggs

Prep time: 5 minutes
Cook time: 9 minutes
Servings: 5
Ingredients:
- 7 eggs
- ½ cup almond milk
- 1 tablespoon butter
- 1 teaspoon basil
- ¼ cup fresh parsley
- 1 teaspoon salt
- 1 teaspoon paprika
- 4 ounces sliced bacon
- 1 tablespoon cilantro

Preparation:
1. Beat the eggs in a mixing bowl and whisk well. Add the almond milk, basil, salt, paprika, and cilantro. Stir the mixture well.
2. Chop the bacon and parsley. Set the Ninja Foodi to "Sauté" mode and add the bacon. Cook it for 3 minutes.
3. Add the whisked egg mixture, and cook for 5 additional minutes. Stir the eggs carefully using a wooden spoon or spatula.
4. Sprinkle the eggs with the chopped parsley, and cook it for 4 minutes.
5. When the eggs are cooked, remove them from the pressure cooker.
Nutrition Values Per Serving: Calories 289, Fat 23.7, Carbs 2.6, Protein 16.9

Soft-Boiled Eggs

Prep time: 15 minutes
Cook time: 15 minutes
Servings: 6
Ingredients:
- 2 cups water
- 1 avocado, pitted
- 4 eggs
- 1 teaspoon paprika
- ½ teaspoon ground black pepper
- 1 sweet bell pepper
- 1 teaspoon salt
- 3 tablespoons heavy cream
- 3 ounces lettuce leaves

Preparation:
1. Put the eggs and water in the pressure cooker and close the lid.
2. Set the pressure cooker mode to "Pressure", and cook for 15 minutes.
3. Remove the eggs from the pressure cooker, and transfer them to an ice bath.
4. Chop the avocado, and remove the seeds from bell pepper. Dice the bell peppers and Peel the eggs and chop them. Combine the chopped ingredients together in a mixing bowl.
5. Sprinkle the mixture with the paprika, ground black pepper, salt, and stir.
6. Transfer the mixture in the lettuce leaves, sprinkle them with the cream, and serve.
Nutrition Values Per Serving: Calories 168, Fat 12.9, Carbs 6.75, Protein 7

Low Carb Morning Casserole

Prep time: 5 minutes
Cook time: 10 minutes
Servings: 3
Ingredients:
- 3 ounces cauliflower hash brown, cooked
- 3 eggs, whisked
- ¾ cup almond milk
- 2 ounces chorizo, chopped
- 1 ounce mozzarella, sliced
- ⅓ teaspoon chili flakes
- ½ teaspoon butter

Preparation:
1. Melt the butter and whisk it together with the chili flakes, chorizo, almond milk, and eggs.
2. Add hash brown and stir gently.
3. Place the egg mixture in the cake pan and place in the Ninja Foodi.
4. Cook on Air Crisp at 365 degrees F for 8 minutes.
5. Then add sliced mozzarella on the top and cook for 2 minutes more, or until you get the desired doneness.
6. Enjoy!
Nutrition Values Per Serving: Calories 326, Fat 28.2, Carbs 5.8, Protein 14.7

Sausage Cheese Frittata

Prep Time: 15 minutes
Cook time: 20 minutes
Servings: 2
Ingredients:
- ¼ lb. breakfast sausage, cooked and crumbled
- 4 eggs, beaten
- ½ cup cheddar cheese, shredded
- 1 red bell pepper, diced
- 1 green onion, chopped
- Cooking spray

Preparation:
1. Mix the eggs, sausage, cheese, onion and bell pepper.
2. Spray a small baking pan with oil. Pour the egg mixture into the pan.
3. Set the basket inside the Ninja Foodi. Close the crisping lid.
4. Select Air Crisp mode. Cook at 360 degrees F for almost 20 minutes.
5. Serve warm.
Nutrition Values Per Serving: Calories: 380,Fat: 27.4g, Carbs: 2.9g, Protein: 31.2g

Morning Sausage Meal

Prep Time: 10 minutes
Cook time: 20 minutes
Servings: 6
Ingredients:
- 4 whole eggs
- 4 sausages, cooked and sliced
- 2 tablespoons butter
- ½ cup mozzarella cheese, grated
- ½ cup cream

Preparation:

1. Take a suitable bowl and mix everything.
2. Add egg mix to your Ninja Foodi, top with cheese and sausage slices.
3. Lock pressure lid and select "Bake/Roast" mode and cook for 20 minutes at 345 degrees F.
4. Serve and enjoy!
Nutrition Values Per Serving: Calories: 180, Fat: 12g, Carbs: 4g, Protein: 12g

Mason Jar Omelet

Prep time: 10 minutes
Cook time: 7 minutes
Servings: 4
Ingredients:
- 4 eggs, whisked
- ¼ cup cream
- ½ teaspoon salt
- 2 ounces bacon, chopped
- 1 teaspoon butter, melted
- 1 cup water, for cooking

Preparation:
1. Mix up together whisked eggs, cream, salt, and chopped bacon. Add melted butter and stir the mixture.
2. Pour egg mixture in the mason jars. Pour 1 cup of water in the pressure cooker and insert trivet.
3. Place mason jars on the trivet. Close the lid and cook an omelet for 7 minutes on High-Pressure mode.
4. Then use quick pressure release. Chill the meal little before serving.
Nutrition Values Per Serving: Calories 234, Fat 18, Carbs 1.2, Protein 16.2

Creamy Pumpkin Slow Cook

Prep time: 10 minutes
Cook time: 15 minutes
Servings: 5
Ingredients:
- 1 cup almond milk
- 1 cup water
- 1 pound pumpkin
- 1 teaspoon cinnamon
- ½ teaspoon cardamom
- ½ teaspoon turmeric
- ⅓ cup coconut flakes
- 2 teaspoons Erythritol

Preparation:
1. Peel the pumpkin and chop it roughly. Transfer the chopped pumpkin in the pressure cooker and add almond milk and water.
2. Sprinkle the mixture with the cinnamon, cardamom, turmeric, and Erythritol.
3. Add coconut flakes and stir the mixture well.
4. Close the pressure cooker lid, and set the mode to "Sauté". Cook for 15 minutes.
5. When the cooking time ends, blend the mixture until smooth using a hand blender.
6. Ladle the pumpkin slow cook in the serving bowls and serve.
Nutrition Values Per Serving: Calories 163, Fat 13.5, Carbs 13.1, Protein 2.3

Zucchini Quiche

Prep time: 15 minutes
Cook time: 40 minutes
Servings: 6
Ingredients:
- 3 green zucchinis
- 7 ounces puff pastry
- 2 onions
- 1 cup dill
- 2 eggs
- 3 tablespoons butter
- ½ cup cream
- 6 ounces cheddar cheese
- 1 teaspoon salt
- 1 teaspoon paprika

Preparation:
1. Wash the zucchini and grate the vegetables. Peel the onions and chop them.
2. Grate the cheddar cheese. Whisk the eggs in the mixing bowl.
3. Roll out the puff pastry. Spread the pressure cooker basket with the butter and transfer the dough to there.
4. Add grated zucchini and chopped onions, and sprinkle the vegetable mixture with the salt and paprika.
5. Chop the dill and add it to the quiche. Sprinkle the dish with the grated cheese and egg mixture, and pour the cream on top.
6. Close the pressure cooker lid, and set the mode to "Steam". Cook the quiche for 40 minutes.
7. When the cooking time ends, check if the dish is cooked and remove it from the pressure cooker. Let the dish cool briefly and serve.
Nutrition Values Per Serving: Calories 398, Fat 28.4, Carbs 25.82, Protein 12

Broccoli Quiche

Prep Time: 20 minutes
Cook time: 22 minutes
Servings: 2
Ingredients:
- 1 cup water
- 2 cups broccoli florets
- 1 carrot, chopped
- 1 cup cheddar cheese, grated
- ¼ cup Feta cheese, crumbled
- ¼ cup milk
- 2 eggs
- 1 teaspoon parsley
- 1 teaspoon thyme
- Salt and black pepper, to taste

Preparation:
1. Pour the water inside the Ninja Foodi. Place the basket inside.
2. Put the carrots and broccoli in the Ninja Foodi. Cover the cooker with the lid.
3. Set it to "Pressure" cooking mode. Cook at high for 2 minutes.
4. Release the pressure quickly. Crack all the eggs in a suitable bowl and beat.
5. For seasoning, add salt, pepper, parsley and thyme.
6. Put the vegetables on a small baking pan.

7. Layer with the cheese and pour in the beaten eggs. Place in the Ninja Foodi.
8. Select Air Crisp mode. Seal the crisping lid.
9. Cook at 350 degrees F for almost 20 minutes.
10. Enjoy!
Nutrition Values Per Serving: Calories: 401, Fat: 28g, Carbs: 13g, Protein: 26g

Milky Tomato Omelet

Prep time: 8 minutes
Cook time: 9 minutes
Servings: 6
Ingredients:
- 5 eggs
- ½ cup coconut milk
- 4 tablespoons tomato paste
- 1 teaspoon salt
- 1 tablespoon turmeric
- ½ cup cilantro
- 1 tablespoon butter
- 4 ounces Parmesan cheese

Preparation:
1. Whisk the eggs with the coconut milk and tomato paste in the mixing bowl.
2. Add salt and turmeric and stir the mixture. Grate the Parmesan cheese and add it to the egg mixture.
3. Mince the cilantro and add it to the egg mixture. Add the butter in the pressure cooker and pour in the egg mixture.
4. Close the pressure cooker lid, and set the mode to "Steam". Cook for 9 minutes.
5. Open the pressure cooker to let the omelet rest. Transfer it to serving plates and enjoy.
Nutrition Values Per Serving: Calories 189, Fat 14.6, Carbs 4.9, Protein 11.7

Keto Cheddar Bites

Prep time: 6 minutes
Cook time: 12 minutes
Servings: 4
Ingredients:
- 4 eggs
- ¼ cup heavy cream
- 3 ounces Cheddar cheese, shredded
- 3 ounces shrimps, peeled, cooked
- ½ teaspoon salt
- ½ cup water

Preparation:
1. Beat the eggs in the bowl and whisk well.
2. Add heavy cream, salt, and cheese. Stir it.
3. Chop the shrimps roughly and add in egg mixture.
4. Pour the egg mixture into the muffin molds.
5. Add water in the pot.
6. Place the muffins molds on the rack.
7. Cover the molds with the foil well.
8. Close the lid and seal it.
9. Cook the bites on Pressure mode at HI for 12 minutes. (Natural pressure release)
10. Discard the foil from bites and transfer them on the serving plates. Taste it!
Nutrition Values Per Serving: Calories 200, Fat 14.6, Carbs 1.1, Protein 15.8

Breakfast Muffins

Prep time: 10 minutes
Cook time: 15 minutes
Servings: 2
Ingredients:
- 1 tablespoon cream cheese
- 1 teaspoon butter
- 1 egg, beaten
- 1 tablespoon almond flour
- 2 ounces Cheddar cheese, grated
- ¼ teaspoon ground black pepper
- ½ teaspoon salt
- ½ teaspoon paprika
- ½ cup water (for cooking on High)

Preparation:
1. Mix up together the cream cheese, butter, egg, almond flour, cheese, ground black pepper, salt, and paprika.
2. Whisk the mixture until smooth.
3. After this, pour ½ cup of water in the pot. Insert the rack.
4. Transfer the batter in the prepared muffins molds and place on the rack.
5. Cover the muffins with the foil and close the lid.
6. Make sure you seal the lid and cook on Pressure mode (High) for 15 minutes.
7. Then make the quick pressure release for 5 minutes.
8. Chill the muffins little and serve!
Nutrition Values Per Serving: Calories 203, Fat 17, Carbs 1.9, Protein 11.1

Chicken Omelet

Prep Time: 10 minutes
Cook Time: 16 minutes
Servings: 2
Ingredients:
- 1 teaspoon butter
- 1 small yellow onion, chopped
- ½ jalapeño pepper, seeded and chopped
- 3 eggs
- Black pepper and salt, as required
- ¼ cup cooked chicken, shredded

Directions:
1. Select the "Sauté/Sear" setting of Ninja Foodi and place the butter into the pot.
2. Press the "Start/Stop" button to initiate cooking and heat for about 2-3 minutes.
3. Add the onion and cook for about 4-5 minutes.
4. Add the jalapeño pepper and cook for about 1 minute.
5. Meanwhile, in a suitable, add the eggs, salt, and black pepper and beat well.
6. Press the "Start/Stop" button to pause cooking and stir in the chicken.
7. Top with the egg mixture evenly.
8. Close the Ninja Foodi's lid with a crisping lid and select "Air Crisp."
9. Set its cooking temperature to 355 degrees F for 5 minutes.
10. Press the "Start/Stop" button to initiate cooking.
11. Open the Ninja Foodi's lid and transfer the omelette onto a plate.

12. Cut into equal-sized wedges and serve hot.
Nutritional Values Per Serving: Calories: 153, Fat: 9.1g, Carbs: 4g, Protein: 13.8g

Aromatic Keto Coffee

Prep time: 10 minutes
Cook time: 5 minutes
Servings: 4
Ingredients:
- 4 teaspoons butter
- 2 cups water
- 4 teaspoons instant coffee
- 1 tablespoon Erythritol
- ⅓ cup heavy cream
- 1 teaspoon ground cinnamon
- ½ teaspoon vanilla extract

Preparation:
1. Pour water, heavy cream, ground cinnamon, and vanilla extract in the cooker.
2. Add instant coffee and stir well until homogenous. Close and seal the lid. Cook the coffee mixture on high Pressure mode for 4 minutes. Then allow natural pressure release for 10 minutes.
3. Open the lid and add butter. Stir well and pour coffee in the serving cups.
Nutrition Values Per Serving: Calories 71, Fat 7.5, Carbs 0.8, Protein 0.3

Spicy Bacon Bites

Prep time: 6 minutes
Cook time: 20 minutes
Servings: 8
Ingredients:
- 10 ounces Romano cheese
- 6 ounces sliced bacon
- 1 teaspoon oregano
- 5 ounces puff pastry
- 1 teaspoon butter
- 2 egg yolks
- 1 teaspoon sesame seeds

Preparation:
1. Chop Romano cheese into small cubes. Roll the puff pastry using a rolling pin.
2. Whisk the egg yolks. Sprinkle them with the oregano and sesame seeds.
3. Cut the puff pastry into the squares, and place an equal amount of butter on every square. Wrap the cheese cubes in the sliced bacon.
4. Place the wrapped cheese cubes onto the puff pastry squares. Make the "bites" of the dough and brush them with the egg yolk mixture.
5. Transfer the bites in the pressure cooker. Close the lid, and set the pressure cooker mode to "Steam". Cook for 20 minutes.
6. When the cooking time ends, remove the dish from the pressure cooker and place on a serving dish.
Nutrition Values Per Serving: Calories 321, Fat 24.4, Carbs 10.9, Protein 16

Avocado Stuffed Eggs

Prep Time: 10 minutes
Cook time: 5 minutes
Servings: 6
Ingredients:
- ½ tablespoon fresh lemon juice
- 1 medium ripe avocado, peeled, pitted and chopped
- 6 eggs, boiled, peeled and cut in half length-wise
- Salt to taste
- ½ cup fresh watercress, trimmed

Preparation:
1. Place cook & crisp basket at the bottom of your Ninja Foodi. Add water.
2. Add watercress on the basket and Lock the Ninja Foodi's lid.
3. Cook on "Pressure" mode at High for almost 3 minutes, then quick release the pressure and drain the watercress.
4. Remove egg yolks and transfer them to a suitable bowl.
5. Add watercress, avocado, lemon juice, salt into the bowl and mash with a fork.
6. Place egg whites in a serving bowl and fill them with the watercress and avocado dish.
7. Serve!
Nutrition Values Per Serving: Calories: 132, Fat: 10g, Carbs: 3g, Protein: 5g

Bell Pepper Frittata

Prep Time: 15 minutes
Cook Time: 18 minutes
Servings: 2
Ingredients:
- 1 tablespoon olive oil
- 1 chorizo sausage, sliced
- 1½ cups bell peppers, seeded and chopped
- 4 large eggs
- Black pepper and salt, as required
- 2 tablespoons feta cheese, crumbled
- 1 tablespoon fresh parsley, chopped

Directions:
1. Select the "Sauté/Sear" setting of Ninja Foodi and place the butter into the pot.
2. Press the "Start/Stop" button to initiate cooking and heat for about 2-3 minutes.
3. Add the sausage and bell peppers and cook for 6-8 minutes or until golden brown.
4. Meanwhile, in a suitable bowl, add the eggs, salt, and black pepper and beat well.
5. Press the "Start/Stop" button to pasue cooking and place the eggs over the sausage mixture, followed by the cheese and parsley.
6. Close the Ninja Foodi's lid with a crisping lid and select "Air Crisp".
7. Set its cooking temperature to 355 degrees F for 10 minutes.
8. Press the "Start/Stop" button to initiate cooking.
9. Open the Ninja Foodi's lid and transfer the frittata onto a platter.
10. Cut into equal-sized wedges and serve hot.
Nutritional Values Per Serving: Calories: 398, Fat: 31g, Carbs: 8g, Protein: 22.9g

Poached Tomato Eggs

Prep time: 5 minutes
Cook time: 5 minutes
Servings: 4
Ingredients:
- 4 eggs
- 3 medium tomatoes
- 1 red onion
- 1 teaspoon salt
- 1 tablespoon olive oil
- ½ teaspoon white pepper
- ½ teaspoon paprika
- 1 tablespoon fresh dill

Preparation:
1. Spray the ramekins with the olive oil inside. Beat the eggs in a mixing bowl and add an equal amount to each ramekin.
2. Combine the paprika, white pepper, fresh dill, and salt together in a mixing bowl and stir the mixture.
3. Dice the red onion and tomatoes and combine. Add the seasonings and stir the mixture.
4. Sprinkle the eggs with the tomato mixture. Transfer the eggs to the pressure cooker.
5. Close the lid, and set the pressure cooker mode to "Steam". Cook for 5 minutes.
6. Remove the dish from the pressure cooker and rest briefly. Let it rest for a few minutes and dish immediately.
Nutrition Values Per Serving: Calories 194, Fat 13.5, Carbs 8.45, Protein 10

Spinach Egg Omelet

Prep time: 6 minutes
Cook time: 6 minutes
Servings: 5
Ingredients:
- 2 cups spinach
- 8 eggs
- ½ cup almond milk
- 1 teaspoon salt
- 1 tablespoon olive oil
- 1 teaspoon ground black pepper
- 4 ounces Parmesan cheese

Preparation:
1. Add the eggs to a mixing bowl and whisk them. Chop the spinach and add it to the egg mixture.
2. Add the almond milk, salt, olive oil, and ground black pepper. Stir the mixture well.
3. Transfer the egg mixture to the pressure cooker and close the lid.
4. Set the pressure cooker mode to "Steam", and cook for 6 minutes. Grate the cheese.
5. When the cooking time ends, remove the omelet from the pressure cooker and transfer it to a serving plate.
6. Sprinkle the dish with the grated cheese and serve.
Nutrition Values Per Serving: Calories 257, Fat 20.4, Carbs 3.4, Protein 17.1

Carrot Meal

Prep Time: 10 minutes
Cook time: 4 minutes
Servings: 4
Ingredients:
- 1 and a ½-pound carrots, chopped
- 1 tablespoon butter at room temperature
- 1 tablespoon agave nectar
- ¼ teaspoon sea salt
- 1 cup water

Preparation:
1. Clean and peel your carrots properly. Roughly chop them into small pieces.
2. Pour 1 cup of water into Ninja Foodi's cooking pot.
3. Place the carrots in a cook & crisp basket and place the basket in the Ninja Foodi.
4. Seal the Ninja's lid and cook on "Pressure" mode at High for 4 minutes. Do a quick release to remove the steam.
5. Transfer the carrots to a deep bowl and use an immersion blender to blend the carrots.
6. Add butter, nectar, salt, and puree. Taste the puree and season more if needed.
7. Enjoy!
Nutrition Values Per Serving: Calories: 143, Fat: 9g, Carbs: 16g, Protein: 2g

Cauliflower Pancake

Prep time: 10 minutes
Cook time: 10 minutes
Servings: 2
Ingredients:
- 7 ounces cauliflower
- 2 eggs, whisked
- 2 tablespoons almond flour
- 1 tablespoon flax meal
- 1 teaspoon butter
- 1 teaspoon chili flakes
- 1 teaspoon dried dill

Preparation:
1. Grind the cauliflower and mix it up with the whisked eggs, almond flour, flax meal, chili flakes, and dried dill. Stir the mixture well.
2. Preheat Ninja Foodi on Sauté mode and add butter. Melt it.
3. Place cauliflower mixture in the cooker with the help of the spoon (to get pancake shape) and cook for 4 minutes from each side.
Nutrition Values Per Serving: Calories 161, Fat 11.2, Carbs 8.4, Protein 9.9

Egg Turkey Cups

Prep Time: 10 minutes
Cook time: 10 minutes
Servings: 4
Ingredients:
- 8 tablespoons turkey sausage, cooked and crumbled, divided
- 8 tablespoons frozen spinach, chopped and divided
- 8 teaspoons shredded cheddar cheese, divided

- 4 eggs
Preparation:
1. Add a layer of the sausage, spinach and cheese on each muffin cup.
2. Crack the egg open on top. Seal the crisping lid. Select Air Crisp mode.
3. Cook at 330 degrees F for almost 10 minutes.
4. Serve warm.
Nutrition Values Per Serving: Calories: 171, Fat: 13.3g, Carbs: 0.5g, Protein: 11.9g

Tofu with Mushrooms

Prep Time: 10 minutes
Cook time: 10 minutes
Servings: 2
Ingredients:
- 8 tablespoons parmesan cheese, shredded
- 2 cups fresh mushrooms, chopped
- 2 blocks tofu, pressed and cubed
- Salt and black pepper, to taste
- 8 tablespoons butter

Preparation:
1. Take a suitable bowl and mix in tofu, salt, and pepper
2. Set your Ninja Foodi to Sauté mode and add seasoned tofu, Sauté for 5 minutes
3. Add mushroom, cheese and Sauté for 3 minutes.
4. Lock the crisping lid and cook on the "Air Crisp" mode for 3 minutes at 350 degrees F.
5. Transfer to a serving plate and enjoy!
Nutrition Values Per Serving: Calories: 211, Fat: 18g, Carbs: 2g, Protein: 11g

Morning Pancakes

Prep Time: 10 minutes
Cook Time: 10 minutes
Servings: 4
Ingredients:
- 2 cups cream cheese
- 2 cups almond flour
- 6 large whole eggs
- ¼ teaspoon salt
- 2 tablespoons butter
- ¼ teaspoon ground ginger
- ½ teaspoon cinnamon powder

Directions:
1. Take a large bowl and add cream cheese, eggs, 1 tablespoon butter. Blend on high until creamy
2. Slow add flour and keep beating
3. Add salt, ginger, cinnamon
4. Keep beating until fully mixed
5. Select "Sauté" mode on your Ninja Foodi and grease stainless steel insert
6. Add butter and heat it up
7. Add ½ cup batter and cook for 2-3 minutes, flip and cook the other side
8. Repeat with the remaining batter. Enjoy.
Nutritional Values Per Serving: Calories: 432, Fat: 40g, Carbs: 3g, Protein: 14g

Cinnamon French Toast

Prep Time: 15 minutes
Cook time: 10 minutes
Servings: 2
Ingredients:
- 2 eggs, beaten
- ¼ cup milk
- ¼ cup brown sugar
- 1 tablespoon honey
- 1 teaspoon cinnamon
- ¼ teaspoon nutmeg
- 4 slices whole meal bread, julienned

Preparation:
1. In a suitable bowl, mix everything except the bread.
2. Dip each strip in the mixture. Place the bread strips on the Ninja Foodi basket.
3. Place basket inside the pot. Cover with the crisping lid. Select Air Crisp mode.
4. Cook at 320 degrees F for almost 10 minutes.
5. Serve warm.
Nutrition Values Per Serving: Calories: 295, Fat: 6.1g, Carbs: 50g, Protein: 11.9g

Sweet Crepes

Prep Time: 5 minutes
Cook time: 10 minutes
Servings: 4
Ingredients:
- 1 ½ teaspoons Splenda
- 3 eggs
- 3 tablespoons coconut flour
- ½ cup heavy cream
- 3 tablespoons coconut oil, melted and divided

Preparation:
1. Mix in 1 ½ tablespoons coconut oil, Splenda, eggs, salt in a suitable bowl.
2. Add coconut flour and keep beating. Stir in heavy cream, beat well.
3. Set your Ninja Foodi to Sauté mode and add ¼ of the mixture.
4. Sauté for 2 minutes on each side. Repeat until all ingredients are used.
5. Enjoy!
Nutrition Values Per Serving: Calories: 145, Fat: 13g, Carbs: 4g, Protein: 4g

Garlicky Potatoes

Prep Time: 1 hour 10 minutes
Cook time: 20 minutes
Servings: 2
Ingredients:
- 2 potatoes, scrubbed, rinsed and diced
- 1 tablespoon olive oil
- Salt to taste
- ¼ teaspoon garlic powder

Preparation:
1. Put the potatoes in a suitable bowl of cold water. Soak for 45 minutes.
2. Pat the potatoes dry with a paper towel. Toss in olive oil, salt and garlic powder.

3. Place in the Ninja Foodi basket. Seal the crisping lid. Select Air Crisp mode.
4. Cook at 400 degrees F for almost 20 minutes. Flip the potatoes when cooked halfway through.
5. Serve warm.
Nutrition Values Per Serving: Calories: 208, Fat: 7.2g, Carbs: 34g, Protein: 3.6g

Spinach Casserole

Prep Time: 10 minutes
Cook Time: 5 minutes
Servings: 1
Ingredients:
- 4 whole eggs
- 1 tablespoons milk
- 1 tomato, diced
- ½ cup spinach
- ¼ teaspoon salt
- ¼ teaspoon black pepper

Directions:
1. Take a baking pan small enough to fit Ninja Foodi and grease it with butter.
2. Take a medium bowl and whisk in eggs, milk, salt, pepper, add veggies to the bowl and stir.
3. Pour egg mixture into the baking pan and lower the pan into the Ninja Foodi.
4. Close crisping lid and Air Crisp for 325 degrees F for 7 minutes.
5. Remove the pan from eggs, and enjoy hot.
Nutritional Values Per Serving: Calories: 78, Fat: 5g, Carbs: 1 g, Protein: 7 g

Stuffed Buns with Egg

Prep time: 8 minutes
Cook time: 10 minutes
Servings: 6
Ingredients:
- 3 large keto bread rolls
- 4 eggs
- 7 ounces cheddar cheese
- 1 teaspoon salt
- ½ teaspoon red chili flakes
- ½ teaspoon sour cream
- 1 tablespoon butter

Preparation:
1. Cut the keto bread rolls in half. Hollow out the center of the bread half partially.
2. Combine the salt, pepper flakes, and sour cream together and stir gently.
3. Add the eggs to a mixing bowl and whisk. Add the butter in the pressure cooker.
4. Pour the eggs equally into the keto bread roll halves.
5. Transfer the bread in the pressure cooker.
6. Sprinkle the dish with the spice mixture. Grate the cheddar cheese and sprinkle the bread with the grated cheese.
7. Close the lid, and set the pressure cooker mode to "Steam". Cook for 10 minutes. Let the dish rest before serving it.
Nutrition Values Per Serving: Calories 259, Fat 19.2, Carbs 2.6, Protein 17.5

Bacon Eggs

Prep time: 7 minutes
Cook time: 7 minutes
Servings: 4
Ingredients:
* 7 ounces sliced bacon
* 4 eggs, boiled
* 1 teaspoon cilantro
* ½ cup spinach
* 2 teaspoons butter
* ½ teaspoon ground white pepper
* 3 tablespoons heavy cream

Preparation:
1. Lay the bacon flat and sprinkle it with the ground white pepper and cilantro on both sides of the slices and stir the mixture.
2. Peel the eggs, and wrap them in the spinach leaves. Wrap the eggs in the sliced bacon.
3. Set the pressure cooker mode to "Sauté" and transfer the wrapped eggs.
4. Add butter and cook for 10 minutes.
5. When the cooking time ends, remove the eggs from the pressure cooker and sprinkle them with the cream. Serve the dish immediately.

Nutrition Values Per Serving: Calories 325, Fat 28.4, Carbs 5.24, Protein 15

Avocado Bacon Bombs

Prep time: 10 minutes
Cook time: 10 minutes
Servings: 4
Ingredients:
* 1 avocado, peeled, cored
* 4 ounces bacon, sliced
* 1 tablespoon almond flour
* 1 tablespoon flax meal
* ½ teaspoon salt

Preparation:
1. Blend together avocado, almond flour, flax meal, and salt. When the mixture is smooth, transfer it in the mixing bowl.
2. Make the medium size balls from it and wrap in the bacon.
3. Secure the balls with the toothpicks. After this, transfer the bombs in the cooker and set to Air Crisp mode.
4. Close the lid and cook the meal for 10 minutes.

Nutrition Values Per Serving: Calories 303, Fat 25.8, Carbs 6.7, Protein 13.3

Mushroom Omelets

Prep Time: 15 minutes
Cook time: 8 minutes
Servings: 2
Ingredients:
* 2 eggs
* ¼ cup milk
* 1 tablespoon red bell pepper, chopped
* 1 slice ham, diced
* 1 tablespoon mushrooms, chopped
* Salt to taste
* ¼ cup cheese, shredded

Preparation:
1. Whisk the eggs and milk in a suitable bowl. Add the ham and vegetables. For seasoning, add the salt.
2. Pour the mixture into a small pan. Place the pan inside the Ninja Foodi's insert.
3. Seal the crisping lid. Select Air Crisp mode. Cook at 350 degrees F for almost 8 minutes.
4. Before it is fully cooked, sprinkle the cheese on top.
5. Serve warm.

Nutrition Values Per Serving: Calories: 177, Fat: 11g, Carbs: 7.1g, Protein: 13.1g

Crispy Egg Toast

Prep Time: 15 minutes
Cook time: 9 minutes
Servings: 1
Ingredients:
* 1 slice bread
* 1 egg
* Salt and black pepper, to taste
* Cooking spray

Preparation:
1. Spray a small baking pan with oil. Place the bread inside the pan.
2. Make a medium-sized hole in the center of the bread slice.
3. Crack open the egg and put it inside the hole.
4. Cover the Ninja Foodi with the crisping lid. Select Air Crisp mode.
5. Cook at 330 degrees F for almost 6 minutes. Flip the toast and cook for 3 more minutes.
6. Serve warm.

Nutrition Values Per Serving: Calories: 92, fat: 5.2g, Carbs: 5g, Protein: 6.2g

Mushroom Stir Fry

Prep Time: 10 minutes
Cook time: 15 minutes
Servings: 8
Ingredients:
* 1 pound white mushrooms stems trimmed
* 2 tablespoons unsalted butter
* ½ teaspoon salt
* ¼ cup water

Preparation:
1. Quarter medium mushrooms and cut any large mushrooms into eight.
2. Put mushrooms, butter, and salt in your Ninja Foodi's inner pot.
3. Add water and lock pressure lid, making sure to seal the valve.
4. Cook on "Pressure" mode at High for 5 minutes, quick release pressure once did.
5. Once done, set your pot to Sauté mode on HIGH and bring the mix to a boil over 5 minutes until all the water evaporates.
6. Once the liquid has evaporated, stir for 1 minute until slightly browned.
7. Enjoy!

Nutrition Values Per Serving: Calories: 50, Fat: 4g, Carbs: 2g, Protein: 2g

Migas

Prep time: 10 minutes
Cook time: 10 minutes
Servings: 6
Ingredients:
- 10 eggs
- 1 jalapeno pepper
- 8 ounces tomatoes
- 1 tablespoon chicken stock
- 7 ounces cheddar cheese
- 2 white onions
- 2 cups tortilla chips
- 1 sweet bell pepper
- ½ cup beef stock
- 1 teaspoon salt

Preparation:
1. Whisk the eggs in the mixing bowl. Chop the jalapeno peppers and tomatoes. Grate the cheddar cheese. Peel the onions and chop them. Crush the tortilla chips. Chop the bell peppers.
2. Combine the jalapeno pepper, tomatoes, onion, and chopped bell pepper together and stir the mixture.
3. Set the pressure cooker mode to "Sauté", and transfer the vegetable mixture. Cook it for 5 minutes.
4. Add the whisked eggs mixture. Add the stocks, salt, and grated cheese. Mix up the mixture well, and cook it for 4 minutes.
5. Add the crushed tortilla chips, and cook for 1 minute more. Stir it and serve.
6. Note: Only add salt if using low-sodium chicken and beef stock, otherwise, you can omit the salt.!

Nutrition Values Per Serving: Calories 295, Fat 19.3, Carbs 9.27, Protein 21

Creamy Soufflé

Prep time: 10 minutes
Cook time: 20 minutes
Servings: 6
Ingredients:
- 3 eggs
- 1 cup cream
- 6 ounces cottage cheese
- 4 tablespoons butter
- ⅓ cup dried apricots
- 1 tablespoon sour cream
- 2 tablespoons sugar
- 1 teaspoon vanilla extract

Preparation:
1. Whisk the eggs and combine them with cream. Transfer the cottage cheese to a mixing bowl, and mix it well using a hand mixer.
2. Add the whisked eggs, butter, sour cream, sugar, and vanilla extract. Blend the mixture well until smooth.
3. Add the apricots, and stir the mixture well. Transfer the soufflé in the pressure cooker and close the lid.
4. Set the pressure cooker mode to Sauté, and cook for 20 minutes.
5. When the cooking time ends, let the soufflé cool little and serve.

Nutrition Values Per Serving: Calories 266, Fat 21.1, Carbs 11.72, Protein 8

Almond Quinoa Porridge

Prep Time: 10 minutes
Cook Time: 1 minute
Servings: 6
Ingredients:
- 1¼ cups water
- 1 cup almond milk
- 1½ cups uncooked quinoa, rinsed
- 1 tablespoon choc zero maple syrup
- 1 cinnamon stick
- Pinch of salt

Directions:
1. In the Ninja Foodi's insert, add all ingredients and stir to combine well.
2. Close the Ninja Foodi's pressure lid and place the pressure valve in the "Seal" position.
3. Select "Pressure" mode and set it to "Hi" for 1 minute.
4. Press the "Start/Stop" button to initiate cooking.
5. Now turn the pressure valve to "Vent" and do a "Quick" release.
6. Open the Ninja Foodi's lid, and with a fork, fluff the quinoa.
7. Serve warm.

Nutritional Values Per Serving: Calories: 186, Fat: 2.6 g, Carbs: 4.8 g, Protein: 6 g

Ninja Foodi Eggs with Spinach

Prep Time: 10 minutes
Cook Time: 25 minutes
Servings: 4
Ingredients:
- 2 tablespoons olive oil
- 4 eggs
- ¼ cup scallion, chopped
- 10 cups chopped baby spinach
- Salt and black pepper, to taste

Directions:
1. Add oil and scallion in the pot of Ninja Foodi Multi-cooker and cook for 5 minutes with an open lid.
2. Add in pepper, salt and spinach and cook for 5-minutes.
3. Make fourwells in the mixture and crack eggs in each well.
4. Close the Crisping Lid and select "Bake".
5. Press the "Start/Stop" button and bake for 15 minutes at 400 degrees F.
6. Take out, serve and enjoy!

Nutritional Values Per Serving: Calories: 142, Fat: 11.7g, Carbs: 3.5g, Protein: 7.8g

Brussels Sprouts Bacon Hash

Prep Time: 10 minutes
Cook Time: 20 minutes
Servings: 4
Ingredients:
- ½ lb. brussels sprouts, sliced in half
- 4 slices bacon, chopped
- ½ red onion, chopped
- salt, to taste
- black pepper, to taste

Directions:
1. Toss all the ingredients into the Ninja Foodi cooking pot.
2. Secure the Ninja Foodi lid and turn its pressure handle to 'SEAL' position.
3. Select mode for 20 minutes at HI.
4. Once done, release the steam naturally then remove the lid.
5. Serve fresh.

Nutritional Values Per Serving:
Calories 121, Total Fat 9 g, Total Carbs 13.8 g, Protein 4.3 g

Apricot Oatmeal

Prep Time: 10 minutes
Cook Time: 8 hours
Servings: 8
Ingredients:
- 2 cups steel-cut oats
- ⅓ cup dried apricots, chopped
- ½ cup dried cherries
- 1 teaspoon ground cinnamon
- 4 cups milk
- 4 cups water
- ¼ teaspoon liquid stevia

Directions:
1. In the Ninja Foodi's insert, place all ingredients and stir to combine.
2. Close the Ninja Foodi's lid with a pressure lid and select "Slow Cook."
3. Set on "LO" for 6-8 hours.
4. Press the "Start/Stop" button to initiate cooking.
5. Open the Ninja Foodi's lid and serve warm.

Nutritional Values Per Serving: Calories: 148, Fat: 3.5g, Carbs: 4.2 g, Protein: 5.9 g

Ninja Foodi Cinnamon Tea

Prep Time: 5 minutes
Cook Time: 12 minutes
Servings: 2
Ingredients:
- 1 cup water
- 1 teaspoon black tea
- 2 cinnamon sticks
- 4 black peppercorns
- ½ cup fat-free cream

Directions:
1. Add water, peppercorns and cinnamon in the pot Ninja Foodi Multi-cooker.
2. Boil for about 10 minutes and add in cream.
3. Close the pressure Lid and select "Pressure".

4. Press the "Start/Stop" button and cook for about 2 minutes at LOW pressure.
5. Open the lid and strain the tea.
6. Serve hot and enjoy!

Nutritional Values Per Serving: Calories: 62, Fat: 0.8g, Carbs: 5.4g, Protein: 8.5g

Cauliflower Meal

Prep Time: 10 minutes
Cook Time: 4 minutes
Servings: 4
Ingredients:
- 1 cauliflower head, florets
- ½ cup vegetable stock
- 2 garlic cloves, minced
- Black pepper and salt to taste
- ⅓ cup grated parmesan
- 1 tablespoon parsley, chopped
- 3 tablespoons olive oil

Directions:
1. Take a suitable and add oil, salt, pepper, garlic, cauliflower and toss well.
2. Transfer the mix to Ninja Foodi cooking basket.
3. Add stock and stir.
4. Lock and secure the Ninja Foodi's pressure lid, turn the pressure valve to SEAL position. Set the unit to Pressure mode. Then cook on "HIGH" pressure for 4 minutes.
5. Add parsley, cheese, and toss.
6. Serve and enjoy a healthy breakfast.

Nutritional Values Per Serving: Calories: 120, Fat: 2g, Carbs: 4g, Protein: 3g

Ham Breakfast Casserole

Prep Time: 10 minutes
Cook Time: 10 minutes
Servings: 4
Ingredients:
- 4 whole eggs
- 1 tablespoons milk
- 1 cup ham, cooked and chopped
- ½ cup cheddar cheese, shredded
- ¼ teaspoon salt
- ¼ teaspoon black pepper

Directions:
1. Take a baking pan small enough to fit into your Ninja Foodi bowl, and grease it well with butter
2. Take a medium bowl and whisk in eggs, milk, salt, pepper and add ham, cheese, and stir
3. Pour mixture into baking pan and lower the pan into your Ninja Foodi
4. Set your Ninja Foodi Air Crisp mode and Air Crisp for 325 degrees F for 7 minutes
5. Remove pan from eggs and enjoy.

Nutritional Values Per Serving: Calories: 169, Fat: 13g, Carbohydrates: 1g, Protein: 12g

Cashew Porridge

Prep Time: 10 minutes
Cook Time: 10 minutes
Servings: 6
Ingredients:
- 1 cup pecans, halved
- 1 cup cashew nuts, raw and unsalted
- 4 teaspoons coconut oil, melted
- 2 cups of water

Directions:
1. Add 1 and ½ cups of water and place a steamer rack in your Ninja Foodi.
2. Trim the core of the cauliflower head and cut it into florets.
3. Take a small bowl and mix with olive oil, salt, cumin, and paprika, then drizzle over cauliflower.
4. Close the Ninja Foodi's pressure lid. Turn the pressure release valve to the SEAL position. Set the unit to Pressure mode.
5. Cook for 4 minutes on Hi.
6. Quick-release the Pressure.
7. Garnish with cilantro.
8. Serve and enjoy.

Nutritional Values Per Serving: Calories: 70, Fat: 6g, Carbs: 1 g, Protein: 3g

Flaxseeds Granola

Prep Time: 15 minutes
Cook Time: 2½ hours
Servings: 16
Ingredients:
- ½ cup sunflower kernels
- 5 cups mixed nuts, crushed
- 2 tablespoons ground flax seeds
- ¼ cup olive oil
- ½ cup unsalted butter
- 1 teaspoon ground cinnamon
- 1 cup choc zero maple syrup

Directions:
1. Grease the Ninja Foodi's insert.
2. In the greased Ninja Foodi's insert, add sunflower kernels, nuts, flax seeds, oil, butter, and cinnamon and stir to combine.
3. Close the Ninja Foodi's lid with a pressure lid and select "Slow Cook."
4. Set on "HI" for 2½ hours.
5. Press the "Start/Stop" button to initiate cooking.
6. Stir the mixture after every 30 minutes.
7. Open the Ninja Foodi's lid and transfer the granola onto a large baking sheet.
8. Add the maple syrup and stir to combine.
9. Set aside to cool completely before serving.
10. You can preserve this granola in an airtight container.

Nutritional Values Per Serving: Calories: 189, Fat: 10 g, Carbs: 7.7 g, Protein: 4.6 g

Nutmeg Pumpkin Porridge

Prep Time: 15 minutes
Cook Time: 5 hours
Servings: 8
Ingredients:
- 1 cup unsweetened almond milk
- 2 pounds pumpkin, peeled and cubed into ½-inch size
- 6-8 drops liquid stevia
- ½ teaspoon ground allspice
- 1 tablespoon ground cinnamon
- 1 teaspoon ground nutmeg
- ¼ teaspoon ground cloves
- ½ cup walnuts, chopped

Directions:
1. In the Ninja Foodi's insert, place ½ cup of almond milk and remaining ingredients and stir to combine.
2. Close the Ninja Foodi's lid with a crisping lid and select "Slow Cook".
3. Set on "LO" for 4-5 hours.
4. Press the "Start/Stop" button to initiate cooking.
5. Open the Ninja Foodi's lid and stir in the remaining almond milk.
6. With a potato masher, mash the mixture completely.
7. Divide the porridge into serving bowls evenly.
8. Serve warm with the topping of walnuts.

Nutritional Values Per Serving: Calories: 96, Fat: 5.5g, Carbs: 11.2g, Protein: 3.3g

Ninja Foodi Ham Muffins

Prep Time: 10 minutes
Cook Time: 20 minutes
Servings: 4
Ingredients:
- 4 eggs
- ½ cup cooked ham, crumbled
- ½ cup red bell pepper, seeded and chopped
- 1 tablespoon water
- Salt and black pepper, to taste

Directions:
1. Add eggs, salt, pepper and water in a bowl. Mix well.
2. Now, add in red bell pepper and crumbled ham. Mix well and set aside.
3. Pour the mixture in greased muffin-tins and place them in the pot of Ninja Foodi Multicooker.
4. Select "Bake" and close the Crisping Lid.
5. Press the "Start/Stop" button and bake for 20 minutes at 350 degrees F.
6. Take out, serve and enjoy!

Nutritional Values Per Serving: Calories: 95, Fat: 5.9g, Carbs: 2.1g, Protein: 8.5g

Chapter 2-Snacks and Appetizers Recipes

Veggies Dredged in Cheese

Prep time: 10 minutes
Cook time: 30 minutes
Servings: 4
Ingredients:
- 2 onions, sliced
- 2 tomatoes, sliced
- 2 zucchinis, sliced
- 2 teaspoons olive oil
- 2 cups cheddar cheese, grated
- 2 teaspoons mixed dried herbs
- Salt and pepper to taste

Preparation:
1. Arrange all the listed ingredients to your Ninja Foodi.
2. Top with olive oil, herbs, cheddar, salt and pepper.
3. Lock lid and Air Crisp for 30 minutes at 350 degrees F.
4. Serve and enjoy!
Nutrition Values Per Serving: Calories: 305, Fat: 22g, Carbs: 9g, Protein: 15g

Bowl Full of Broccoli Salad

Prep time: 10 minutes
Cook time: 5 minutes
Servings: 4
Ingredients:
- 1 pound broccoli, cut into florets
- 2 tablespoons balsamic vinegar
- 2 garlic cloves, minced
- 1 teaspoon mustard seeds
- 1 teaspoon cumin seeds
- Salt and pepper to taste
- 1 cup cottage cheese, crumbled

Preparation:
1. Add 1 cup of water to your Ninja Foodi. Place cook & crisp basket.
2. Place broccoli in basket and lock lid, cook on Pressure mode at HI for 5 minutes.
3. Quick release pressure and remove lid.
4. Toss broccoli with other ingredients and serve. Enjoy!
Nutrition Values Per Serving: Calories: 95, Fat: 3.1g, Carbs: 10g, Protein: 2g

Buffalo Wings

Prep Time: 10 minutes
Cook time: 6 hours
Servings: 4
Ingredients:
- 1 bottle (12 ounces) hot pepper sauce
- ½ cup melted ghee
- 1 tablespoon dried oregano
- 2 teaspoons garlic powder
- 1 teaspoon onion powder
- 5 pounds chicken wing sections

Preparation:
1. Mix ghee, hot sauce, oregano, garlic powder, onion powder in a suitable bowl.
2. Add chicken wings and toss to coat.
3. Pour this mix into Ninja Foodi's insert and cook on "Slow Cook" mode with LOW heat for 6 hours.
4. Serve and enjoy!
Nutrition Values Per Serving: Calories: 529, Fat: 4g, Carbs: 1g, Protein: 31g

Simple Treat of Garlic

Prep time: 10 minutes
Cook time: 5 minutes
Servings: 4
Ingredients:
- 1 tablespoon extra-virgin olive oil
- 2 garlic cloves, minced
- 2 large-sized Belgian endive, halved lengthwise
- ½ cup apple cider vinegar
- ½ cup broth
- Salt and pepper to taste
- 1 teaspoon cayenne pepper

Preparation:
1. Set your Ninja Foodi to Sauté mode and add oil, let the oil heat up.
2. Add garlic and cook for 30 seconds unto browned.
3. Add endive, vinegar, broth, salt, pepper, and cayenne.
4. Lock lid and cook on Pressuire mode at LOW for 2 minutes. Quick release pressure and serve. Enjoy!
Nutrition Values Per Serving: Calories: 91, Fat: 6g, Carbs: 3g, Protein: 2g

Buttered Up Garlic and Fennel

Prep time: 10 minutes
Cook time: 5 minutes
Servings: 4
Ingredients:
- ½ stick butter
- 2 garlic cloves, sliced
- ½ teaspoon salt
- 1 and ½ pounds fennel bulbs, cut into wedges
- ¼ teaspoon ground black pepper
- ½ teaspoon cayenne
- ¼ teaspoon dried dill weed
- ⅓ cup dry white wine
- ⅔ cup stock

Preparation:
1. Set your Ninja Foodi to Sauté mode and add butter, let it heat up.
2. Add garlic and cook for 30 seconds. Add rest of the ingredients.
3. Lock lid and cook on Pressure mode at LOW for 3 minutes. Remove lid and serve. Enjoy!
Nutrition Values Per Serving: Calories: 111, Fat: 6g, Carbs: 2g, Protein: 2g

Creamy Fudge Meal

Prep Time: 10 minutes + chill times
Cook time: 10-20 minutes
Servings: 20
Ingredients:
- ½ teaspoon organic vanilla extract
- 1 cup heavy whip cream
- 2 ounces butter, soft
- 2 ounces 70% dark chocolate, finely chopped

Preparation:
1. Set your Ninja Foodi to Sauté mode and add vanilla, heavy cream. Sauté for 5 minutes.
2. Add butter and chocolate and Sauté for 2 minutes. Transfer to serving the dish.
3. Chill for few hours and enjoy!
Nutrition Values Per Serving: Calories: 292, Fat: 26g, Carbs: 8g, Protein: 5g

Cider Dipped Chili

Prep Time: 10 minutes
Cook time: 11 minutes
Servings: 4
Ingredients:
- 1 pound green chilies
- 1 and ½ cups apple cider vinegar
- 1 teaspoon pickling salt
- 1 and ½ teaspoons date paste
- ¼ teaspoon garlic powder

Preparation:
1. Add the above-mentioned ingredients to the Ninja Foodi's insert.
2. Seal the lid and cook on "Pressure" mode at High for 10 minutes
3. Release the pressure naturally.
4. Spoon the mix into washed jars and cover the slices with a bit of cooking liquid.
5. Add vinegar to submerge the chilly.
6. Enjoy!
Nutrition Values Per Serving: Calories: 3.1, Fat: 0g, Carbs: 0.6g, Protein: 0.1g

Saucy Chicken Thighs

Prep Time: 10 minutes
Cook time: 5-7 hours
Servings: 4
Ingredients:
- 3 pounds boneless, skinless chicken thighs
- ½ cup low-sodium chicken broth
- 2 cups cherry tomatoes, halved
- 4 garlic cloves, minced
- 2 teaspoons garlic salt
- ¼ teaspoon ground white pepper
- 2 tablespoons fresh basil, chopped
- 2 tablespoons fresh oregano, chopped

Preparation:
1. Add the chicken and all the listed ingredients to your Ninja Foodi and mix gently.
2. Lock the Ninja Foodi's lid and cook on "Slow Cook" mode with Low Heat for 5-7 hours.
3. Serve and enjoy!
Nutrition Values Per Serving: Calories: 247, Fat: 5g, Carbs: 15g, Protein: 34g

Excellent Bacon and Cheddar Frittata

Prep time: 10 minutes
Cook time: 10 minutes
Serving: 6
Ingredients:
- 6 whole eggs
- 2 tablespoons milk
- ½ cup bacon, cooked and chopped
- 1 cup broccoli, cooked
- ½ cup shredded cheddar cheese
- ¼ teaspoon salt
- ¼ teaspoon ground black pepper

Preparation:
1. Take a baking pan (small enough to fit into your Ninja Foodi) bowl, and grease it well with butter.
2. Take a medium sized bowl and add eggs, milk, salt, pepper, bacon, broccoli, and cheese. Stir well.
3. Pour mixture into your prepared baking pan and lower pan into your Foodi, close Crisping lid.
4. Air Crisp for 7 minutes at 375 degrees F. Remove pan and enjoy!
Nutrition Values Per Serving: Calories: 269, Fat: 20g, Carbs: 3g, Protein: 19g

Orange Cauliflower Salad

Prep Time: 10 minutes
Cook time: 10 minutes
Servings: 4
Ingredients:
- 1 small-sized cauliflower, florets
- 1 Romanesco cauliflower, florets
- 1 pound broccoli florets
- 2 seedless oranges, peeled and sliced

For vinaigrette
- 1 orange, juiced and zest
- 4 anchovies
- 1 hot pepper, sliced and chopped
- 1 tablespoon capers
- 4 tablespoons extra virgin olive oil
- Salt as needed
- Pepper as needed

Preparation:
1. Add broccoli, cauliflower florets to your Ninja Foodi.
2. Seal the lid and cook on "Pressure" mode at High for 7 minutes.
3. Once done, quick-release the pressure and remove the lid.
4. Make the vinaigrette by mixing the hot pepper, anchovies, olive oil, capers, pepper, salt, and mix well.
5. Strain the veggies out and mix with vinaigrette and the orange slices.
6. Enjoy!
Nutrition Values Per Serving: Calories: 163, Fat: 11g, Carbs: 15g, Protein: 3g

Bacon-Wrapped Drumsticks

Prep Time: 10 minutes
Cook time: 8 hours
Servings: 6
Ingredients:
- 12 chicken drumsticks
- 12 slices thinly-cut bacon

Preparation:
1. Wrap each chicken drumsticks in bacon. Place drumsticks in your Ninja Foodi's insert.
2. Place lid and cook "Slow Cook" cooking mode with LOW heat for 8 hours.
3. Serve and enjoy!
Nutrition Values Per Serving: Calories: 202, Fat: 8g, Carbs: 3g, Protein: 30g

Pork Packed Jalapeno

Prep time: 10 minutes
Cook time: 10 minutes
Serving: 6
Ingredients:
- 2 pounds pork sausage, ground
- 2 cups parmesan cheese, shredded
- 2 pounds large sized jalapeno peppers sliced lengthwise and seeded
- 2 (8 ounces packages), cream cheese, softened
- 2 (8 ounces) bottles, ranch dressing

Preparation:
1. Take a bowl and add pork sausage, cream cheese, ranch dressing and mix well.
2. Slice jalapeno in half, remove seeds and clean them.
3. Stuff sliced jalapeno pieces with pork mixture.
4. Place peppers in crisping basket and transfer basket to your Ninja Foodi.
5. Lock Crisping lid and cook on Air Crisp mode for 10 minutes at 350 degrees F.
6. Cook in batches if needed, serve and enjoy!
Nutrition Values Per Serving: Calories: 609, Fat: 50g, Carbs: 10g, Protein: 29g

Nutty Brussels Sprouts

Prep Time: 10 minutes
Cook time: 3 minutes
Servings: 4
Ingredients:
- 1 pound Brussels sprouts
- ¼ cup pine nuts
- 1 tablespoon olive oil
- 1 pomegranate
- ½ teaspoon salt
- 1 pepper, grated

Preparation:
1. Remove outer leaves and trim the stems off the washed Brussels sprouts.
2. Cut the largest ones in uniform halves.
3. Add 1 cup of water to the Ninja Foodi.
4. Place cook & crisp basket and add sprouts in the basket.
5. Seal the lid and cook on "Pressure" mode at High for 3 minutes.

6. Release the pressure naturally.
7. Transfer the sprouts to the serving dish and dress with olive oil, pepper, and salt.
8. Sprinkle toasted pine nuts and pomegranate seeds!
9. Serve warm and enjoy!
Nutrition Values Per Serving: Calories: 118, Fat: 10g, Carbs: 7g, Protein: 3g

Crispy Zucchini Fries

Prep Time: 10 minutes
Cook time: 10 minutes
Servings: 4
Ingredients:
- 1-2 pounds of zucchini, sliced into 2 and ½ inch sticks
- Salt to taste
- 1 cup cream cheese
- 2 tablespoons olive oil

Preparation:
1. Add zucchini in a colander and season with salt, add cream cheese and mix.
2. Add oil into your Ninja Foodie's pot and add zucchini.
3. Lock the Crisping Lid and set the temperature to 365 degrees F and timer to 10 minutes.
4. Let it cook for 10 minutes and take the dish out once done, enjoy!
Nutrition Values Per Serving: Calories: 374, Fat: 36g, Carbs: 6g, Protein: 7g

Cheesy Chicken Parmesan

Prep Time: 10 minutes
Cook time: 20 minutes
Servings: 4
Ingredients:
- 1 spaghetti squash
- 1 cup marinara sauce
- 1 pound chicken, cooked and cubed
- 16 ounces mozzarella

Preparation:
1. Split the squash in halves and remove the seeds.
2. Add 1 cup of water to the Ninja Foodi and place a trivet on top.
3. Add the squash halves on the trivet. Seal the Ninja's lid and cook on Pressure mode at High for 20 minutes.
4. Do a quick release. Remove the squashes and shred them using a fork into spaghetti portions.
5. Pour sauce over the squash and give it a nice mix.
6. Top them with the cubed chicken and top with mozzarella.
7. Broil for 1-2 minutes and broil until the cheese has melted.
8. Serve warm.
Nutrition Values Per Serving: Calories: 127, Fat: 8g, Carbs:11g, Protein:5g

Braised Kale Salad

Prep Time: 5 minutes
Cook time: 8 minutes
Servings: 4
Ingredients:
- 10 ounces kale, chopped
- 1 tablespoon ghee
- 1 medium onion, sliced
- 3 medium carrots, cut into half-inch pieces
- 5 garlic cloves, peeled and chopped
- ½ cup chicken broth
- Fresh ground pepper
- Vinegar as needed
- ½ teaspoon red pepper flakes

Preparation:
1. Set your pot to Sauté mode and add ghee, allow the ghee to melt.
2. Add chopped onion and carrots and Sauté for a while.
3. Add garlic and sauté for a while. Pile the kale on top.
4. Pour chicken broth and season with pepper.
5. Seal the lid and cook on "Pressure" mode at High for 8 minutes.
6. Release the pressure naturally over 10 minutes and remove the lid.
7. Add vinegar and sprinkle a bit more pepper flakes.
8. Enjoy!
Nutrition Values Per Serving: Calories: 41, Fat: 2g, Carbs: 5g, Protein: 2g

Cheesy Mushroom Appetizer

Prep Time: 10 minutes
Cook time: 20 minutes
Servings: 6
Ingredients:
- 24 mushrooms, caps and stems diced
- 1 cup cheddar cheese, shredded
- ½ orange bell pepper, diced
- ½ onion, diced
- 4 bacon slices, diced
- ½ cup sour cream

Preparation:
1. Set your Ninja Foodie to Sauté mode and add mushroom stems, onion, bacon, bell pepper and Sauté for 5 minutes.
2. Add 1 cup of cheese, sour cream and cook for 2 minutes.
3. Stuff mushrooms with cheese and vegetable mixture and top with cheddar cheese
4. Transfer them to your cook & crisp basket and lock the crisping lid.
5. Cook on "Air Crisp" mode for 8 minutes at 350 degrees F.
6. Serve and enjoy!
Nutrition Values Per Serving: Calories: 288, Fat: 6g, Carbs: 3g, Protein: 25g

Stuffed Egg Whites

Prep Time: 10 minutes
Cook time:3 minutes
Servings: 4

Ingredients:
- ½ tablespoon fresh lemon juice
- 1 medium ripe avocado, peeled and pitted, chopped
- 6 organic eggs, boiled, peeled and cut half
- Salt to taste
- ½ cup fresh watercress, trimmed

Preparation:
1. Place the Ninja's cook & crisp basket at the bottom of the Ninja Foodi's insert.
2. Add water to the insert and put the watercress in the basket.
3. Lock the Ninja Foodi's lid and at pressure mode cook for 3 minutes.
4. Quick release pressure, then remove the lid.
5. Allow the boiled eggs to cool, peel and cut them in half.
6. Remove egg yolk and transfer to a suitable bowl
7. Add watercress, avocado, lemon juice, salt, and mash well
8. Place egg whites in serving the dish and fill whites with watercress, mix well.
9. Enjoy!
Nutrition Values Per Serving: Calories: 132, Fat: 10g, Carbs: 3g, Protein: 6g

Ninja Foodi Spiced Almonds

Prep Time: 10 minutes
Cook Time: 14 minutes
Servings: 6
Ingredients:
- 2 tablespoons unsweetened applesauce
- 1 cup almonds
- ¼ teaspoon cayenne pepper
- ¼ teaspoon ground cumin
- ½ teaspoon olive oil
- ½ tablespoon water
- ¼ teaspoon ground cinnamon
- ¼ teaspoon red chili powder
- Salt, to taste

Directions:
1. Arrange almonds in Ninja Foodi Multi-cooker and select "Bake".
2. Close the Crisping Lid and press the "Start/Stop" button.
3. Bake for about 10 minutes at 350 degrees F and open the lid.
4. Take out and set aside.
5. Meanwhile, add oil, water and applesauce in a bowl. Mix well.
6. Add in almonds and toss to coat well.
7. Add cinnamon, ground cumin, red chili powder, cayenne pepper and salt in another bowl. Mix well.
8. Arrange almonds again in the Ninja Foodi Multi-cooker and top them with cinnamon mixture.
9. Close the Crisping Lid and press the "Start/Stop" button.
10. Bake them for about 4 minutes at 350 degrees F and open the lid.
11. Take out, serve and enjoy!
Nutritional Values Per Serving: Calories: 98, Fat: 8.4g, Carbs: 4.2g, Protein: 3.4g

Mexican Cheese Frittata

Prep Time: 10 minutes
Cook time: 25 minutes
Servings: 4
Ingredients:
- 4 whole eggs
- 1 cup half and half
- 10 ounces canned green chilies
- ½ -1 teaspoons salt
- ½ teaspoon ground cumin
- 1 cup Mexican blend shredded cheese
- ¼ cup cilantro, chopped

Preparation:
1. Take a suitable bowl and beat eggs and a half and half.
2. Add diced green chilis, salt, cumin and ½ cup of shredded cheese.
3. Pour the mixture into 6 inches greased metal pan and cover with foil.
4. Add 2 cups of water to the Ninja Foodi.
5. Place trivet into the Ninja Foodi's pot and place the pan in the trivet.
6. Seal the lid and cook on "Pressure" mode at High for 20 minutes.
7. Release the pressure naturally over 10 minutes.
8. Scatter half a cup of the cheese on top of your quiche.
9. Enjoy!
Nutrition Values Per Serving: Calories: 257, Fat: 19g, Carbs: 6g, Protein:14g

Crispy Beet Chips

Prep Time: 10 minutes
Cook time: 8 hours
Servings: 8
Ingredients:
- ½ beet, peeled and sliced

Preparation:
1. Arrange beet slices in a single layer in the cook & crisp basket of Ninja Foodi.
2. Place the basket into the Ninja Foodi's pot and close the crisping lid.
3. Set the Ninja Foodi to Dehydrate mode and let it dehydrate for 8 hours at 135 degrees F.
4. Once the dehydrating is done, remove the basket from the pot.
5. Serve.
Nutrition Values Per Serving: Calories: 35, Fat: 0g, Carbs: 8g, Protein: 1g

Ninja Foodi Cheddar Biscuits

Prep Time: 10 minutes
Cook Time: 15 minutes
Servings: 8
Ingredients:
- ¼ teaspoon baking powder
- ¼ cup butter
- ¼ teaspoon ginger powder
- ¼ teaspoon garlic powder
- 4 eggs
- ¼ cup coconut flour, sifted
- 1 cup cheddar cheese
- Salt, to taste

Directions:
1. Add flour, baking powder, garlic powder and salt in a large bowl. Mix well.
2. Now, add butter and eggs in another bowl. Whisk well.
3. Combine the two mixtures and mix properly. Set aside.
4. Place the batter in Ninja Foodi Multi-cooker and press the "Bake" button.
5. Close the Crisping Lid and press the "Start/Stop" button.
6. Bake for 15-minutes at 400 degrees F and open the lid.
7. Take out, serve and enjoy!
Nutritional Values Per Serving: Calories: 155, Fat: 13g, Carbs: 3g, Protein: 6.9g

Ninja Foodi Spicy Peanuts

Prep Time: 5 minutes
Cook Time: 2 hours 40 minutes
Servings: 6
Ingredients:
- ¾ cups peanuts
- 1½ tablespoons chili seasoning mix
- ½ tablespoon butter

Directions:
1. Add peanuts, chili seasoning mix and butter in the pot of Ninja Foodi Multi-cooker. Mix well.
2. Select "Slow Cook" and close the pressure Lid.
3. Press the "Start/Stop" button and cook for about 2 hours and 30 minutes at Lo. Stir after every 30 minutes.
4. Open the lid and cook for 15 minutes.
5. Take out, serve and enjoy!
Nutritional Values Per Serving: Calories: 134, Fat: 11.1g, Carbs: 6.7g, Protein: 5.6g

Ninja Foodi Cod Sticks

Prep Time: 10 minutes
Cook Time: 15 minutes
Servings: 8
Ingredients:
- 1 cup almond flour
- 2 eggs
- 1 cod fillet, thinly sliced
- 2 teaspoons dried parsley, crushed
- ½ teaspoon cayenne pepper
- Salt and black pepper, to taste

Directions:
1. Add eggs in one bowl and all the other ingredients except cod slices in another bowl. Mix well.
2. Dip cod slices first in egg mixture and then in the other mixture. Set aside.
3. Arrange cod slices in Ninja Foodi Multi-cooker and press the "Bake" button.
4. Close the Crisping Lid and press the "Start/Stop" button.
5. Bake for 6 minutes on each side at 350 degrees F and open the lid.
6. Take out, serve and enjoy!
Nutritional Values Per Serving: Calories: 111, Fat: 7.9g, Carbs: 3.2g, Protein: 6.9g

Ninja Foodi Spicy Popcorns

Prep Time: 10 minutes
Cook Time: 5 minutes
Servings: 6
Ingredients:
- 1 cup popping corns
- 2 teaspoons ground turmeric
- ½ teaspoon garlic powder
- 6 tablespoons olive oil
- Salt, to taste

Directions:
1. Heat four tablespoons of olive-oil in a Ninja Foodi Multi-cooker and add popping corns in it.
2. Select "Pressure" and close the pressure Lid.
3. Press the "Start/Stop" button and cook for about 5 minutes at HIGH pressure.
4. Take out and set aside.
5. Meanwhile, add remaining olive oil, turmeric, garlic powder and salt in a bowl. Mix well.
6. Pour the mixture on popcorns and toss to coat well.
7. Serve and enjoy!
Nutritional Values Per Serving: Calories: 143, Fat: 14.1g, Carbs: 5.3g, Protein: 0.3g

Ninja Foodi Spinach Chips

Prep Time: 12 minutes
Cook Time: 10 minutes
Servings: 4
Ingredients:
- ½ teaspoon paprika
- ¼ teaspoon ground cumin
- ¼ teaspoon olive oil
- 2 cups fresh spinach leaves
- Salt, to taste

Directions:
1. Add everything in a large-bowl and mix-well. Set aside.
2. Place spinach leaves in Ninja Foodi Multi-cooker and press the "Bake" button.
3. Close the Crisping Lid and press the "Start/Stop" button.
4. Bake for about 10 minutes at 325 degrees F and open the lid.
5. Take out, serve and enjoy!
Nutritional Values Per Serving: Calories: 7, Fat: 0.4g, Carbs: 0.7g, Protein: 0.5g

Ninja Foodi Spicy Cashews

Prep Time: 10 minutes
Cook Time: 2 hours 45 minutes
Servings: 12
Ingredients:
- 2½ cups cashews
- 3 tablespoons chili seasoning mix
- 1½ tablespoons butter

Directions:
1. Add everything in the pot of Ninja Foodi Multi-cooker and mix well.
2. Close the pressure Lid and select "Slow Cook".
3. Press the "Start/Stop" button and cook for about 2 hours and 30 minutes on LOW TEMP.

4. Open the lid and cook for 15 more minutes.
5. Take out, serve and enjoy!
Serving Suggestions: Top with red chili powder before serving.
Variation Tip: You can add cayenne pepper for a stronger taste.
Nutritional Values Per Serving: Calories: 741, Fat: 61.2g, Carbs: 40.2g, Protein: 18.6g

Ninja Foodi Banana Cookies

Prep Time: 15 minutes
Cook Time: 20 minutes
Servings: 7
Ingredients:
- 1 banana, mashed
- ¼ cup soymilk
- ½ tablespoon canola oil
- ¼ tablespoon baking powder
- 1 cup white flour

Directions:
1. Add mashed bananas, oil and soymilk in a bowl. Mix well.
2. Add in flour and baking powder. Stir properly.
3. Knead the dough and roll it with the help of a rolling pin.
4. Cut the dough into circles and place them in Ninja Foodi Multi-cooker.
5. Select "Bake" and close the Crisping Lid.
6. Press the "Start/Stop" button and bake for about 20 minutes at 400 degrees F.
7. Open the lid and take out.
8. Serve and enjoy!
Nutritional Values Per Serving: Calories: 94, Fat: 1.4g, Carbs: 18.3g, Protein: 2.3g

Roasted Chickpeas

Prep Time: 5 Minutes
Cook Time: 15 Minutes
Servings: 1
Ingredients:
- 50 grams chickpeas
- 1 teaspoon of olive oil
- 1 packet salad dressing
- 1 tablespoon of seasoning mix
- 1 tablespoon parmesan cheese

Directions:
1. Heat your Ninja Foodi Multi-Cooker at 390° F. Rinse the chickpeas, and dry them.
2. Toss in with one tablespoon of extra virgin olive oil.
3. Now again toss with the parmesan cheese and the seasoning mix, make sure you get a nice coating.
4. Now put the chickpeas in the Ninja Foodi Multi-Cooker Cook & Crisp Basket. Cook for about 15 minutes. Make sure you toss it a couple of times.
5. Remove them from the Cook & Crisp Basket and grab them for snacking. Store in an air-tight container!
Nutritional Values Per Serving: Calories: 205, Fat: 12.7g, Carbs: 12.2g, Protein: 6.2g

Ninja Foodi Chickpea Crackers

Prep Time: 15 minutes
Cook Time: 20 minutes
Servings: 5
Ingredients:
- ½ cup chickpea flour
- 1 tablespoon yeast
- ¼ cup water
- ¼ teaspoon sesame oil
- ¼ teaspoon baking powder
- 1 teaspoon toasted sesame seeds
- ¼ teaspoon turmeric
- Salt, to taste

Directions:
1. Add baking powder, chickpea flour, sesame seeds, yeast, salt and turmeric in a bowl. Mix well.
2. Add water and oil gradually in the mixture and mix until proper dough is formed.
3. Cover the dough and set aside till the dough rises.
4. Make square shapes out of the dough and place them in Ninja Foodi Multi-cooker.
5. Select "Bake" and close the Crisping Lid.
6. Press the "Start/Stop" button and bake for about 20 minutes at 350 degrees F.
7. Open the Crisping Lid and take out.
8. Serve and enjoy!
Nutritional Values Per Serving: Calories: 86, Fat: 1.9g, Carbs: 13.4g, Protein: 1.9g

Ninja Foodi Lemon Scones

Prep Time: 10 minutes
Cook Time: 25 minutes
Servings: 3
Ingredients:
- ¾ cup all-purpose flour
- ¼ cup unsweetened soymilk
- 2 tablespoons sugar
- ½ teaspoon lemon extract
- ½ tablespoon sunflower oil
- ½ tablespoon baking powder
- Salt, to taste

Directions:
1. Add wet ingredients in one bowl and dry ingredients in another. Mix well.
2. Combine the two mixtures and mix until dough is formed.
3. Make spheres out of the mixture and press them with tortilla press.
4. Make triangular shapes out of the dough and place them in Ninja Foodi Multi-cooker.
5. Press the "Bake" button and close the Crisping Lid.
6. Press the "Start/Stop" button and bake for 15 minutes at 400 degrees F.
7. Open the Crisping Lid and take out.
8. Serve and enjoy!
Nutritional Values Per Serving: Calories: 175, Fat: 3g, Carbs: 33.4g, Protein: 3.8g

Ninja Foodi Popcorn

Prep Time: 5 Minutes
Cook Time: 10 Minutes
Servings: 14
Ingredients:
- 3 tablespoons oil, whatever kind you like
- ½ cup popcorn kernels
- ½ teaspoon salt
- 4 tablespoons butter, salted and room temp

Directions:
1. Measure out a piece of foil that is 4" larger than the diameter of the Ninja Foodi Multi-Cooker Inner Pot and wide enough to be able to fold into a pouch. Tuck the ends under the lip of the inner pot and make multiple holes with a thin sharp object. I used the pointy end of my cake tester. You don't want the holes too big or the butter will just pour out in places.
2. Add the three tablespoons of oil to the inner pot and half cup of popped corn kernel. Turn the Ninja Foodi Multi-Cooker on High Sear/Sauté and cover with Pressure Lid and turn Vent.
3. While you are waiting for the kernel to pop, cut or spread your butter on the foil.
4. When you hear the kernel pop, add in the remaining un popped kernels and the salt. Stir to combine.
5. Close the foil packet and secure by tucking under the lid of the inner pot. Cover with Pressure Lid. Leave the Sear/Sauté on high until to begin to hear the kernels rapidly popping (less than one second between pops), turn the heat down to Medium/Low. Insert a spatula or wooden spoon and stir the bottom to move the kernels around.
6. Once the popping has slowed down to about one pop every few seconds, turn the Ninja Foodi Multi-Cooker off and stir again. If there is any butter left in the foil, shake it over the popcorn and stir.
7. Serve and enjoy!
Nutritional Values Per Serving: Calories: 78, Fat: 7g, Carbs: 4g, Protein: 1g

Loaded Zucchini Chips

Prep Time: 9 Minutes
Cook Time: 23-25 Minutes
Servings: 6
Ingredients:
- 2 medium-sized zucchinis
- 1 cup toasted bread crumbs
- 1.2 cup grated parmesan
- ½ teaspoon kosher salt
- Chili powder ¼ teaspoon
- Black pepper to taste
- 1 beaten egg
- Oil spray

Directions:
1. Start by cutting the ends of the zucchini and then cut it into a round shape. Place a clean towel on a plate. Then place zucchini chips and sprinkle a little salt. Now place another towel on top and then a heavy pan on top.
2. Let it sit for about 12 to 15 minutes for the extra moisture to be drawn out.
3. On the other hand, mix crumbs, salt, pepper, and parmesan at the end. In a separate bowl beat the egg. Place the bowl with egg, crumb mix, and place side by side.
4. Dip the cut zucchini in the egg bowl with one of your hands, now with the other hand, coat it in the crumbs, and place it on a clean plate. At this step spray the zucchini rounds with a good amount of olive oil and let them sit for about 2 minutes.
5. Now you can either spray or brush the Ninja Foodi Multi-Cooker Basket of the Air Crisp with olive oil.
6. Make sure you place the chips in a single layer.
7. Lastly, bake the zucchini chips for 6 minutes at 375° F.

Nutritional Values Per Serving: Calories: 153, Fat: 6 g, Carbs: 11 g, Protein: 11.5 g

Buffalo Cauliflower Platter

Prep Time: 12 Minutes
Cook Time: 12-17 Minutes
Servings: 4
Ingredients:
- 1 medium-sized cauliflower head
- 1 cup of buffalo sauce
- 1 tablespoon of melted butter
- 1 cup of bread crumbs
- Salt to taste

For Sides
- Carrot sticks
- Celery sticks
- 2 tablespoons orange dressing

Directions:
1. Cut the cauliflower into florets and place them in a mixing bowl.
2. Mix the hot sauce and butter in a separate bowl.
3. Now on top of the cauliflower pieces, pour the hot sauce.
4. Let it marinate for 15 minutes, making sure you keep stirring it from time to time. Now in another shallow dish put the bread crumbs and season it with a bit of salt.
5. Now to coat the cauliflower, dip it in the crumb mixture.
6. Place the cauliflower pieces on the Cook & Crisp Basket and make sure to not overlap them.
7. It is recommended to cook this recipe in two batches so that the cauliflower does not get overcrowded.
8. Set the Air Crisp at 390° F and let it cook for about 12 to 15 minutes.
9. Serve these cauliflower buffalo bites with optional orange dressing, carrot, and celery sticks!

Nutritional Values Per Serving: Calories: 201, Fat: 10.1g, Carbs: 18.5g, Protein: 5.8g

Air Crisped Chicken Nuggets

Prep Time: 10 Minutes
Cook Time: 8-10 Minutes
Servings: 6
Ingredients:
- 1 pound minced chicken
- Salt and pepper to taste
- 1 tablespoon olive oil
- 5 tablespoons of season bread crumbs
- 1 tablespoon of panko mix
- 1 tablespoon parmesan cheese (grated)

Directions:
1. At 320° F, preheat the Ninja Foodi Multi-Cooker at Air Crisp Mode for 8 minutes.
2. In a bowl add bread crumbs, panko mix, parmesan cheese, and olive oil.
3. For the seasoning, dump in salt and pepper on the chicken.
4. To ensure the olive oil is evenly coated on all the chicken, put the olive oil well if needed.
5. Shape up the small pieces of chicken that pop out of the batter.
6. Don't add too many chicken chunks at a time into the breadcrumb mixture for the coating purpose. Then place it on the Cook & Crisp Basket and give a slight olive oil spray on the top.
7. Let it Air Crisp for 8 minutes, make sure to turn it halfway until the color is golden!

Nutrition Information per Serving: Calories: 112, Fat: 3.9g, Carbs: 5.5g, Protein: 10.4g

Chapter 3-Pork, Beef & Lamb Recipes

Broccoli Pork with Rice

Prep time: 5 minutes
Cook time: 14 minutes
Servings: 4
Ingredients:
- 1 head broccoli, cut into florets
- 1 tablespoon extra-virgin olive oil
- ¼ teaspoon black pepper
- ¼ teaspoon sea salt
- 1 cup long-grain white rice
- 1 cup water
- 1 trimmed pork tenderloin, cut into 1-inch pieces
- 1 cup teriyaki sauce
- Sesame seeds to garnish

Preparation:
1. In a mixing bowl, combine the broccoli with the olive oil. Season with the ground black pepper and salt.
2. In another bowl, combine the sauce and pork until evenly coated.
3. Take Ninja Foodi multi-cooker, arrange it over a cooking platform, and open the top lid.
4. In the pot, add the water and rice.
5. Seal the Ninja Foodi by locking it with the pressure lid, ensure to keep the pressure release valve locked/sealed.
6. Select "pressure" mode and select the "HI" . Then, set timer to 2 minutes and press "stop/start", it will start the cooking process by building up inside pressure.
7. When the timer goes off, quick release pressure by adjusting the pressure valve to the vent. After pressure gets released, open the pressure lid.
8. Over the rice, arrange the reversible rack and place the pork and broccoli over the rack.
9. Seal the multi-cooker by locking it with the crisping lid, ensure to keep the pressure release valve locked/sealed.
10. Select "broil" mode. Then, set timer to 12 minutes and press "Stop/Start", it will start the cooking process by building up inside pressure.
11. When the timer goes off, quick release pressure by adjusting the pressure valve to the vent.
12. After pressure gets released, open the pressure lid.
13. Serve the pork mixture warm with the cooked rice and some sesame seeds on top.
Nutrition Values Per Serving: Calories: 453, Fat 9.5g, Carbs: 52g, Protein: 39g

Instant Lamb Steaks

Prep time: 3 Minutes
Cook time: 7-8 Minutes
Servings: 1
Ingredients:
- 1 pound lamb steaks
- Olive oil

Dry Ingredients:
- Salt to taste
- Black pepper to taste
- 1 teaspoon paprika powder
- 1 tablespoon garlic powder
- 1 tablespoon ginger powder
- ¼ teaspoon red chili flakes
- 1 teaspoon five-spice powder
- 1 teaspoon oregano

Preparations:
1. Take out the steaks from the refrigerator and allow them to defrost.
2. Preheat the Ninja Foodi at Air Crisp mode at 390° F. Pat dry the lamb steaks and rub them with olive oil.
3. Combine all dry ingredients in a bowl. Press each side of the steaks into the dry mixture then place it in the Ninja Foodi cook & crisp basket.
4. Air Crisp the lamb sticks at medium-rare for 7 to 8 minutes. Instant bread meat treatment can be used to check the internal temperature at 145 degrees F. Dish out the steaks and serve!
Nutrition Values Per Serving: Calories 647, Fat 43.4g, Carbs 8.2g, Protein 1.9g

Pulled Pork

Prep time: 15 minutes
Cook time: 38 minutes
Servings: 6
Ingredients:
- 2 pounds boneless pork shoulder, cut into 1-inch cubes
- 3 tablespoons fresh lemon juice
- 6 garlic cloves, crushed
- 2 teaspoons fresh lemon zest, grated
- 1 teaspoon dried oregano
- 1½ teaspoons red chili powder
- 1 teaspoon ground cumin
- Salt and ground black pepper, as required
- ½ large onion, peeled
- ½ cup homemade chicken broth

Preparation:
1. In the pot of Ninja Foodi, place the pork shoulder, lemon juice, garlic, lemon zest, oregano, chili powder, cumin, salt and black pepper and stir to combine. Top with the onion and broth.
2. Close the Ninja Foodi with pressure lid and place the pressure valve to "Seal" position.
3. Set to Pressure mode at HI for 20 minutes. Press "Start/Stop" to begin cooking. Switch the valve to "Vent" and do a "Quick" release. Remove the onion from the pot and shred the meat.
4. Select "Sear/Sauté" setting of Ninja Foodi and press "Start/Stop" to begin cooking. Cook for about 15 minutes, stirring occasionally.
5. Press "Start/Stop" to stop cooking.
6. Serve hot.
Nutrition Values Per Serving: Calories: 236 Fat: 5.7g Carbs: 3.3g Protein: 40.6g

Honey Glazed Ham

Prep time: 15 minutes
Cook time: 40 minutes
Servings: 4
Ingredients:
- 1 pound/10½ ounces sugar-free ham
- 1 cup homemade chicken broth
- 2 tablespoons French mustard
- 1 tablespoon yacon syrup

Preparation:
1. Place the ham at room temperature for about 30 minutes before cooking.
2. In a bowl, mix together the whiskey, mustard, and yacon syrup.
3. Place the ham in a baking pan with half of the yacon syrup mixture and coat well.
4. Arrange the cook & crisp basket in the pot of Ninja Foodi.
5. Close the Ninja Foodi with crisping lid and select "Air Crisp".
6. Set the temperature to 320 degrees F for 5 minutes.
7. Press "Start/Stop" to begin preheating.
8. After preheating, open the lid.
9. Place the baking pan into the cook & crisp basket.
10. Close the Ninja Foodi with crisping lid and select "Air Crisp".
11. Set the temperature to 320 degrees F for 40 minutes.
12. Press "Start/Stop" to begin cooking.
13. After 15 minutes of cooking, flip the side of ham and top with the remaining yacon syrup mixture.
14. Place the ham onto a platter for about 10 minutes before slicing.
15. Cut into desired size slices and serve.
Nutrition Values Per Serving: Calories: 279 Fat: 14.5g Carbs: 8.7g Protein: 27g

Cabbage & Pork Stew

Prep time: 15 minutes
Cook time: 7½ hours
Servings: 8
Ingredients:
- 2½ pounds boneless country-style pork ribs
- 2½ cups cabbage, chopped
- 2 cups tomatoes, chopped finely
- 1 medium onion, chopped
- 2 garlic cloves, minced
- 2 tablespoons olive oil
- 4 cups homemade chicken broth
- 1 tablespoon fresh oregano, minced
- Salt and ground black pepper, as required
- 3 tablespoons fresh lime juice

Preparation:
1. In the pot of Ninja Foodi, add all ingredients and mix well. Close the Ninja Foodi with crisping lid and select "Slow Cook". Set on "Low" for 7½ hours. Press "Start/Stop" to begin cooking.
2. Transfer pork into large bowl and with 2 forks, shred the meat. Return the shredded pork into the pot and mix well.
3. Serve hot with the drizzling of lime juice.
Nutrition Values Per Serving: Calories: 299 Fat: 15.8g Carbs: 5.4g Protein: 31.2g

Eastern Lamb Stew

Prep time: 1 hour and 30 minutes
Cook time: 60 minutes
Servings: 4
Ingredients:
- 2 tablespoons olive oil
- 1½ pounds lamb stew meat, sliced into cubes
- 1 onion, diced
- 6 garlic cloves, chopped
- 1 teaspoon cumin
- 1 teaspoon coriander
- 1 teaspoon turmeric
- 1 teaspoon cinnamon
- Black pepper and salt to taste
- 2 tablespoons tomato paste
- ¼ cup red wine vinegar
- 2 tablespoons choc zero maple syrup
- 1¼ cups chicken broth
- 15 oz. chickpeas, rinsed and drained

Preparation:
1. Set to Sauté mode in the Ninja Foodi. Stir in the oil. Sauté onion for 3 minutes.
2. Add the lamb and seasonings. Cook for 5 minutes, stirring frequently.
3. Stir in the rest of the ingredients. Cover the pot. Set the pressure to HI.
4. Cook on Pressure mode at High for 50 minutes. Release the pressure naturally.
5. Serve with quinoa.
6. Freeze and serve the next day for a more intense flavor.
Nutritional Values Per Serving: Calories: 867, Fat: 26.6g, Carbs: 87.4g, Protein: 71.2g

Braised Lamb Shanks

Prep time: 20 minutes
Cook time: 46 minutes
Servings: 4
Ingredients:
- 2 tablespoons olive oil
- 4 lamb shanks
- Black pepper and salt to taste
- 4 cloves garlic, minced
- ¾ cup dry red wine
- 1 teaspoon dried basil
- ¾ teaspoons dried oregano
- 28 ounces crushed tomatoes

Preparation:
1. Set the Ninja Foodi to sauté. Stir in the oil. Season the lamb with black pepper and salt.
2. Cook until brown. Remove and set aside. Add the garlic and cook for 15 seconds.
3. Pour in the wine. Simmer for 2 minutes. Stir in the basil, oregano and tomatoes.
4. Put the lamb back to the pot. Seal the pot. Setto Pressure mode at HI.
5. Cook for 45 minutes. Release the pressure naturally.
6. Serve over polenta.
Nutritional Values Per Serving: Calories: 790, Fat: 31g, Carbs: 18.3g, Protein: 96.8g

Roasted Lamb

Prep time: 7 Minutes
Cook time: 25 Minutes
Servings: 4
Ingredients
- 283-gram lamb leg
- 1 tablespoon ginger garlic paste
- 1 teaspoon black pepper
- 1 tablespoon rosemary
- 1 tablespoon olive oil
- 1 tablespoon dried thyme

Preparation:
1. Preheat the Ninja Foodi at Air Crisp Mode at 390° F.
2. Mix olive oil with rosemary, black pepper, ginger garlic paste, and thyme in a bowl. Pat dry the lamb roast leg and then rub the herb oil mixture until it is well-coated. Let it rest to infuse the flavors.
3. Place it carefully in the Ninja Foodi cook & crisp basket and Air Crisp it for 15 minutes.
4. It's recommended to check the temperature with a meat thermometer to ensure that it's cooked according to your preference.
5. Cook it for another 8 to 10 minutes and then wrap it with kitchen foil for 5 minutes and leave it to rest before serving!
Nutrition Values Per Serving: Calories 321, Fat 11.2g, Carbs 49.3g, Protein 21.8g

Lemony Pork Butt

Prep time: 45 minutes
Cook time: 38 minutes
Servings: 5
Ingredients:
- 2 pounds pork butt, cut into 2-inch pieces
- Salt and ground black pepper, as required
- 2-3 tablespoons fresh lemon juice
- 1 yellow onion, peeled and cut in half
- ½ cup homemade chicken broth

Preparation:
1. Season the pork butt with salt and black pepper generously.
2. In the pot of Ninja Foodi, place the pork butt. Place the lemon juice over pork butt.
3. Place the onion and broth over the pork. Close the Ninja Foodi with pressure lid and place the pressure valve to "Seal" position. Select "Pressure" and set to "High" for 20 minutes. Press "Start/Stop" to begin cooking.
4. Switch the valve to "Vent" and do a "Quick" release.
5. Remove the onion from the pot. Select "Sear/Sauté" setting of Ninja Foodi and cook for about 10 minutes. Press "Start/Stop" to stop cooking.
6. Now, close the Ninja Foodi with crisping lid and select "Broil" for 8 minutes. Press "Start/Stop" to begin cooking.
7. Serve hot.
Nutrition Values Per Serving: Calories: 304, Fat: 10.3g, Carbs: 1.9g, Protein: 47.7g

Jamaican Pulled Pork

Prep time: 15 minutes
Cook time: 55 minutes
Servings: 12
Ingredients:
- 4 pounds pork shoulder
- Olive oil cooking spray
- ¼ cup sugar-free Jamaican jerk spice blend
- 1 tablespoon butter
- ½ cup homemade beef broth

Preparation:
1. Spray the pork shoulder with the cooking spray and then, rub with Jamaican Jerk spice blend evenly.
2. Select "Sear/Sauté" setting of Ninja Foodi and place the butter into the pot. Press "Start/Stop" to begin cooking and heat for about 2-3 minutes.
3. Add the pork shoulder and cook, uncovered for about 10 minutes or until browned completely. Press "Start/Stop" to stop cooking and stir in the broth.
4. Close the Ninja Foodi with pressure lid and place the pressure valve to "Seal" position.
5. Select "Pressure" and set to "High" for 45 minutes. Press "Start/Stop" to begin cooking.
6. Switch the valve to "Vent" and do a "Quick" release.
7. With 2 forks, shred the meat and serve hot.
Nutrition Values Per Serving: Calories: 479, Fat: 36.3g, Carbs: 0.1g, Protein: 35.6g

Delicious Pork & Bacon Chili

Prep time: 15 minutes
Cook time: 6 hours 8 minutes
Servings: 8
Ingredients:
- 1 teaspoon olive oil
- 2 pounds ground pork
- 8 thick bacon slices, chopped
- 1 (14-ounce) can diced tomatoes, drained
- 1 onion, chopped
- 3 small green bell peppers, chopped
- 1 (6-ounce) can sugar-free tomato sauce
- 2 tablespoons red chili powder
- ¼ teaspoon garlic powder
- ¼ teaspoon onion powder
- Salt and ground black pepper, as required

Preparation:
1. Select "Sear/Sauté" setting of Ninja Foodi and place the oil into the pot.
2. Press "Start/Stop" to begin cooking and heat for about 2-3 minutes. Add the pork and cook for about 6-8 minutes or until browned completely.
3. Press "Start/Stop" to stop cooking and stir in the remaining ingredients.
4. Close the Ninja Foodi with crisping lid and select "Slow Cook". Set on "Low" for 6 hours. Press "Start/Stop" to begin cooking.
5. Serve hot.
Nutrition Values Per Serving: Calories: 290, Fat: 20.1g, Carbs: 6.7g, Protein: 22.1g

Smothered Pork Chops

Prep Time: 10 minutes
Cook time: 28 minutes
Servings: 4
Ingredients:
- 6 ounces boneless pork loin chops
- 1 tablespoon paprika
- 1 teaspoon garlic powder
- 1 teaspoon onion powder
- 1 teaspoon black pepper
- 1 teaspoon salt
- ¼ teaspoon cayenne pepper
- 2 tablespoon coconut oil
- ½ of a sliced medium onion
- 6 ounces baby Bella mushrooms, sliced
- 1 tablespoon of butter
- ½ cup whip cream
- ¼ teaspoon xanthan gum
- 1 tablespoon parsley, chopped

Preparation:
1. Mix garlic powder, paprika, onion powder, black pepper, salt, and cayenne pepper.
2. Rub the seasoning all over the meat.
3. Reserve the remaining spice mixture.
4. Set your Ninja Foodi to Sauté mode and add coconut oil to heat.
5. Brown the chops 3 minutes per sides.
6. Add sliced onion to the base of your Ninja Foodi along with mushrooms.
7. Top with the browned pork chops, then seal the lid to cook for 10 minutes on High pressure.
8. Release the pressure and remove the lid. Transfer the pork chops to a plate.
9. Set your Ninja Foodi to Sauté mode and whisk in remaining spices mix, heavy cream, and butter
10. Sprinkle ¼ teaspoon of xanthan gum and stir.
11. Simmer for 3-5 minutes and remove the heat.
12. Serve warm with the pork.
Nutrition Values Per Serving: Calories: 481, Fat: 32g, Carbs: 6g, Protein: 39g

Caramelized Pork Butt

Prep time: 45 minutes
Cook time: 38 minutes
Servings: 6
Ingredients:
- 2 tablespoons olive oil
- 2 pounds pork butt, cut in 1-inch pieces
- Salt and ground black pepper, as required
- 4 tablespoons Erythritol
- 3 garlic cloves, minced
- 2 tablespoons red boat fish sauce
- ½ cup water
- ½ cup homemade chicken broth
- 1 small onion, sliced

Preparation:
1. Select "Sear/Sauté" setting of Ninja Foodi and place the butter into the pot. Press "Start/Stop" to begin cooking and heat for about 2-3 minutes.
2. Add the pork, salt and black pepper and cook for about 4-5 minutes or until browned completely.

3. Add the Erythritol and cook for about 2 minutes or until golden brown, stirring continuously. Stir in the garlic and cook for about 1 minute. Press "Start/Stop" to stop cooking and stir in the fish sauce, broth and water.
4. Close the Ninja Foodi with the pressure lid and place the pressure valve to "Seal" position. Select "Pressure" mode and set to "High" for 20 minutes. Press "Start/Stop" to begin cooking.
5. Switch the valve to "Vent" and do a "Natural" release. Select "Sear/Sauté" setting of Ninja Foodi and stir in the onions.
6. Cook for about 5-10 minutes or until desired thickness of sauce.
7. Press "Start/Stop" to stop cooking and serve hot.
Nutrition Values Per Serving: Calories: 347, Fat: 14.9g, Carbs: 1.7g, Protein: 49g

Sausage & Pork Meatloaf

Prep time: 15 minutes
Cook time: 25 minutes
Servings: 4
Ingredients:
- 14 ounces lean ground pork
- 1 gluten-free chorizo sausage, chopped finely
- 1 small onion, chopped
- 1 garlic clove, minced
- 2 tablespoons fresh cilantro, chopped
- 3 tablespoons pork rinds, crushed
- 1 organic egg
- Salt and ground black pepper, as required
- 2 tablespoons fresh mushrooms, sliced thinly
- 2 tablespoons olive oil

Preparation:
1. In a large bowl, add all ingredients except mushrooms and mix until well combined.
2. In a baking pan, place the beef mixture and with the back of a spatula, smooth the surface.
3. Top with mushroom slices and gently, press into the meatloaf.
4. Drizzle with oil evenly.
5. Arrange the "Reversible Rack" in the pot of Ninja Foodi.
6. Close the Ninja Foodi with crisping lid and select "Air Crisp".
7. Set the temperature to 390 degrees F for 5 minutes.
8. Press "Start/Stop" to begin preheating.
9. After preheating, open the lid.
10. Place the pan over the "Reversible Rack".
11. Close the Ninja Foodi with crisping lid and select "Air Crisp".
12. Set the temperature to 390 degrees F for 25 minutes.
13. Press "Start/Stop" to begin cooking.
14. Cut the meatloaf in desires size wedges and serve.
Nutrition Values Per Serving: Calories: 320, Fat: 25.6g, Carbs: 2.1g, Protein: 21.1g

Zesty Pork Meatballs

Prep time: 15 minutes
Cook time: 5 minutes
Servings: 8
Ingredients:
For Meatballs:
- 1½ pounds ground pork
- 2 tablespoons fresh ginger, grated
- 1 tablespoon garlic, minced
- 1 tablespoon lemongrass paste
- 1 teaspoon fresh lime zest, grated
- 2 tablespoons fresh lime juice
- 1 tablespoon low-sodium soy sauce
- ½ tablespoon chili paste
- Salt, as required

For Sauce:
- 1½ cups homemade beef broth
- 1 tablespoon low-sodium soy sauce
- ½ tablespoon red boat fish sauce

Preparation:
1. For meatballs: in a large bowl, add all the ingredients and with your hands, mix until well combined.
2. Make golf ball-sized meatballs from the mixture and arrange onto a large parchment paper-lined baking sheet.
3. Freeze for about 20 minutes.
4. In the pot of Ninja Foodi, place the meatballs and top with broth, soy sauce and fish sauce.
5. Close the Ninja Foodi with the pressure lid and place the pressure valve to "Seal" position.
6. Set to Pressure mode at HI for 5 minutes.
7. Press "Start/Stop" to begin cooking.
8. Switch the valve to "Vent" and do a "Natural" release.
9. Serve hot.
Nutrition Values Per Serving: Calories: 192 Fat: 13.3g Carbs: 2.2g Protein: 16.

Deliciously Spicy Pork Salad Bowl

Prep time: 10 minutes
Cook time: 90 minutes
Servings: 6
Ingredients:
- 4 pounds pork shoulder
- Butter as needed
- 2 teaspoons salt
- 2 cups chicken stock
- 1 teaspoon smoked paprika powder
- 1 teaspoon garlic powder
- 1 teaspoon black pepper
- 1 pinch dried oregano leaves
- 4 tablespoons coconut oil
- 6 garlic cloves

Preparation:
1. Remove rind from pork and cut meat from bone, slice into large chunks.
2. Trim fat off met.
3. Set your Foodi to Sauté mode and add oil, let it heat up.
4. Once the oil is hot, layer chunks of meat in the bottom of the pot and sauté for around 30 minutes until browned.

5. While the meat is being browned, peel garlic cloves and cut into small chunks.
6. Once the meat is browned, transfer it to a large sized bowl.
7. Add a few tablespoons of chicken stock to the pot an deglaze it, scraping off browned bits.
8. Transfer browned bits to the bowl with meat chunks.
9. Repeat if any more meat is left.
10. Once done, add garlic, oregano leaves, smoked paprika, garlic powder, pepper and salt to the meat owl and mix it up.
11. Add all chicken stock to pot and bring to a simmer over Sauté mode.
12. Once done, return seasoned meat to the pot and lock lid, cook on high pressure for 45 minutes. Release pressure naturally over 10 minutes.
13. Open lid and shred the meat using fork, transfer shredded meat to a bowl and pour cooking liquid through a mesh to separate fat into the bowl with shredded meat.
14. Serve with lime and enjoy!
Nutrition Values Per Serving: Calories: 307, Fat: 23g, Carbs: 8g, Protein: 15g

Beef Cooked in Mango-Turmeric Spice

Prep time: 4 minutes
Cook time: 50 minutes
Servings: 2
Ingredients:
- 1 pound beef shin, cut into chunks
- ½ teaspoon ground cinnamon
- ¼ teaspoon ground cloves
- 1 teaspoon dried mango powder
- 1 teaspoon ground turmeric
- ½ teaspoon ground cumin
- 3 cloves of garlic, minced
- 1 tablespoon lemon juice
- 1 teaspoon honey
- 12 cardamom pods, bashed
- Salt and pepper to taste
- 2 tablespoons ghee
- 1 cup onions, cut into wedges
- 2 green chilies, sliced
- 2 tomatoes, chopped
- 1 cup water

Preparation:
1. In a mixing bowl, combine the first 11 ingredients and allow to marinate in the fridge for at least 2 hours.
2. Set the Ninja Foodi to Sear/Sauté mode on the Ninja Foodi and add the ghee. Stir in the marinated beef and sear on both sides for at least 5 minutes.
3. Stir in the rest of the ingredients.
4. Install pressure lid. Close Ninja Foodi, set to Pressure mode at high, and set time to 45 minutes.
5. Once done cooking, do a quick release.
6. Serve and enjoy.
Nutrition Values Per Serving: Calories 463, fat: 20g, Carbs: 19.3g, protein: 51.5g

Cheesy Pork Sausage

Prep time: 15 minutes
Cook time: 20 minutes
Servings: 6
Ingredients:
- 2 pounds gluten-free pork sausages, casing removed and crumbled
- 16 ounces sugar-free marinara sauce
- 10 ounces Parmesan cheese, shredded
- 16 ounces mozzarella cheese, shredded

Preparation:
1. Close the Ninja Foodi with crisping lid and select "Bake/Roast".
2. Set the temperature to 360 degrees F for 5 minutes.
3. Press "Start/Stop" to begin preheating.
4. After preheating, open the lid.
5. Grease the pot of Ninja Foodi generously.
6. In the prepared pot, arrange half of the sausages and top with half of the marinara sauce, followed by half of the mozzarella and Parmesan cheese.
7. Repeat the layer once.
8. Close the Ninja Foodi with crisping lid and select "Bake/Roast".
9. Set the temperature to 360 degrees F for 20 minutes.
10. Press "Start/Stop" to begin cooking.
11. Serve hot.
Nutrition Values Per Serving: Calories: 916, Fat: 68g, Carbs: 9g, Protein: 65g

Tasty Ground Pork Soup

Prep time: 15 minutes
Cook time: 30 minutes
Servings: 6
Ingredients:
- 1 tablespoon olive oil
- 1½ pounds ground pork
- 1 onion, chopped
- 2 cups carrots, peeled and chopped
- 2 cups green beans, trimmed and cut into pieces
- 5 cups homemade chicken broth
- ⅔ cup low-sodium soy sauce
- Ground black pepper, as required

Preparation:
1. Select "Sear/Sauté" setting of Ninja Foodi and place the butter into the pot. Press "Start/Stop" to begin cooking and heat for about 2-3 minutes.
2. Add the pork and cook for about 5 minutes or until browned completely. Press "Start/Stop" to stop cooking and stir in the remaining ingredients.
3. Close the Ninja Foodi with pressure lid and place the pressure valve to "Seal" position. Select "Pressure" and set to "High" for 25 minutes.
4. Press "Start/Stop" to begin cooking. Switch the valve to "Vent" and do a "Quick" release.
5. Serve hot.
Nutrition Values Per Serving: Calories: 303, Fat: 19.4g, Carbs: 9g, Protein: 23.8g

Sweet & Sour Pork Butt

Prep time: 70 minutes
Cook time: 1 hour
Servings: 6
Ingredients:
- 1 tablespoon garlic, minced
- ¼ cup red boat fish sauce
- 1 tablespoon fresh lime juice
- 2 tablespoons Erythritol
- 1 teaspoon five-spice powder
- Ground black pepper, as required
- 2½ pounds pork butt

Preparation:
1. For sauce: in a bowl, place the pork butt and top with the sauce evenly. Close the Ninja Foodi with the pressure lid and place the pressure valve to "Seal" position.
2. Select "Pressure" and set to "High" for 60 minutes. Press "Start/Stop" to begin cooking. Switch the valve to "Vent" and do a "Natural" release.
3. With tongs, place the pork butt onto a cutting board for about 5 minutes.
4. Cut into desired sized slices and serve with the topping of pan sauce.
Nutrition Values Per Serving: Calories: 283, Fat: 9.5g, Carbs: 0.4g, Protein: 46.2g

Cheddar Meatballs

Prep time: 15 minutes
Cook time: 14 minutes
Servings: 2
Ingredients:
- ½ pound ground pork
- 1 onion, chopped
- 1 teaspoon garlic paste
- 2 tablespoons fresh basil, chopped
- 1 teaspoon mustard
- 1 teaspoon yacon syrup
- 1 tablespoon Cheddar cheese, grated
- Salt and ground black pepper, as required

Preparation:
1. In a bowl, add all ingredients and mix until well combined.
2. Make small equal-sized balls from the mixture.
3. Arrange the greased cook & crisp basket in the pot of Ninja Foodi.
4. Close the Ninja Foodi with crisping lid and select "Air Crisp".
5. Set the temperature to 390 degrees F for 5 minutes.
6. Press "Start/Stop" to begin preheating.
7. After preheating, open the lid.
8. Place the meatballs into the cook & crisp basket.
9. Close the Ninja Foodi with crisping lid and select "Air Crisp".
10. Set the temperature to 390 degrees F for 14 minutes.
11. Press "Start/Stop" to begin cooking.
12. Serve hot.
Nutrition Values Per Serving: Calories: 205, Fat: 5.7g, Carbs: 5.4g, Protein: 31.5g

Southern-Style Lettuce Wraps

Prep time: 10 minutes
Cook time: 30 minutes
Servings: 6
Ingredients:
- 3 pounds boneless pork shoulder, cut into 1- to 2-inch cubes
- 2 cups light beer
- 1 cup brown sugar
- 1 teaspoon chipotle chiles in adobo sauce
- 1 cup barbecue sauce
- 1 head iceberg lettuce, quartered and leaves separated
- 1 cup roasted peanuts, chopped or ground
- Cilantro leaves

Preparation:
1. Place the pork, beer, brown sugar, chipotle, and barbecue sauce in the pot. Assemble pressure lid, making sure the pressure release valve is in the seal position.
2. Select pressure and set to HI. Set the timer to 30 minutes. Select Start/Stop to begin.
3. When pressure cooking is complete, quick release the pressure by turning the pressure release valve to the Vent position. Carefully remove lid when unit has finished releasing pressure.
4. Using a silicone-tipped utensil, shred the pork in the pot. Stir to mix the meat in with the sauce.
5. Place a small amount of pork in a piece of lettuce. Top with peanuts and cilantro to serve.
Nutrition Values Per Serving: Calories: 811, Fat 58g, Carbs: 22g, Protein: 45g

Bacon-Wrapped Hot Dogs

Prep time: 15 minutes
Cook time: 15 minutes
Servings: 3
Ingredients:
- 4 beef hot dogs
- 4 bacon strips
- Cooking spray
- 4 bakery hot dog buns, split and toasted
- ½ red onion, chopped
- 1 cup sauerkraut, rinsed and drained

Preparation:
1. Place cook & crisp basket in pot. Close crisping lid. Select Air Crisp, set temperature to 360°F, and set time to 5 minutes. Select Start/Stop to begin preheating.
2. Wrap each hot dog with 1 strip of bacon, securing it with toothpicks as needed.
3. Once unit has preheated, open lid and coat the basket with cooking spray. Place the hot dogs in the basket in a single layer. Close crisping lid.
4. Select Air Crisp, set temperature to 360°F, and set time to 15 minutes. Select Start/Stop to begin.
5. After 10 minutes, open lid and check doneness. If needed, continue cooking until it reaches your desired doneness.
6. When cooking is complete, place the hot dog in the buns with the onion and sauerkraut. Top, if desired, with condiments of your choice, such as yellow mustard, ketchup, or mayonnaise.
Nutrition Values Per Serving: Calories: 336, Fat: 17g, Carbs: 27g, Protein: 20g

Beef Pork Chili

Prep Time: 10 minutes
Cook time: 35 minutes
Servings: 4
Ingredients:
- 1 pound ground beef
- 1 pound ground pork
- 3 tomatillos, chopped
- 1 teaspoon garlic powder
- 1 jalapeno pepper
- 1 tablespoon ground cumin
- 1 tablespoon Chilli powder
- Salt as needed

Preparation:
1. Set your Ninja Foodi to Sauté mode and add beef and pork. Sauté until brown.
2. Add onion, garlic, tomatillo, tomato paste, jalapeno, cumin, water, Chilli powder, and mix well.
3. Seal the lid and cook on "Pressure" mode on High for 35 minutes.
4. Release the Pressure naturally, then remove the lid.
5. Serve and enjoy!
Nutrition Values Per Serving: Calories: 325, Fat: 23g, Carbs: 6g, Protein: 20g

Special "Swiss" Pork chops

Prep time: 5 minutes
Cook time: 18 minutes
Servings: 4
Ingredients:
- ½ cup Swiss cheese, shredded
- 4 pork chops, bone-in
- 6 bacon strips, cut in half
- Salt and pepper to taste
- 1 tablespoon butter

Preparation:
1. Season pork chops with salt and pepper
2. Set your Foodi to Sauté mode and add butter, let the butter heat up.
3. Add pork chops and sauté for 3 minutes on each side.
4. Add bacon strips and Swiss cheese.
5. Lock lid and cook on low pressure for 15 minutes.
6. Release pressure naturally over 10 minutes.
7. Transfer steaks to serving platter, serve and enjoy!
Nutrition Values Per Serving: Calories: 483, Fat: 40g, Carbs:0.7g, Protein: 27g

Beef Pot Pie

Prep time: 6 minutes
Cook time: 25 minutes
Servings: 2
Ingredients:
- 1 ½ tablespoons butter
- ½ cup diced onion
- ½ cup diced celery
- 2 cloves garlic, minced
- 6 ounces beef
- 1 teaspoon dried thyme
- ¾ cup potatoes, diced
- ⅓ cup carrots, diced
- ⅓ cup frozen peas
- ¼ cups beef broth
- 2 tablespoons milk
- 1 tablespoon cornstarch + 1 ½ tablespoons water
- ½ box puff pastry
- 1 egg white

Preparation:
1. Set the Ninja Foodi to Sauté mode and heat the butter. Sauté the onion, celery and garlic until fragrant. Add the beef and sear button for 5 minutes.
2. Stir in the thyme, potatoes, carrots, frozen peas, beef broth and milk.
3. Install pressure lid. Close Ninja Foodi, set to Pressure mode at HI, and set time to 10 minutes.
4. Once done cooking, do a quick release.
5. Ladle into two ramekins and cover the top of the ramekins with puff pastry. Brush the top with egg whites.
6. Place in Ninja Foodi, bake at 350 degreesF for 10 minutes or until tops are lightly browned.
Nutrition Values Per Serving: Calories 328, fat: 15.3g, Carbs: 26.6g, protein: 20.8g

Classic Pork Meal with Green Bean

Prep time: 5 minutes
Cook time: 25 minutes
Servings: 4
Ingredients:
- 2 pounds pork stew meat, cut into small cubes
- 1 tablespoon avocado oil
- 1 pound green beans, trimmed and halved
- 2 minced garlic cloves
- 1 tablespoon basil, chopped
- 1 teaspoon chili powder
- ¾ cup veggie stock
- A pinch of black pepper and salt

Preparation:
1. Take Ninja Foodi, arrange it over a cooking platform, and open the top lid.
2. In the pot, add the oil, Select "Sear/Sauté" mode and select "MD: HI" level.
3. Press "Stop/Start". After about 4-5 minutes, the oil will start simmering.
4. Add the meat, garlic, and stir-cook for about 4-5 minutes to brown evenly.
5. Add the remaining ingredients, stir well.

6. Seal the multi-cooker by locking it with the pressure lid, ensure to keep the pressure release valve locked/sealed.
7. Select "pressure" mode and select the "HI" pressure level. Then, set timer to 20 minutes and press "Stop/Start", it will start the cooking process by building up inside pressure.
8. When the timer goes off, naturally release inside pressure for about 8-10 minutes. Then, quick-release pressure by adjusting the pressure valve to the vent.
9. After pressure gets released, open the pressure lid.
10. Serve warm.
Nutrition Values Per Serving: Calories: 403, Fat: 15.5g, Carbs: 18g, Protein: 53.5g

Beef 'n Mushrooms in Thick Sauce

Prep time: 5 minutes
Cook time: 30 minutes
Servings: 2
Ingredients:
- ½ tablespoon butter
- ½ pound beef chunks
- Salt and pepper to taste
- ½ cup onions, chopped
- ½ tablespoon garlic, minced
- 1 carrot, sliced diagonally
- ¼ cup chopped celery
- ⅓ cup mushrooms, halved
- 1 medium potato, peeled and quartered
- 1 tablespoon Worcestershire sauce
- 1 tablespoon tomato paste
- ½ cup chicken broth
- 1 tablespoon all-purpose flour + 1 tablespoon water

Preparation:
1. Set the Ninja Foodi to Sauté mode and melt the butter. Sear the beef chunks and season with salt and pepper to taste. Add the onions and garlic until fragrant.
2. Stir in the carrots, celery, mushrooms and potatoes.
3. Add the Worcestershire sauce, tomato paste, and chicken broth. Season with more salt and pepper to taste.
4. Install pressure lid. Close Ninja Foodi, set to Pressure mode at High, and set time to 30 minutes.
5. Once done cooking, do a quick release.
6. Open the lid and set the Ninja Foodi to Sauté mode. Stir in the all-purpose flour and allow to simmer until the sauce thickens.
7. Serve and enjoy.
Nutrition Values Per Serving: Calories 539, Fat: 13.1g, Carbs: 61.3g, Protein 43.9g

Healthy 'n Tasty Meatloaf

Prep time: 7 minutes
Cook time: 20 minutes
Servings: 2
Ingredients:
- ¾ pound ground beef
- ¾ cup bread crumbs
- ⅓ cup parmesan cheese
- 2 small eggs, beaten
- 1 tablespoon minced garlic
- 1 teaspoon steak seasoning
- Salt and pepper to taste
- 1 ½ teaspoons sear button sugar
- ¼ cup ketchup
- ½ tablespoon mustard
- 1 teaspoon Worcestershire sauce

Preparation:
1. Place a trivet in the Ninja Foodi and pour a cup of beef broth.
2. In a mixing bowl, mix together the beef, bread crumbs, cheese, eggs, garlic, and steak seasoning. Season with salt and pepper to taste.
3. Pour meat mixture in a heat-proof pan and place on top of the trivet. Cover top with foil.
4. Install pressure lid. Close Ninja Foodi, set to Steam mode, and set time to 20 minutes.
5. While waiting for the meatloaf to cook, combine in a saucepan the sugar, ketchup, mustard, and Worcestershire sauce. Mix until the sauce becomes thick.
6. Once done cooking, do a quick release.
7. Remove the meatloaf from the Ninja Foodi and allow to cool.
8. Serve with sauce and enjoy.
Nutrition Values Per Serving: Calories 574, Fat: 32.7g, Carbs: 23.2g, protein: 46.6g

Tangy Pork Carnitas

Prep time: 10 minutes
Cook time: 25 minutes
Servings: 6
Ingredients:
- 2 pounds pork shoulder, bone-in
- 2 tablespoons butter, melted
- 2 oranges, juiced
- Ground black pepper and salt to taste
- 1 teaspoon garlic powder
- 5-6 warmed carnitas

Preparation:
1. Season the pork with salt, garlic powder, and black pepper.
2. Take Ninja Foodi multi-cooker, arrange it over a cooking platform, and open the top lid.
3. In the pot, add the butter, Select "Sear/Sauté" mode and select "MD: HI" pressure level.
4. Press "Stop/Start." After about 4-5 minutes, the butter will start simmering.
5. Add the meat and stir cook for about 2-3 minutes to brown evenly. Stir in orange juice.
6. Seal the multi-cooker by locking it with the pressure lid, ensure to keep the pressure release valve locked/sealed.
7. Select "Pressure" mode and select the "HI" pressure level. Then, set timer to 15 minutes

and press "Stop/Start", it will start the cooking process by building up inside pressure.
8. When the timer goes off, naturally release inside pressure for about 8-10 minutes. Then, quick-release pressure by adjusting the pressure valve to the vent.
9. Select "Broil" mode. Then, set timer to 15 minutes and press "Stop/Start", it will start the cooking process by building up inside pressure.
10. When the timer goes off, quick release pressure by adjusting the pressure valve to the vent.
11. After pressure gets released, open the pressure lid.
12. Shred the meat and remove the bones. Add the mixture over the carnitas, fold and serve warm.
Nutrition Values Per Serving: Calories: 486, Fat: 32g, Carbs: 9g, Protein: 34g

Beef Stew Recipe from Ethiopia

Prep time: 6 minutes
Cook time: 55 minutes
Servings: 2
Ingredients:
- 1 pound beef stew meat, cut into chunks
- ¼ teaspoon turmeric powder
- 1 tablespoon garam masala
- 1 tablespoon coriander powder
- 1 teaspoon cumin
- ¼ teaspoon ground nutmeg
- 2 teaspoons smoked paprika
- ¼ teaspoon black pepper
- 2 tablespoons ghee
- 1 onion, chopped
- 1 tablespoon ginger, grated
- 2 cloves of garlic, grated
- 1 tablespoon onions
- 3 tablespoons tomato paste
- ½ teaspoon sugar
- Salt and pepper to taste
- 1 cup water

Preparation:
1. In a mixing bowl, combine the first 8 ingredients and allow to marinate in the fridge for at least 4 hours.
2. Set the Ninja Foodi to Sauté mode and heat the oil. Sauté the onion, ginger, and garlic until fragrant. Stir in the marinated beef and allow to sear button for 3 minutes.
3. Stir in the rest of the ingredients.
4. Install pressure lid. Close Ninja Foodi, set to Pressure mode at High, and set time to 50 minutes.
5. Once done cooking, do a quick release.
6. Serve and enjoy.
Nutrition Values Per Serving: Calories 591, Fat: 23.4g, Carbs: 11.5g, protein: 83.5g

Indian Beef Meal

Prep Time: 10 minutes
Cook time: 20 minutes
Servings: 4
Ingredients:
- ½ yellow onion, chopped
- 1 tablespoon olive oil
- 2 garlic cloves, minced
- 1 jalapeno pepper, chopped
- 1 cup cherry tomatoes, quartered
- 1 teaspoon fresh lemon juice
- 1-2 pounds grass-fed ground beef
- 1-2 pounds fresh collard greens, trimmed and chopped

Spices
- 1 teaspoon cumin, ground
- ½ teaspoon ginger, ground
- 1 teaspoon coriander, ground
- ½ teaspoon fennel seeds, ground
- ½ teaspoon cinnamon, ground
- Salt and black pepper, to taste
- ½ teaspoon turmeric, ground

Preparation:
1. Set your Ninja Foodi to Sauté mode, add garlic and onion, then sauté for 3 minutes.
2. Add Jalapeno pepper, beef, spices and stir well.
3. Lock the Ninja Foodi's lid and cook on "Pressure" mode on low for 15 minutes.
4. Release pressure naturally and remove the lid.
5. Add tomatoes and collard, sauté for 3 minutes
6. Stir in lemon juice, salt, and black pepper, then mix well.
7. Serve and enjoy!
Nutrition Values Per Serving: Calories: 409, Fat: 16g, Carbs: 5g, Protein: 56g

Perfect Sichuan Pork Soup

Prep time: 10 minutes
Cook time: 20 minutes
Servings: 6
Ingredients:
- 2 tablespoons olive oil
- 1 tablespoon garlic, minced
- 1 tablespoon fresh ginger, minced
- 2 tablespoons coconut aminos
- 2 tablespoons black vinegar
- 1-2 teaspoons stevia
- 1-2 teaspoons salt
- ½ onion, sliced
- 1 pound pork shoulder, cut into 2-inch chunks
- 2 pepper corns, crushed
- 3 cups water
- 3-4 cups bok choy, chopped
- ¼ cup fresh cilantro, chopped

Preparation:
1. Preheat your Ninja Foodi by setting it to Sauté mode on HIGH temperature.
2. Once the inner pot it hot enough, add oil and let heat until shimmering.
3. Add garlic and ginger and Saute for 1-2 minutes.

4. Add coconut aminos, vinegar, sweetener, pepper corn, salt, onion, pork, water and stir.
5. Lock lid and cook on Pressure mode at High for 20 minutes.
6. Release pressure naturally over 10 minutes.
7. Open lid and add bok choy, close lid and let it cook in the remaining heat for 10 minutes.
8. Ladle soup into serving bowl and serve with topping of cilantro.
9. Enjoy!
Nutrition Values Per Serving: Calories: 256, Fat: 20g, Carbs: 5g, Protein: 14g

Potatoes, Beefy-Cheesy Way

Prep time: 5 minutes
Cook time: 25 minutes
Servings: 2
Ingredients:
- ½ pound ground beef
- 2 large potatoes, peeled and chopped
- ¾ cup cheddar cheese, shredded
- ¼ cup chicken broth
- ½ tablespoon Italian seasoning mix
- Salt and pepper to taste

Preparation:
1. Set the Ninja Foodi to Sauté mode and stir in the beef. Sear the meat until some of the oil has rendered.
2. Add the rest of the ingredients.
3. Install pressure lid.
4. Close Ninja Foodi, set to Pressure mode at High, and set time to 20 minutes.
5. Once done cooking, do a quick release.
Nutrition Values Per Serving: Calories 801, Fat: 35.6g, Carbs: 66.8g, protein: 53.4g

Authentic Beginner Friendly Pork Belly

Prep time: 10 minutes
Cook time: 40 minutes
Servings: 4
Ingredients:
- 1 pound pork belly
- ½-1 cup white wine vinegar
- 1 garlic clove
- 1 tablespoon olive oil
- Salt and pepper to taste

Preparation:
1. Set your Ninja Foodi to "Sauté" mode and add oil, let it heat up.
2. Add pork and sear for 2-3 minutes until both sides are golden and crispy.
3. Add vinegar until about a quarter inch, season with salt, pepper and garlic.
4. Add garlic clove and Saute until the liquid comes to a boil.
5. Lock lid and cook on high pressure for 40 minutes.
6. Once done, quick release pressure.
7. Slice the meat and serve with the sauce.
8. Enjoy!
Nutrition Values Per Serving: Calories: 331, Fat: 21g, Carbs: 2g, Protein: 19g

Pork and Eggplant Casserole

Prep time: 20 minutes
Cook time: 3 hours
Servings: 10
Ingredients:
- 2 cups eggplant cubed
- Salt, as required
- 1 tablespoon olive oil
- 2 pounds lean ground pork
- 2 teaspoons Worcestershire sauce
- 2 teaspoons mustard
- Ground black pepper, as required
- 28 ounces canned diced tomatoes drained
- 16 ounces canned tomato sauce
- 2 cups mozzarella cheese, grated
- 2 tablespoons fresh parsley, chopped
- 1 teaspoon dried oregano

Preparation:
1. Select "Sear/Sauté" setting of Ninja Foodi and place the butter into the pot.
2. Press "Start/Stop" to begin cooking and heat for about 2-3 minutes.
3. Add the pork and cook for about 5 minutes or until browned completely.
4. In a colander, place the eggplant and sprinkle with salt.
5. Set aside for about 30 minutes.
6. Transfer the eggplant into bowl and mix with olive oil.
7. In another bowl, add the pork, Worcestershire sauce, mustard, salt and black pepper and mix well.
8. In the greased pot of Ninja Foodi, place the pork mixture and top with eggplant.
9. Spread tomatoes and sauce over eggplant and sprinkle with cheese, followed by parsley and oregano.
10. Close the Ninja Foodi with crisping lid and select "Slow Cook".
11. Set on "High" for 3 hours.
12. Press "Start/Stop" to begin cooking.
13. Serve hot.
Nutrition Values Per Serving: Calories: 192, Fat: 6.1g, Carbs: 7.3g, Protein: 22.1g

Healthy Cranberry BBQ Pork

Prep time: 10 minutes
Cook time: 45 minutes
Servings: 4
Ingredients:
- 3-4 pounds pork shoulder, boneless, fat trimmed
- 3 tablespoons liquid smoke
- 2 tablespoons tomato paste
- 2 cups fresh cranberries
- ¼ cup hot sauce
- ⅓ cup blackstrap molasses
- ½ cup water
- ½ cup apple cider vinegar
- 1 teaspoon salt
- 1 tablespoons adobo sauce
- 1 cup tomato puree
- 1 chipotle pepper in adobo sauce, diced

Preparation:
1. Cut pork against halves/thirds and keep it on the side.

2. Set your Ninja Foodi to "Sauté" mode and let it heat up.
3. Add cranberries and water to the pot.
4. Let them simmer for 4-5 minutes until cranberries start to pop, add rest of the sauce ingredients and simmer for 5 minutes more.
5. Add pork to the pot and lock lid.
6. Cook on high pressure for 40 minutes.
7. Quick release pressure.
8. Use fork to shred the pork and serve on your favorite greens.
Nutrition Values Per Serving: Calories: 250, Fat: 17g, Carbs: 5g, Protein: 15g

Ninja Foodi Minced Beef with Tomatoes

Prep Time: 10 minutes
Cook Time: 10 hours
Servings: 4
Ingredients:
- ¾ cup chopped tomatoes
- ½ cup water
- ½ pound minced beef
- 1½ tablespoons mixed herbs
- Salt and black pepper, to taste

Directions:
1. Mix all the ingredients in a Ninja Foodi Multi-cooker and select "Slow Cook".
2. Close the pressure Lid and press the "Start/Stop" button.
3. Cook for about 8-hours on LOW TEMP and open the lid.
4. Take out, serve and enjoy!
Nutritional Values Per Serving: Calories: 116, Fat: 3.7g, Carbs: 2.3g, Protein: 17.7g

Ninja Foodi Steak Fajitas
Prep Time: 10 minutes
Cook Time: 8 hours
Servings: 3
Ingredients:
- 1 pound beef, trimmed and sliced
- 1¼ cups salsa
- 1 tablespoon fajita seasoning
- ½ bell pepper, sliced
- ½ onion, sliced
- Salt and black pepper, to taste

Directions:
1. Place salsa in the bottom of Ninja Foodi Multi-cooker and top it with fajita seasoning, onion, beef, bell pepper, salt and pepper.
2. Stir well and select "Slow Cook".
3. Close the pressure Lid and cook for about 8 hours.
4. Open the lid and take out.
5. Serve and enjoy!
Nutritional Values Per Serving: Calories: 369, Fat: 9.9g, Carbs: 20.3g, Protein: 49.9g

St. Patty's Corned Beef Recipe

Prep time: 6 minutes
Cook time: 60 minutes
Servings: 2
Ingredients:
- 2 cloves of garlic, chopped
- ½ onion, quartered
- 1 ¼ pounds corned beef brisket, cut in large slices
- 3 ounces Beer
- 1 cup water
- 2 small carrots, roughly chopped
- 1 small potato, chopped
- ½ head cabbage, cut into four pieces

Preparation:
1. In the Ninja Foodi, place the garlic, onion, corned beef brisket, beer, and water. Season with salt and pepper to taste.
2. Install pressure lid. Close Ninja Foodi, set to Pressure mode at HI, and set time to 50 minutes.
3. Once done cooking, do a quick release. Open the lid and take out the meat. Shred the meat using fork and place it back into the Ninja Foodi.
4. Stir in the vegetables.
5. Install pressure lid. Close the lid and seal the vent and set to Pressure mode. Cook for another 10 minutes. Do quick release.
Nutrition Values Per Serving: Calories 758, Fat: 44.7g, Carbs: 45.8g, protein: 43.1g

Beefy Stew Recipe from Persia

Prep time: 6 minutes
Cook time: 20 minutes
Servings: 2
Ingredients:
- 1 tablespoon vegetable oil
- 1 onion, chopped
- 2 cloves garlic, minced
- ¾ pound beef stew meat, cut into chunks
- ½ tablespoon ground cumin
- ¼ teaspoon saffron threads
- ½ teaspoon turmeric
- ¼ teaspoon ground cinnamon
- ¼ teaspoon ground allspice
- Salt and pepper to taste
- 2 tablespoons tomato paste
- ½ can split peas, rinsed and drained
- 2 cups bone broth
- 1 can crushed tomatoes
- 2 tablespoons lemon juice, freshly squeezed

Preparation:
1. Set the Ninja Foodi to Sauté mode. Heat the oil and sauté the onion and garlic until fragrant.
2. Add cumin, saffron, turmeric, cinnamon, and allspice. Stir in the beef and sear button for 3 minutes. Season with salt and pepper to taste.
3. Pour in the rest of the ingredients.
4. Install pressure lid. Close Ninja Foodi, set to Pressure mode at HI, and set time to 20 minutes.
5. Once done cooking, do a quick release.
Nutrition Values Per Serving: Calories 466, Fat: 14g, Carbs: 36g, Protein: 49g

Mexican Beef Short Ribs

Prep Time: 10 minutes
Cook time: 35 minutes
Servings: 4
Ingredients:
- 2 and ½ pounds boneless beef short ribs
- 1 tablespoon Chilli powder
- 1 and ½ teaspoons salt
- 1 tablespoon fat
- 1 medium onion, thinly sliced
- 1 tablespoon tomato sauce
- 6 garlic cloves, peeled and smashed
- ½ cup roasted tomato salsa
- ½ cup bone broth
- Fresh black pepper
- ½ cup cilantro, minced
- 2 radishes, sliced

Preparation:
1. Mix beef, salt, Chilli powder in a suitable bowl.
2. Set the Ninja Foodi to Sauté mode, add butter to melt.
3. Add garlic, tomato paste, then sauté for 30 seconds
4. Add beef stock and fish sauce on top.
5. Lock the Ninja Foodi's lid and cook on "Pressure" mode on HIGH for 35 minutes.
6. Naturally, release pressure, then remove the lid.
7. Enjoy!
Nutrition Values Per Serving: Calories: 308, Fat: 18g, Carbs: 21g, Protein: 38g

Adobo Beef Steak

Prep Time: 5 minutes
Cook time: 25 minutes
Servings: 4
Ingredients:
- 2 cups water
- 8 steaks, cubed, 28 ounces pack
- Black pepper to taste
- 1 and ¾ teaspoons adobo seasoning
- 1 can (8 ounces) tomato sauce
- ⅓ cup green pitted olives
- 2 tablespoons brine
- 1 small red pepper
- ½ a medium onion, sliced

Preparation:
1. Chop onions and peppers into ¼-inch strips
2. Season the beef with pepper and adobo.
3. Add to the Ninja Foodi's insert, then add remaining ingredients and close the Ninja's lid.
4. Cook on "Pressure" mode for 25 minutes on HIGH.
5. Release pressure naturally, then remove the lid.
6. Serve and enjoy!
Nutrition Values Per Serving: Calories: 429, Fat: 24g, Carbs: 11g, Protein: 31g

Tomato Beef Stew

Prep Time: 11 minutes
Cook time: 10 minutes
Servings: 4
Ingredients:
- 1 pound beef roast
- 4 cups beef broth
- 2 tomatoes, chopped
- ½ white onion, chopped
- 3 garlic cloves, chopped
- 1 carrot, chopped
- 2 celery stalks, chopped
- ¼ teaspoon salt
- ⅛ teaspoon black pepper

Preparation:
1. Add beef roast along with all ingredients to your Ninja Foodi's inset.
2. Cover the Foodi's lid and seal it for pressure cooking.
3. Cook on "Pressure" mode for 10 minutes on HIGH.
4. Release pressure naturally, then remove the lid.
5. Serve and enjoy!
Nutrition Values Per Serving: Calories: 529, Fat: 4g, Carbs: 1g, Protein: 31g

Jamaican Pork Meal

Prep Time: 10 minutes
Cook time: 30 minutes
Servings: 4
Ingredients:
- ½ cup beef stock
- 1 tablespoon olive oil
- ¼ cup Jamaican jerk spice blend
- 4 ounces pork shoulder

Preparation:
1. Rub roast with olive oil and spice blend.
2. Set your Ninja Foodi to Sauté mode and add meat, brown all sides.
3. Pour beef broth and seal the lid.
4. Cook on "Pressure" cook mode at High for 30 minutes.
5. Release the pressure completely then re-move the lid and shred the meat.
6. Serve warm.
Nutrition Values Per Serving: Calories: 308, Fat: 18g, Carbs: 5g, Protein: 31g

Onion Pork Chops

Prep Time: 10 minutes
Cook time: 20 minutes
Servings: 4
Ingredients:
- 4 pork chops
- 10 ounces French Onion Soup
- ½ cup sour cream
- 10 ounces chicken broth

Preparation:
1. Add pork chops and broth to your Ninja Foodi's insert.
2. Lock the Ninja Foodi's lid and cook on "Pres-sure" mode at High for 12 minutes

3. Release pressure naturally over 10 minutes, then remove the lid.
4. Whisk sour cream and French Onion Soup and pour mixture over pork
5. Set your Ninja Foodi to Sauté mode and cook for 6-8 minutes more
6. Serve and enjoy!
Nutrition Values Per Serving: Calories: 356, Fat: 26g, Carbs: 7g, Protein: 21g

Ranch Beef Roast

Prep Time: 10 minutes
Cook time: 60 minutes
Servings: 4
Ingredients:
- 3 pounds beef roast
- 1 tablespoon olive oil
- 2 tablespoons ranch dressing
- 1 jar pepper rings, with juices
- 8 tablespoons butter
- 1 cup water

Preparation:
1. Set your Ninja Foodi to Sauté mode and add 1 tablespoon of oil.
2. Once the oil is hot, add roast and sear on both sides.
3. Add water, reserved juice, seasoning mix, and pepper rings on top of the beef.
4. Seal the lid and cook on "Pressure" mode on HIGH for 60 minutes.
5. Release the pressure naturally over 10 minutes.
6. Cut the beef with salad sheers and enjoy with pureed cauliflower.
7. Enjoy!
Nutrition Values Per Serving: Calories: 365, Fat: 18g, Carbs: 12g, Protein: 16g

New York Steak

Prep Time: 10 minutes
Cook time: 9 minutes
Servings: 4
Ingredients:
- 24 ounces NY strip steak
- ½ teaspoon black pepper
- 1 teaspoon salt

Preparation:
1. Add steaks on a metal trivet, place it on your Ninja Foodi.
2. For seasoning, add salt and black pepper on top.
3. Add 1 cup water to the Ninja Foodi's pot.
4. Cover the Foodi's lid and seal it for pressure cooking.
5. Cook on "Pressure" mode for 1 minute on HIGH.
6. Release pressure naturally, then remove the lid.
7. Place crisping lid and cook on the "Air Crisp" mode for 8 minutes for a medium-steak.
8. Serve and enjoy!
Nutrition Values Per Serving: Calories: 503, Fat: 46g, Carbs: 1g, Protein: 46g

Lemon Pork Cutlets

Prep Time: 10 minutes
Cook time: 5 minutes
Servings: 4
Ingredients:
- ½ cup hot sauce
- ½ cup water
- 2 tablespoons butter
- ⅓ cup lemon juice
- 1 pound pork cutlets
- ½ teaspoon paprika

Preparation:
1. Add pork cutlets and all other listed ingredients to the Ninja Foodi
2. Lock the Ninja Foodi's lid and cook on "Pressure" mode at High for 5 minutes.
3. Now release the cooker's pressure naturally for 10 minutes, then remove the lid.
4. Gently mix and serve warm.
Nutrition Values Per Serving: Calories: 414, Fat: 21g, Carbs: 3g, Protein: 50g

Kale Sausage Soup

Prep Time: 5-10 minutes
Cook time: 10 minutes
Servings: 4
Ingredients:
- ½ diced onion
- 2 cups chicken broth
- 1 pound chopped sausage roll
- 1 tablespoon olive oil
- 2 cups almond milk
- ½ cup parmesan cheese
- 3 cups chopped kale fresh
- 28 ounces tomatoes, crushed
- 1 tablespoon minced garlic
- 1 teaspoon oregano, dried
- ¼ teaspoon salt

Preparation:
1. Preheat your Ninja Foodi on "Sear/Sauté" mode.
2. Add the sausage and stir-cook to brown evenly.
3. Stir in spices, onions, kale, tomatoes, milk, and chicken broth, then mix well.
4. Select "Pressure" mode with high pressure level and seal the lid.
5. Naturally, release inside pressure for about 8-10 minutes.
6. Serve warm with the cheese on top.
7. Enjoy.
Nutrition Values Per Serving: Calories: 162, Fat: 11g, Carbs: 2g, Protein: 19g

Beef Meatballs with Marinara Sauce

Prep Time: 10 minutes
Cook time: 11 minutes
Servings: 4
Ingredients:
- 2 cups ground beef
- 1 egg, beaten

- 1 teaspoon taco seasoning
- 1 tablespoon sugar-free marinara sauce
- 1 teaspoon garlic, minced
- ½ teaspoon salt

Preparation:
1. Mix ground beef with egg, taco seasoning and the rest of the ingredients in a bowl.
2. Make golf-ball sized meatballs out of this mixture and put them in a single layer in the Air fryer's Basket.
3. Cover the crisping lid and cook on "Air Crisp" mode for 11 minutes at 350 degrees F.
4. Serve immediately and enjoy!
Nutrition Values Per Serving: Calories: 205, Fat: 12g, Carbs: 2g, Protein: 19g

Saucy Lamb Roast

Prep Time: 10 minutes
Cook time: 60 minutes
Servings: 4
Ingredients:
- 2 pounds lamb roasted Wegmans
- 1 cup beef broth
- 1 cup onion soup
- Salt and black pepper, to taste

Preparation:
1. Place your lamb roast in your Ninja Foodi pot
2. Add beef broth, onion soup, salt and black pepper.
3. Cover the Foodi's lid and seal it for pressure cooking.
4. Cook on "Pressure" mode for 55 minutes on HIGH.
5. Release pressure naturally, then remove the lid.
6. Serve and enjoy!
Nutrition Values Per Serving: Calories: 211, Fat: 7g, Carbs: 2g, Protein: 30g

Herbed Pork Chops

Prep Time: 10 minutes
Cook time: 30 minutes
Servings: 4
Ingredients:
- 2 tablespoons ghee
- 2 tablespoons Dijon mustard
- 4 pork chops
- Salt and black pepper, to taste
- 1 tablespoon fresh rosemary, chopped

Preparation:
1. Take a suitable bowl and add pork chops, cover with Dijon mustard and carefully sprinkle rosemary, salt, and black pepper.
2. Let it marinate for 2 hours.
3. Add ghee and marinated pork chops to your Ninja Foodi pot.
4. Cover the Foodi's lid and seal it for pressure cooking.
5. Cook on "Pressure" mode for 30 minutes on Low.
6. Release pressure naturally, then remove the lid.
7. Serve and enjoy!
Nutrition Values Per Serving: Calories: 315, Fat: 26g, Carbs: 1g, Protein: 18g

Ninja Foodi Pork Shoulder Roast

Prep Time: 10 minutes
Cook Time: 10 hours
Servings: 14
Ingredients:
* 4 pounds pork shoulder roast
* 4 carrots, peeled and sliced
* 4 onions, sliced
* 4 tablespoons Italian seasonings
* Salt and black pepper, to taste

Directions:
1. Add pork shoulder, Italian seasonings, salt and pepper in a large bowl. Mix-well and set aside for about 4 hours.
2. Now, place carrots and onions in the bottom of Ninja Foodi Multi-cooker and add marinated pork shoulder in it.
3. Select "Slow Cook" and close the pressure Lid.
4. Press the "Start/Stop" button and cook for about 10 hours on low TEMP.
5. Open the pressure Lid and take out.
6. Serve and enjoy!
Nutritional Values Per Serving: Calories: 365, Fat: 27.6g, Carbs: 5.1g, Protein: 22.3g

Ninja Foodi Carrot & Pork Stew

Prep Time: 10 minutes
Cook Time: 8 hours
Servings: 4
Ingredients:
* 1 pound pork meat, trimmed
* 1½ onions, sliced thinly
* 3 carrots, sliced thinly
* ¾ cup vegetable broth
* Salt and black pepper, to taste

Directions:
1. Add everything in a Ninja Foodi Multi-cooker and mix well.
2. Select "Slow Cook" and press the "Start/Stop" button.
3. Close the pressure Lid and cook for about 8 hours.
4. Open the lid and take out.
5. Serve and enjoy!
Nutritional Values Per Serving: Calories: 465, Fat: 34.8g, Carbs: 21.2g, Protein: 17.1g

Ninja Foodi Mushroom & Beef Stew

Prep Time: 10 minutes
Cook Time: 8 hours
Servings: 5
Ingredients:
* 1 pound beef, chopped
* 1½ onions, chopped
* 1 cup mushrooms, sliced
* ½ cup vegetable broth
* Salt and black pepper, to taste

Directions:

1. Add everything in a Ninja Foodi Multi-cooker and select "Slow Cook".
2. Close the pressure Lid and press the "Start/Stop" button.
3. Cook for about 8-hours on LOW TEMP and open the lid.
4. Take out, serve and enjoy!
Nutritional Values Per Serving: Calories: 224, Fat: 6g, Carbs: 11.9g, Protein: 29.8g

Ninja Foodi Beef Casserole

Prep Time: 10 minutes
Cook Time: 8 hours
Servings: 3
Ingredients:
* ½ pound beef steak, chopped
* ½ cup chopped tomatoes
* ½ onion, chopped
* ¼ cup beef broth
* Salt and black pepper, to taste

Directions:
1. Add everything in a Ninja Foodi Multi-cooker and select "Slow Cook".
2. Cover the lid and press the "Start/Stop" button.
3. Cook for about 8-hours on LOW TEMP and open the lid.
4. Take out, serve and enjoy!
Nutritional Values Per Serving: Calories: 156, Fat: 4.9g, Carbs: 3g, Protein: 23.8g

Ninja Foodi Lamb & Kale Stew

Prep Time: 10 minutes
Cook Time: 6 hours 5 minutes
Servings: 10
Ingredients:
* 3 pounds lamb meat, cubed
* 1 teaspoon dried thyme
* 1 celery stalk, chopped
* 2 tablespoons olive oil
* 1 teaspoon dried basil
* 1 cup chopped tomatoes
* 2 onions, chopped
* ½ cup chopped carrots
* 2 cups water
* 2 garlic cloves, minced
* 10 cups fresh kale, chopped
* Salt and black pepper, to taste

Directions:
1. Heat oil in the pot of Ninja Foodi Multi-cooker and add lamb, salt and pepper in it.
2. Select "Slow Cook" and press the "Start/Stop" button.
3. Cook for about 5 minutes and take out. Set aside.
4. Now, add lamb with all the other ingredients in a Ninja Foodi Slow Cook and close the pressure Lid.
5. Cook for about 6 hours at HIGH TEMP and open the lid.
6. Take out, serve and enjoy!
Nutritional Values Per Serving: Calories: 350, Fat: 20.9g, Carbs: 10.6g, Protein: 27.8g

Cheesy Beef Meatloaf

Prep Time: 5-10 minutes
Cook time: 70 minutes
Servings: 6
Ingredients:
- ¼ cup tomato puree or crushed tomatoes
- 1 pound lean ground beef
- ½ cup onion, chopped
- 2 garlic cloves, minced
- ½ cup green bell pepper, chopped
- 2 eggs, beaten
- 1 cup cheddar cheese, grated
- 3 cups spinach, chopped
- 1 teaspoon dried thyme, crushed
- 6 cups mozzarella cheese, grated
- Black pepper to taste

Preparation:
1. Grease a baking pan with cooking spray.
2. Mix all the listed ingredients except cheese and spinach.
3. Place the prepared mixture over the wax paper, top it with spinach, cheese, and roll it to make a meatloaf.
4. Remove wax paper and add the rolled meatloaf to the baking pan.
5. Add water to the Ninja Foodi's pot and place a reversible rack inside the pot.
6. Place the pan on the rack.
7. Select "Bake/Roast" mode and adjust the 380 degrees F.
8. Then, set the timer to 70 minutes and hit "Stop/Start."
9. Serve warm.

Nutrition Values Per Serving: Calories: 426, Fat: 17g, Carbs: 5.5g, Protein: 49g

Ninja Foodi Beef Chili

Prep Time: 10 minutes
Cook Time: 6 hours
Servings: 3
Ingredients:
- ¾ pound lean ground beef
- ¼ tablespoon garlic, minced
- ½ tablespoon dried basil
- ¼ onion, chopped
- 1 tablespoon tomato paste
- ½ tablespoon chili powder
- ¼ cup chicken broth
- ½ tablespoon balsamic vinegar
- 2 tablespoons water
- ¾ tablespoon capers
- ½ tablespoon dried thyme
- ¼ tablespoon cayenne pepper
- Salt, to taste

Directions:
1. Add everything in a Ninja Foodi Multi-cooker and select "Slow Cook".
2. Press the "Start/Stop" button and close the pressure Lid.
3. Cook for about 6 hours on low TEMP and open the lid.
4. Take out and serve hot.

Nutritional Values Per Serving: Calories: 231, Fat: 7.6g, Carbs: 3.5g, Protein: 35.5g

Ninja Foodi Ground Beef Soup

Prep Time: 20 minutes
Cook Time: 21 minutes
Servings: 6
Ingredients:
- 1 pound lean ground beef
- 1 ginger, minced
- ½ pound fresh mushrooms, sliced
- 1 onion, chopped
- 2 tablespoons soy sauce
- 1 garlic clove, minced
- 4 cups chicken broth
- Salt and black pepper, to taste

Directions:
1. Add beef in a large Ninja Foodi Multi-cooker, press the "Broil" button and cook for about 2 minutes.
2. Press the "Start/Stop" button and stir in mushrooms, garlic and onion and cook for about 4 minutes.
3. Add in remaining ingredients and cook for 15 minutes on low heat.
4. Take out, serve and enjoy!

Nutritional Values Per Serving: Calories: 186, Fat: 5.8g, Carbs: 4.4g, Protein: 27.9g

Ninja Foodi Spinach Beef Soup

Prep Time: 10 minutes
Cook Time: 30 minutes
Servings: 4
Ingredients:
- 1 tablespoon olive oil
- 4 cups spinach, chopped
- 1 onion, chopped
- 4 cups chicken broth
- 1 pound ground beef
- 1 teaspoon ground ginger
- 1 cup chopped carrots
- Salt and black pepper, to taste

Directions:
1. Add oil and beef in Ninja Foodi Multi-cooker and select "Pressure".
2. Press the "Start/Stop" button and cook for about 5-minutes.
3. Add in broth, spinach, carrots, onions, ginger, salt and pepper. Mix well.
4. Cook for about 25 minutes at LO and take out.
5. Serve and enjoy!

Nutritional Values Per Serving: Calories: 310, Fat: 12.1g, Carbs: 7.6g, Protein: 40.7g

Ninja Foodi Lamb & Carrot Stew

Prep Time: 10 minutes
Cook Time: 9 hours
Servings: 3
Ingredients:
- ¾ pound lamb chops, trimmed
- ½ cup vegetable broth
- 2½ carrots, chopped
- 1 onion, chopped
- Salt and black pepper, to taste

Directions:
1. Add all the ingredients in Ninja Foodi Multi-cooker and mix well. Select "Slow Cook".
2. Cover the pressure Lid and press the "Start/Stop" button.
3. Cook for about 9 hours on LOW TEMP and open the lid.
4. Serve and enjoy!
Nutritional Values Per Serving: Calories: 320, Fat: 8.6g, Carbs: 24.6g, Protein: 34.8g

Ninja Foodi Filling Beef Dish

Prep Time: 10 minutes
Cook Time: 10 minutes
Servings: 4
Ingredients:
- 2 tablespoons olive oil
- 4 garlic cloves, minced
- 1 pound beef sirloin steak, chopped
- 3 tablespoons low-sodium soy sauce
- 2 cups fresh kale, chopped
- 2 cups carrots, chopped
- Salt and pepper, to taste

Directions:
1. Heat olive oil in Ninja Foodi Multi-cooker and select "Pressure".
2. Sauté garlic in it for about 1 minute and press the "Start/Stop" button.
3. Add in black pepper and beef. Stir well and cook for about 4 minutes at LO.
4. Stir in kale, soy sauce, salt and carrots and cook for about 5 minutes.
5. Take out and serve hot.
Nutritional Values Per Serving: Calories: 318, Fat: 14.1g, Carbs: 10.7g, Protein: 36.8g

Ninja Foodi Lamb Chops with Tomatoes

Prep Time: 10 minutes
Cook Time: 8 hours
Servings: 4
Ingredients:
- 1 pound lamb chops
- 3 tablespoons mixed herbs
- 1 cup water
- 1½ cups chopped tomatoes
- Salt and black pepper, to taste

Directions:
1. Mix everything in Ninja Foodi Multi-cooker and cover the lid.
2. Select "Slow Cook" and press the "Start/Stop" button.
3. Cook for about 8 hours at low TEMP and open the lid.
4. Take out, serve and enjoy!
Nutritional Values Per Serving: Calories: 258, Fat: 8.9g, Carbs: 10.2g, Protein: 34.2g

Ninja Foodi Plum & Beef Salad

Prep Time: 20 minutes
Cook Time: 10 minutes
Servings: 6
Ingredients:
- 2 pounds beef, trimmed
- 2 teaspoons unsweetened applesauce
- 8 plums, thinly sliced
- 4 tablespoons olive oil
- Salt and black pepper, to taste

Directions:
1. Add 1 tablespoon salt, olive oil and pepper in a large bowl. Mix well.
2. Add in beef and toss to coat well.
3. Place beef in Ninja Foodi Multi-cooker and select "Pressure".
4. Close the pressure Lid and press the "Start/Stop" button.
5. Cook for about 5 minutes at LO per side and open the lid.
6. Take out the beef in a bowl and add in remaining ingredients. Mix properly.
7. Serve and enjoy!
Nutritional Values Per Serving: Calories: 402, Fat: 19g, Carbs: 10.9g, Protein: 46.5g

Elegant Chicken Stock

Prep time: 10 minutes
Cook time: 2hours
Servings: 4
Ingredients:
- 2 pounds meaty chicken bones
- ¼ teaspoon salt
- 3 and ½ cups water

Preparation:
1. Place chicken parts in Ninja Foodi and season with salt.
2. Add water, place the pressure cooker lid and seal the valve, cook on Pressure mode at HI for 90 minutes.
3. Release the pressure naturally over 10 minutes.
4. Line a colander with cheesecloth and place it over a large bowl, pour chicken parts and stock into the colander and strain out the chicken and bones.
5. Let the stock cool and let it peel off any layer of fat that might accumulate on the surface.
6. Use as needed!
Nutrition Values Per Serving: Calories: 51, Fat: 3g, Carbs: 1g, Protein: 6g

Cabbage and Chicken Meatballs

Prep time: 10 minutes + 30 minutes
Cook time: 4-6 minutes
Servings: 4
Ingredients:
- 1 pound ground chicken
- ¼ cup heavy whip cream
- 2 teaspoons salt
- ½ teaspoon ground caraway seeds
- 1 and ½ teaspoons fresh ground black pepper, divided
- ¼ teaspoon ground allspice
- 4-6 cups green cabbage, thickly chopped
- ½ cup almond milk
- 2 tablespoons unsalted butter

Preparation:
1. Transfer meat to a bowl and add cream, 1 teaspoon of salt, caraway, ½ teaspoon of pepper, allspice and mix it well.
2. Let the mixture chill for 30 minutes.
3. Once the mixture is ready, use your hands to scoop the mixture into meatballs.
4. Add half of your balls to Ninja Foodi pot and cover with half of the cabbage.
5. Add remaining balls and cover with rest of the cabbage.
6. Add milk, pats of butter, season with salt and pepper.
7. Lock lid and cook on Pressure mode at HI for 4 minutes.
8. Quick release pressure.
9. Unlock lid and serve.
10. Enjoy!
Nutrition Values Per Serving: Calories: 294, Fat: 26g, Carbs: 4g, Protein: 12g

Taiwanese Chicken Delight

Prep time: 5 minutes
Cook time: 10 minutes
Servings: 4
Ingredients:
- 6 dried red chilis
- ¼ cup sesame oil
- 2 tablespoons ginger
- ¼ cup garlic, minced
- ¼ cup red wine vinegar
- ¼ cup coconut aminos
- Salt as needed
- 1.2 teaspoon xanthan gum (for the finish)
- ¼ cup Thai basil, chopped

Preparation:
1. Set your Ninja Foodi to Sauté mode and add ginger, chilis, garlic and sauté for 2 minutes.
2. Add remaining ingredients.
3. Lock lid and cook on Pressure mode at HI for 10 minutes.
4. Quick release pressure.
5. Serve and enjoy!
Nutrition Values Per Serving: Calories: 307, Fat: 15g, Carbs: 7g, Protein: 31g

Lemon and Chicken Extravaganza

Prep time: 5 minutes
Cook time: 18 minutes
Servings: 4
Ingredients:
- 4 bone-in, skin on chicken thighs
- Salt and pepper to taste
- 2 tablespoons butter, divided
- 2 teaspoons garlic, minced
- ½ cup herbed chicken stock
- ½ cup heavy whip cream
- ½ a lemon, juiced

Preparation:
1. Season your chicken thighs generously with salt and pepper.
2. Set your Ninja Foodi to Sauté mode and add oil, let it heat up.
3. Add thigh, sauté both sides for 6 minutes.
4. Remove thigh to a platter and keep it on the side.
5. Add garlic, cook for 2 minutes.
6. Whisk in chicken stock, heavy cream, lemon juice and gently stir.
7. Bring the mix to a simmer and reintroduce chicken.
8. Lock lid and cook for 10 minutes on Pressure mode at HI.
9. Release pressure over 10 minutes.
10. Serve and enjoy!
Nutrition Values Per Serving: Calories: 294, Fat: 26g, Carbs: 4g, Protein: 12g

Shredded Up Salsa Chicken

Prep time: 5 minutes
Cook time: 20 minutes
Servings: 4
Ingredients:
- 1 pound chicken breast, skin and bones removed
- ¾ teaspoon cumin
- ½ teaspoon salt
- Pinch of oregano
- Pepper to taste
- 1 cup chunky salsa Keto friendly

Preparation:
1. Season chicken with spices and add to Ninja Foodi.
2. Cover with salsa and lock lid, cook on Pressure mode for 20 minutes.
3. Quick release pressure.
4. Add chicken to a platter and shred the chicken.
5. Serve and enjoy!

Nutrition Values Per Serving: Calories: 125, Fat: 3g, Carbs: 2g, Protein: 22g

Sensational Lime and Chicken Chili

Prep time: 10 minutes
Cook time: 23 minutes
Servings: 6
Ingredients:
- ¼ cup cooking wine (Keto-Friendly)
- ½ cup organic chicken broth
- 1 onion, diced
- 1 teaspoon salt
- ½ teaspoon paprika
- 5 garlic cloves, minced
- 1 tablespoon lime juice
- ¼ cup butter
- 2 pounds chicken thighs
- 1 teaspoon dried parsley
- 3 green chilies, chopped

Preparation:
1. Set your Ninja Foodi to Sauté mode and add onion and garlic.
2. Sauté for 3 minutes, add remaining ingredients.
3. Lock lid and cook on Pressure mode at HI for 20 minutes.
4. Release pressure naturally over 10 minutes
5. Serve and enjoy!

Nutrition Values Per Serving: Calories: 282, Fat: 15g, Carbs: 6g, Protein: 27g

Delightful Cheese Casserole

Prep time: 10 minutes
Cook time: 30 minutes
Servings: 8
Ingredients:
- 6 ounces cheddar cheese
- 1 zucchini
- ½ cup ground chicken
- 4 ounces Parmesan cheese
- 3 tablespoons butter
- 1 teaspoon paprika
- 1 teaspoon salt
- 1 teaspoon basil
- 1 teaspoon cilantro
- ½ cup fresh dill
- ⅓ cup tomato juice
- ½ cup cream
- 2 red sweet bell peppers

Preparation:
1. Grate cheddar cheese. Chop the zucchini and combine it with the ground chicken.
2. Sprinkle the mixture with the paprika, salt, basil, cilantro, tomato juice, and cream. Stir the mixture well. Transfer it to the pressure cooker.
3. Chop the dill, sprinkle the mixture in the pressure cooker, and add the butter. Chop the Parmesan cheese and add it to the pressure cooker.
4. Chop the bell peppers and add them too. Sprinkle the mixture with the grated cheddar cheese and close the lid.
5. Set the pressure cooker mode to "Sauté", and cook for 30 minutes.
6. When the cooking time ends, let the casserole chill briefly and serve.

Nutrition Values Per Serving: Calories 199, Fat 14.7, Carbs 6.55, Protein 11

Amazing Duck Pot Pie

Prep time: 10 minutes
Cook time: 50 minutes
Servings: 8
Ingredients:
- 7 ounces keto dough
- 1 teaspoon onion powder
- 1 pound duck breast
- ½ teaspoon anise
- 1 cup green beans
- 1 cup cream
- 1 egg
- 1 teaspoon salt

Preparation:
1. Place the duck breast on the trivet and transfer the trivet into the pressure cooker.
2. Set the pressure cooker to "Steam" mode. Steam the duck for 25 minutes.
3. When the cooking time ends, remove the duck from the pressure cooker and shred it well. Place the shredded duck in the mixing bowl.
4. Add onion powder, anise, cream, salt, and green beans and stir well. Beat the egg. Roll the keto dough and cut it into two parts.
5. Put the one part of the bread dough into the pressure cooker and make the pie crust.
6. Transfer filling in the pie crust and cover it with the second part of the dough.
7. Spread the pie with the whisked egg and close the lid. Cook the dish on "Pressure" mode for 25 minutes.
8. When the cooking time ends, let the pot pie rest briefly.
9. Transfer it to a serving plate, cut it into slices and serve.

Nutrition Values Per Serving: Calories 194, Fat 5.6, Carbs 7.8, Protein 28

Mexico's Favorite Chicken Soup

Prep time: 5 minutes
Cook time: 20 minutes
Servings: 4
Ingredients:
- 2 cups chicken, shredded
- 4 tablespoons olive oil
- ½ cup cilantro, chopped
- 8 cups chicken broth
- ⅓ cup salsa
- 1 teaspoon onion powder
- ½ cup scallions, chopped
- 4 ounces green chilies, chopped
- ½ teaspoon habanero, minced
- 1 cup celery root, chopped
- 1 teaspoon cumin
- 1 teaspoon garlic powder
- Salt and pepper to taste

Preparation:
1. Add all ingredients to Ninja Foodi.
2. Stir and lock lid, cook on Pressure mode at HI for 10 minutes.
3. Release pressure naturally over 10 minutes.
4. Serve and enjoy!

Nutrition Values Per Serving: Calories: 204, Fat: 14g, Carbs: 4g, Protein: 14g

Spicy Hot Paprika Chicken

Prep time: 10 minutes
Cook time: 5 minutes
Servings: 4
Ingredients:
- 4 pieces (4 ounces each) chicken breast, skin on
- Salt and pepper as needed
- 1 tablespoon olive oil
- ½ cup sweet onion, chopped
- ½ cup heavy whip cream
- 2 teaspoons smoked paprika
- ½ cup sour cream
- 2 tablespoons fresh parsley, chopped

Preparation:
1. Lightly season the chicken with salt and pepper.
2. Set your Ninja Foodi to Sauté mode and add oil, let the oil heat up.
3. Add chicken and sear both sides until properly browned, should take about 15 minutes.
4. Remove chicken and transfer them to a plate.
5. Take a skillet and place it over medium heat, add onion and sauté for 4 minutes until tender.
6. Stir in cream, paprika and bring the liquid simmer.
7. Return chicken to the skillet and alongside any juices.
8. Transfer the whole mixture to your Ninja Foodi and lock lid, cook on Pressure mode at HI for 5 minutes.
9. Release pressure naturally over 10 minutes.
10. Stir in sour cream, serve and enjoy!

Nutrition Values Per Serving: Calories: 389, Fat: 30g, Carbs: 4g, Protein: 25g

Hot Turkey Cutlets

Prep time: 10 minutes
Cook time: 15 minutes
Servings: 4
Ingredients:
- 1 teaspoon Greek seasoning
- 1 pound turkey cutlets
- 2 tablespoons olive oil
- 1 teaspoon turmeric powder
- ½ cup almond flour

Preparation:
1. Take a bowl and add Greek seasoning, turmeric powder, almond flour and mix well.
2. Dredge turkey cutlets in the bowl and let it sit for 30 minutes.
3. Set your Ninja Foodi to Sauté mode and add oil, let it heat up.
4. Add cutlets and sauté for 2 minutes.
5. Lock lid and cook on Pressure mode at LO for 20 minutes.
6. Release pressure naturally over 10 minutes.
7. Take the dish out, serve and enjoy!

Nutrition Values Per Serving: Calories: 340, Fat: 19g, Carbs: 3.7g, Protein: 36g

Pulled-Up Keto-Friendly Chicken Tortilla's

Prep time: 15 minutes
Cook time: 15 minutes
Servings: 4
Ingredients:
- 1 tablespoon avocado oil
- 1 pound pastured organic boneless chicken breasts
- ½ cup orange juice
- 2 teaspoons gluten-free Worcestershire sauce
- 1 teaspoon garlic powder
- 1 teaspoon salt
- ½ teaspoon chili powder
- ½ teaspoon paprika

Preparation:
1. Set your Ninja Foodi to Sauté mode and add oil, let the oil heat up.
2. Add chicken on top, take a bowl and add remaining ingredients mix well.
3. Pour the mixture over chicken.
4. Lock lid and cook on Pressure mode at HI for 15 minutes.
5. Release pressure naturally over 10 minutes.
6. Shred the chicken and serve over salad green shell such as cabbage or lettuce.
7. Enjoy!

Nutrition Values Per Serving: Calories: 338, Fat: 23g, Carbs: 10g, Protein: 23g

Ham-Stuffed Generous Turkey Rolls

Prep time: 10 minutes
Cook time: 20 minutes
Servings:8
Ingredients:
- 4 tablespoons fresh sage leaves
- 8 ham slices
- 8 (6 ounces each) turkey cutlets
- Salt and pepper to taste
- 2 tablespoons butter, melted

Preparation:
1. Season turkey cutlets with salt and pepper.
2. Roll turkey cutlets and wrap each of them with ham slices tightly.
3. Coat each roll with butter and gently place sage leaves evenly over each cutlet.
4. Transfer them to your Ninja Foodi.
5. Lock lid and select the "Bake/Roast" mode, bake for 10 minutes at 360 degrees F.
6. Open the lid and gently give it a flip, lock lid again and bake for 10 minutes more.
7. Once done, serve and enjoy!
Nutrition Values Per Serving: Calories: 467, Fat: 24g, Carbs: 1.7g, Protein: 56g

The Great Hainanese Chicken

Prep time: 20 minutes
Cook time: 4 hours
Servings: 4
Ingredients:
- 1 ounce ginger, peeled
- 6 garlic cloves, crushed
- 6 bundles cilantro/basil leaves
- 1 teaspoon salt
- 1 tablespoon sesame oil
- 3 (1 and ½ pounds each) chicken meat, ready to cook

For Dip
- 2 tablespoons ginger, minced
- 1 teaspoon garlic, minced
- 1 tablespoon chicken stock
- 1 teaspoon sesame oil
- ½ teaspoon sugar
- Salt to taste

Preparation:
1. Add chicken, garlic, ginger, leaves, and salt in your Ninja Food.
2. Add enough water to fully submerge chicken, lock lid cook on Slow Cook mode on LOW for 4 hours.
3. Release pressure naturally.
4. Take chicken out of pot and chill for 10 minutes.
5. Take a bowl and add all the dipping ingredients and blend well in a food processor.
6. Take chicken out of ice bath and drain, chop into serving pieces.
7. Arrange onto a serving platter.
8. Brush chicken with sesame oil.
9. Serve with ginger dip.
10. Enjoy!
Nutrition Values Per Serving: Calories: 535, Fat: 45g, Carbs: 5g, Protein: 28g

Funky-Garlic and Turkey Breasts

Prep time: 10 minutes
Cook time: 19 minutes
Servings: 4
Ingredients:
- ½ teaspoon garlic powder
- 4 tablespoons butter
- ¼ teaspoon dried oregano
- 1 pound turkey breasts, boneless
- 1 teaspoon pepper
- ½ teaspoon salt
- ¼ teaspoon dried basil

Preparation:
1. Season turkey on both sides generously with garlic, dried oregano, dried basil, salt and pepper.
2. Set your Ninja Foodi to Sauté mode and add butter, let the butter melt.
3. Add turkey breasts and sauté for 2 minutes on each side.
4. Lock the lid and select the "Bake/Roast" setting, bake for 15 minutes at 355 degrees F.
5. Serve and enjoy once done!
Nutrition Values Per Serving: Calories: 223, Fat: 13g, Carbs: 5g, Protein: 19g

Stuffed Tomatoes with Ground Chicken

Prep time: 10 minutes
Cook time: 10 minutes
Servings: 6
Ingredients:
- 5 big tomatoes
- 10 ounces ground chicken
- 1 teaspoon ground black pepper
- 1 tablespoon sour cream
- 6 ounces Parmesan cheese
- 1 onion
- 1 tablespoon minced garlic
- 5 tablespoons chicken stock
- 1 teaspoon cayenne pepper

Preparation:
1. Use a paring knife or apple corer to remove the flesh from the tomatoes.
2. Combine the ground chicken, ground black pepper, sour cream, minced garlic, and cayenne pepper together in a mixing bowl.
3. Peel the onion and grate it. Add the onion to the ground chicken mixture and stir well. Fill the tomatoes with the ground chicken mixture.
4. Grate the Parmesan cheese and sprinkle the stuffed tomatoes with the cheese.
5. Set the pressure cooker to "Pressure" mode. Pour the chicken stock into the pressure cooker and add the stuffed tomatoes. Close the pressure cooker lid and cook for 20 minutes.
6. When the cooking time ends, let the dish rest briefly.
7. Transfer the tomatoes to a serving plate and serve.
Nutrition Values Per Serving: Calories 222, Fat 12.4, Carbs 10.55, Protein 18

Chicken and Cauliflower Rice Soup

Prep time: 10 minutes
Cook time: 31 minutes
Servings: 8
Ingredients:
- 1 cup cauliflower rice
- 1 pound chicken drumsticks
- 1 tablespoon salt
- 1 teaspoon curry
- 1 teaspoon dill
- 1 teaspoon ground celery root
- 1 garlic clove
- 3 tablespoons sour cream
- 1 teaspoon cilantro
- 6 cups water
- ½ cup tomato juice
- 1 teaspoon oregano
- 1 tablespoon butter
- 8 ounces kale

Preparation:
1. Combine the salt, curry, dill, ground celery, and cilantro together in a mixing bowl and stir.
2. Peel the garlic clove and slice it. Set the Ninja Foodi to "Pressure" mode.
3. Add the butter into the Ninja Foodi and melt it.
4. Add the sliced garlic and cook the dish for 30 seconds. Add the spice mixture and cook the dish for 10 seconds, stirring constantly.
5. Add the drumsticks, sour cream, water, oregano, tomato juice, and cauliflower rice. Chop the kale and sprinkle the soup with it, stir well, and close the lid.
6. Cook the dish on "Sauté" mode for 30 minutes.
7. When the cooking time ends, open the pressure cooker lid, chill the soup briefly, then ladle it into serving bowls.
Nutrition Values Per Serving: Calories 140, Fat 5.7, Carbs 4.9, Protein 17.1

Tasty Chicken Tart

Prep time: 10 minutes
Cook time: 35 minutes
Servings: 8
Ingredients:
- 1 cup almond flour
- 1 egg
- 7 ounces butter
- 1 teaspoon salt
- 10 ounces ground chicken
- 1 teaspoon olive oil
- 1 red onion
- 1 tablespoon cream
- 1 teaspoon ground pepper
- 4 ounces celery stalk

Preparation:
1. Combine the almond flour and butter together in a mixing bowl.
2. Add the egg and knead the dough. Put the dough in the freezer. Peel the onion and grate it.
3. Combine the onion with the salt, ground chicken, cream, ground pepper. Chop the celery

stalk and add it to the ground chicken mixture and stir.
4. Set the pressure cooker to "Pressure" mode. Spray the pressure cooker with the olive oil.
5. Remove the dough from the freezer and cut it in half. Grate the first part of the dough into the pressure cooker.
6. Add half of the chicken mixture. Grate the remaining dough and add the remaining chicken mixture.
7. Close the pressure cooker lid and cook for 35 minutes.
8. When the dish is cooked, let it rest briefly. Slice the tart and serve.
Nutrition Values Per Serving: Calories 318, Fat 31, Carbs 5, Protein 14.4

Spinach Stuffed Chicken Breasts

Prep time: 15 minutes
Cook time: 30 minutes
Servings: 2
Ingredients:
- 1 tablespoon olive oil
- 1¾ ounces fresh spinach
- ¼ cup ricotta cheese, shredded
- 2 (4-ounce) skinless, boneless chicken breasts
- Salt and ground black pepper, as required
- 2 tablespoons cheddar cheese, grated
- ¼ teaspoon paprika

Preparation:
1. Select the "Sear/Sauté" setting of Ninja Foodi and place the oil into the pot.
2. Press "Start/Stop" to begin cooking and heat for about 2-3 minutes.
3. Add the spinach and cook for about 3-4 minutes.
4. Stir in the ricotta and cook for about 40-60 seconds.
5. Press "Start/Stop" to stop cooking and transfer the spinach mixture into a bowl.
6. Set aside to cool.
7. Cut slits into the chicken breasts about ¼-inch apart but not all the way through.
8. Stuff each chicken breast with the spinach mixture.
9. Sprinkle each chicken breast with salt and black pepper and then with cheddar cheese and paprika.
10. Arrange the greased cook & crisp basket in the pot of Ninja Foodi.
11. Close the Ninja Foodi with a crisping lid and select "Air Crisp".
12. Set the temperature to 390 degrees F for 5 minutes.
13. Press "Start/Stop" to begin preheating.
14. After preheating, open the lid.
15. Place the chicken breasts into the "Cook & Crisp Basket."
16. Close the Ninja Foodi with a crisping lid and select "Air Crisp".
17. Set the temperature to 390 degrees F for 25 minutes.
18. Press "Start/Stop" to begin cooking.
19. Open the lid and serve hot.
Nutrition Values Per Serving: Calories: 279, Fat: 16 g, Carbs: 2.7 g, Protein: 31.4 g

Turkey with Chickpeas & Quinoa

Prep time: 15 minutes
Cook time: 20 minutes
Servings: 4
Ingredients:
- 1½ tablespoons olive oil
- 6 ounces skinless, boneless turkey breast, cubed
- 1 medium onion, chopped
- 1 small sweet potato, peeled and chopped
- 2 garlic cloves, minced
- 1 tablespoon red chili powder
- ¼ teaspoon red pepper flakes, crushed
- ¼ teaspoon ground cumin
- ¼ teaspoon ground coriander
- Salt, to taste
- 1 cup canned chickpeas, rinsed and drained
- ¼ cup uncooked quinoa
- 1 cup tomatoes, chopped finely
- 1½ cups chicken broth
- 1 tablespoon fresh lemon juice
- 2 tablespoons fresh cilantro, chopped

Preparation:
1. Select "Sear/Sauté" setting of Ninja Foodi and place the oil into the pot.
2. Press "Start/Stop" to begin cooking and heat for about 2-3 minutes.
3. Add the turkey and cook for about 5 minutes or until browned completely.
4. With a slotted spoon, transfer the turkey into a bowl.
5. In the pot, add the onion and cook for about 5 minutes.
6. Add the sweet potato and cook for about 5 minutes.
7. Add the garlic and spices and cook for about 1 minute.
8. Press "Start/Stop" to stop cooking and stir in the turkey, chickpeas, quinoa, tomato and broth.
9. Close the Ninja Foodi with the pressure lid and place the pressure valve to "Seal" position.
10. Select "Pressure" and set to "High" for 4 minutes.
11. Press "Start/Stop" to begin cooking.
12. Do a "Natural" release for about 10 minutes and then switch the valve to "Vent" to do a "Quick" release.
13. Open the lid and stir in the lemon juice and cilantro.
14. Serve hot.
Nutrition Values Per Serving: Calories: 390, Fat: 11.5 g, Carbs: 49.8 g, Protein: 24.2 g

Glazed Chicken Drumsticks

Prep time: 15 minutes
Cook time: 25 minutes
Servings: 4
Ingredients:
- ¼ cup Dijon mustard
- 1 tablespoon honey
- 2 tablespoons olive oil
- Salt and ground black pepper, as required
- 4 (6 ounces) chicken drumsticks

Preparation:

1. In a bowl, add all the ingredients except the drumsticks and mix until well combined.
2. Add the drumsticks and coat with the mixture generously.
3. Refrigerate, covered to marinate overnight.
4. In the pot of Ninja Foodi, place 1 cup of water.
5. Arrange the greased cook & crisp basket in the pot of Ninja Foodi.
6. Place the chicken drumsticks into the "Cook & Crisp Basket".
7. Close the Ninja Foodi with the pressure lid and place the pressure valve to the "Seal" position.
8. Select "Pressure" and set it to "High" for 6 minutes.
9. Press "Start/Stop" to begin cooking.
10. Switch the valve to "Vent" and do a "Quick" release.
11. Now, close the Ninja Foodi with a crisping lid and select "Air Crisp."
12. Set the temperature to 320 degrees F for 12 minutes.
13. Press "Start/Stop" to begin cooking.
14. After 12 minutes of cooking, set the temperature to 355 degrees F for 5 minutes.
15. Open the lid and serve hot.
Nutrition Values Per Serving: Calories: 374, Fat: 17.3 g, Carbs: 5.2 g, Protein: 47.5 g

Crispy Duck Patties

Prep time: 10 minutes
Cook time: 15 minutes
Servings: 6
Ingredients:
- 1 tablespoon mustard
- 1 teaspoon ground black pepper
- 9 ounces ground duck
- ½ cup parsley
- 1 teaspoon salt
- 1 tablespoon olive oil
- 1 teaspoon oregano
- 1 teaspoon red pepper
- ½ teaspoon cayenne pepper
- 1 tablespoon flax meal

Preparation:
1. Combine the mustard, ground black pepper, ground duck, salt, oregano, red pepper, cayenne pepper, and flax meal together in a mixing bowl and stir well.
2. Wash the parsley and chop it. Sprinkle the duck mixture with the chopped parsley and stir well.
3. Make medium-sized patties from the duck mixture. Set the Ninja Foodi to "Sauté" mode.
4. Pour the olive oil into the Ninja Foodi. Add the duck patties and cook the dish on Sauté mode for 15 minutes or until browned on both sides.
5. Serve immediately.
Nutrition Values Per Serving: Calories 106, Fat 6.9, Carbs 3.3, Protein 8.6

Warm Chicken Salad

Prep time: 10 minutes
Cook time: 25 minutes
Servings: 7
Ingredients:
- 1 pound boneless chicken
- 1 cup spinach
- 1 tablespoon mayonnaise
- 1 teaspoon lemon juice
- 4 eggs, boiled
- 1 tablespoon chives
- ½ cup dill

Preparation:
1. Put the chicken in the trivet and place the trivet into the pressure cooker.
2. Set the Ninja Foodi to "Steam" mode. Cook the dish for 25 minutes.
3. Peel the eggs and chop them. Chop the spinach and dill.
4. Transfer the chopped greens to a mixing bowl. Add chives and chopped eggs.
5. Sprinkle the mixture with the lemon juice and mayonnaise.
6. When the chicken is cooked, remove it from the pressure cooker and let it rest briefly.
7. Grind the cooked chicken and transfer it to the egg mixture.
8. Mix until smooth and serve.
Nutrition Values Per Serving: Calories 154, Fat 8, Carbs 0.92, Protein 19

Amazing Parsley Duck Legs

Prep time: 10 minutes
Cook time: 30 minutes
Servings: 2
Ingredients:
- 2 garlic cloves, minced
- 1 tablespoon fresh parsley, chopped
- 1 teaspoon five-spice powder
- Salt and ground black pepper, as required
- 2 duck legs

Preparation:
1. In a bowl, mix together garlic, parsley, five-spice powder, salt and black pepper.
2. Rub the duck legs with garlic mixture generously.
3. Arrange the cook & crisp basket in the pot of Ninja Foodi.
4. Close the Ninja Foodi with crisping lid and select "Air Crisp".
5. Set the temperature to 340 degrees F for 5 minutes.
6. Press "Start/Stop" to begin preheating.
7. After preheating, open the lid.
8. Place the duck legs into the cook & crisp basket.
9. Close the Ninja Foodi with crisping lid and select "Air Crisp".
10. Set the temperature to 340 degrees F for 25 minutes.
11. Press "Start/Stop" to begin cooking.
12. After 25 minutes of cooking, set the temperature to 390 degrees F for 5 minutes.
13. Open the lid and serve hot.
Nutrition Values Per Serving: Calories: 434, Fat: 14.4 g, Carbs: 1.1 g, Protein: 70.4 g

Heathy Chicken Meatballs

Prep time: 10 minutes
Cook time: 10 minutes
Servings: 8
Ingredients:
- 1 cup broccoli rice, cooked
- 10 ounces ground chicken
- 1 carrot
- 1 egg
- 1 teaspoon salt
- ½ teaspoon cayenne pepper
- 1 teaspoon olive oil
- 1 tablespoon flax meal
- 1 teaspoon sesame oil

Preparation:
1. Peel the carrot and chop it roughly. Transfer the chopped carrot to a blender and blend it well.
2. Combine the blended carrot and ground chicken together in a mixing bowl and stir.
3. Sprinkle the meat mixture with the broccoli rice, egg, cayenne pepper, salt, and flax meal and combine well.
4. Set the pressure cooker to "Sauté" mode. Pour the olive oil and sesame oil into the pressure cooker.
5. Make meatballs from the meat mixture and place them into the pressure cooker.
6. Cook the dish on Sauté mode for 10 minutes. Stir the meatballs until all the sides are light brown.
7. Remove them from the pressure cooker, drain on paper towel to remove any excess oil, and serve.
Nutrition Values Per Serving: Calories 96, Fat 4.7, Carbs 1.9, Protein 11.5

Bruschetta Chicken Meal

Prep time: 5 minutes
Cook time: 9 minutes
Servings: 4
Ingredients:
- 2 tablespoons balsamic vinegar
- ⅓ cup olive oil
- 2 teaspoons garlic cloves, minced
- 1 teaspoon black pepper
- ½ teaspoon salt
- ½ cup sun-dried tomatoes, in olive oil
- 2 pounds chicken breasts, quartered, boneless
- 2 tablespoons fresh basil, chopped

Preparation:
1. Take a bowl and whisk in vinegar, oil, garlic, pepper, salt.
2. Fold in tomatoes, basil and add breast, mix well.
3. Transfer to fridge and let it sit for 30 minutes.
4. Add everything to Ninja Foodi and lock lid, cook on Pressure mode at HI for 9 minutes.
5. Quick release pressure.
6. Serve and enjoy!
Nutrition Values Per Serving: Calories: 480, Fat: 26g, Carbs: 4g, Protein: 52g

Tomato Ground Chicken Bowl

Prep time: 10 minutes
Cook time: 30 minutes
Servings: 5
Ingredients:
- 1 cup tomatoes
- ½ cup cream
- 1 onion
- 1 teaspoon chili powder
- 3 tablespoons tomato paste
- 1 bell pepper
- 1 jalapeño pepper
- 1 tablespoon olive oil
- 15 ounces ground chicken

Preparation:
1. Peel the onion and dice it. Combine the onion with the chili powder, tomato paste, and cream and stir well.
2. Chop the jalapeño pepper and bell pepper. Wash the tomatoes and chop them.
3. Set the pressure cooker to "Sauté" mode. Place all the ingredients into the pressure cooker.
4. Add ground chicken and combine. Close the pressure cooker lid and cook for 30 minutes.
5. When the cooking time ends, remove the dish from the pressure cooker and stir well.
6. Transfer the dish to serving bowls.

Nutrition Values Per Serving: Calories 220, Fat 14.5, Carbs 7.24, Protein 17

Tasty Chicken Pies

Prep time: 15 minutes
Cook time: 24 minutes
Servings: 8
Ingredients:
- 8 ounces puff pastry
- 4 ounces ground chicken
- 1 teaspoon paprika
- 1 teaspoon ground ginger
- ½ teaspoon cilantro
- 1 egg
- 1 tablespoon butter
- 1 onion
- 1 teaspoon olive oil

Preparation:
1. Roll the puff pastry using a rolling pin. Cut the rolled puff pastry into medium-sized squares. Combine the ground chicken, cilantro, ground ginger, paprika, and egg together in a mixing bowl and stir well.
2. Peel the onion and dice it. Add the onion to the meat mixture and stir well. Place the ground chicken mixture in the middle of every square and wrap them to form the pies.
3. Set the pressure cooker to "Sear/Sauté" mode.
4. Spray the pressure cooker with the olive oil inside and place the chicken pies inside.
5. Close the pressure cooker lid and cook the dish for 24 minutes.
6. When the chicken pies are cooked, remove them from the pressure cooker, let it rest briefly and serve.

Nutrition Values Per Serving: Calories 217, Fat 15.2, Carbs 14.52, Protein 6

Sour Cream Chicken Liver

Prep time: 10 minutes
Cook time: 18 minutes
Servings: 7
Ingredients:
- 1 pound chicken livers
- 1 onion
- 1 teaspoon garlic powder
- 1 tablespoon cilantro
- ¼ cup dill
- 1 teaspoon olive oil
- 1 cup cream
- ¼ cup cream cheese
- 1 teaspoon salt
- 1 teaspoon ground black pepper

Preparation:
1. Chop the chicken livers roughly and place them into the pressure cooker.
2. Set the pressure cooker to "Sauté" mode. Sprinkle the liver with the olive oil and sauté it for 3 minutes, stirring frequently.
3. Combine the sour cream and cream cheese together in a mixing bowl. Sprinkle the mixture with the cilantro, garlic powder, salt, and ground black pepper and stir well.
4. Pour the sour cream mixture into the pressure cooker and stir well.
5. Close the pressure cooker lid and cook the dish on "Sear/Sauté" mode for 15 minutes.
6. When the dish is cooked, let it rest briefly and serve.

Nutrition Values Per Serving: Calories 239, Fat 18.2, Carbs 8.22, Protein 11

Indian Chicken

Prep time: 10 minutes
Cook time: 30 minutes
Servings: 8
Ingredients:
- 1 tablespoon curry paste
- 1 tablespoon lemongrass paste
- ½ cup fresh thyme
- 2 pounds chicken breasts
- 1 cup almond milk
- ½ cup cream
- 1 teaspoon salt
- 1 teaspoon cilantro
- 1 tablespoon olive oil

Preparation:
1. Wash the thyme and chop it. Combine the almond milk with the curry paste and lemongrass paste.
2. Stir the mixture until everything is dissolved. Add cilantro, salt, and cream. Add the chopped thyme and chicken breasts. Let the chicken sit for 10 minutes.
3. Set the pressure cooker to "Sear/Sauté" mode. Transfer the chicken mixture into the pressure cooker and close the lid. Cook the chicken for 30 minutes.
4. When the cooking time ends, remove the dish from the pressure cooker and remove the chicken from the cream mixture, slice it and serve.

Nutrition Values Per Serving: Calories 261, Fat 15.6, Carbs 4.77, Protein 25

Herbed Cornish Hen

Prep time: 15 minutes
Cook time: 16 minutes
Servings: 6
Ingredients:
- ½ cup olive oil
- 1 teaspoon fresh rosemary, chopped
- 1 teaspoon fresh thyme, chopped
- 1 teaspoon fresh lemon zest, grated finely
- ¼ teaspoon sugar
- ¼ teaspoon red pepper flakes, crushed
- Salt and ground black pepper, as required
- 2 pounds Cornish game hen, backbone removed and halved

Preparation:
1. In a large bowl, mix well all ingredients except hen portions.
2. Add the hen portions and coat with marinade generously.
3. Cover and refrigerator for about 2-24 hours.
4. In a strainer, place the hen portions to drain any liquid.
5. Arrange the greased cook & crisp basket in the pot of Ninja Foodi.
6. Close the Ninja Foodi with crisping lid and select "Air Crisp".
7. Set the temperature to 390 degrees F for 5 minutes.
8. Press "Start/Stop" to begin preheating.
9. After preheating, open the lid.
10. Place the hen portions into the cook & crisp basket.
11. Close the Ninja Foodi with crisping lid and select "Air Crisp".
12. Set the temperature to 390 degrees F for 16 minutes.
13. Press "Start/Stop" to begin cooking.
14. Open the lid and place the hen portions onto a cutting board.
15. Cut each portion in 2 pieces and serve hot.
Nutrition Values Per Serving: Calories: 681, Fat: 57.4 g, Carbs: 0.8 g, Protein: 38.2 g

Braised Turkey Breast

Prep time: 15 minutes
Cook time: 30 minutes
Servings: 8
Ingredients:
- 1 celery stalk, chopped
- 1 large onion, chopped
- 1 tablespoon fresh thyme, minced
- 1 tablespoon fresh rosemary, minced
- 14 ounces chicken broth
- 1 (6½-pound) skin-on, bone-in turkey breast
- Salt and ground black pepper, as required
- 3 tablespoons cornstarch
- 3 tablespoons water

Preparation:
1. In the pot of Ninja Foodi, place celery, onion, herbs, and broth.
2. Arrange turkey breast on top and sprinkle with salt and black pepper.
3. Close the Ninja Foodi with the pressure lid and place the pressure valve to "Seal" position.
4. Select "Pressure" and set to "High" for 30 minutes.

5. Press "Start/Stop" to begin cooking.
6. Switch the valve to "Vent" and do a "Quick" release.
7. Open the lid and transfer the turkey breast onto a cutting board.
8. With a slotted spoon, skim off the fat from the surface of broth. Then strain it, discarding solids.
9. In a small bowl, dissolve the cornstarch in water.
10. Return the broth in pot and select "Sear/Sauté" setting of Ninja Foodi.
11. Press "Start/Stop" to begin cooking.
12. Add the cornstarch mixture, stirring continuously and cook for about 3-4 minutes.
13. Press "Start/Stop" to stop cooking and transfer the gravy into a serving bowl.
14. Cut the turkey breast into desired sized slices and serve alongside the gravy.
Nutrition Values Per Serving: Calories: 655, Fat: 26.7 g, Carbs: 5.2 g, Protein: 80.3 g

Butter Chicken Cutlets

Prep time: 15 minutes
Cook time: 25 minutes
Servings: 8
Ingredients:
- 3 tablespoons cream
- 5 tablespoons butter
- 1 teaspoon starch
- 2 tablespoons chicken stock
- 9 ounces ground chicken
- ½ cup dill
- 1 teaspoon ground black pepper
- 1 teaspoon paprika
- 1 teaspoon tomato paste
- 2 eggs
- 3 tablespoons semolina

Preparation:
1. Combine the cream and butter together and whisk.
2. Sprinkle the mixture with the starch, paprika, tomato paste, semolina, and ground black pepper and stir well.
3. Set the pressure cooker to "Sear/Sauté" mode. Chop the dill and add it into the pressure cooker.
4. Add the eggs and ground chicken and combine. Make medium-sized balls from the ground chicken mixture, then flatten them.
5. Pour the chicken stock into the pressure cooker and add the chicken flatten balls.
6. Close the pressure cooker lid and cook for 25 minutes.
7. When the dish is cooked, let it rest briefly and serve.
Nutrition Values Per Serving: Calories 172, Fat 13.4, Carbs 4.32, Protein 9

Raspberries Chicken Fillets

Prep time: 10 minutes
Cook time: 25 minutes
Servings: 8
Ingredients:
- 8 ounces raspberries
- 1 pound boneless chicken breast
- 1 teaspoon sour cream
- ⅓ cup cream
- 6 ounces Parmesan
- 2 tablespoons butter
- 1 teaspoon cilantro
- 1 tablespoon white pepper

Preparation:
1. Pound the chicken breasts with a meat mallet.
2. Set the pressure cooker to "Sauté" mode. Add the butter into the pressure cooker and melt it.
3. Grate the Parmesan cheese. Sprinkle the chicken with the cilantro and white pepper. Place the boneless chicken breasts into the pressure cooker. Sprinkle them with raspberries.
4. Add sour cream and cream. Sprinkle the dish with the grated cheese.
5. Close the pressure cooker lid and cook the dish on "Sear/Sauté" mode for 25 minutes.
6. When the cooking time ends, remove the dish from the pressure cooker, and let it rest, and serve.
Nutrition Values Per Serving: Calories 226, Fat 12.5, Carbs 5, Protein 23.8

Chicken Piccata

Prep time: 10 minutes
Cook time: 17 minutes
Servings: 8
Ingredients:
- 2 tablespoons capers
- 1 ½ pounds boneless chicken breast
- 1 teaspoon ground black pepper
- 3 tablespoons olive oil
- 3 tablespoons butter
- 1 teaspoon salt
- ½ cup lemon juice
- 1 cup chicken stock
- ⅓ cup fresh parsley
- 1 teaspoon oregano
- 1 tablespoon coconut flour
- 1 teaspoon paprika

Preparation:
1. Cut the chicken breast into medium-sized pieces. Sprinkle the chicken with the ground black pepper, salt, oregano, and paprika and stir well.
2. Set the pressure cooker to "Sauté" mode. Pour the olive oil and butter into the pressure cooker.
3. Stir well and sauté it for 1 minute. Add the chicken into the pressure cooker, and cook the chicken for 6 minutes. Stir the chicken frequently.
4. Remove the chicken from the pressure cooker. Add the capers, lemon juice, chicken stock, and coconut flour to the pressure cooker and stir well until smooth. Cook the liquid for 1 minute.
5. Add the cooked chicken and close the pressure cooker lid. Cook for 10 minutes at the "Pressure" mode.
6. When the cooking time ends, release the remaining pressure and open the pressure cooker lid.
7. Serve the chicken piccata immediately.
Nutrition Values Per Serving: Calories 257, Fat 16.3, Carbs 1.6, Protein 25.2

Spicy Whole Turkey

Prep time: 15 minutes
Cook time: 8 hours 5 minutes
Servings: 14
Ingredients:
For Spice Rub:
- 2 teaspoons dried thyme, crushed
- 2 teaspoons ground cumin
- 2 teaspoons paprika
- 2 teaspoons salt
- 1 teaspoon ground white pepper
- 1 teaspoon ground black pepper

For Turkey:
- 1 (8-pound) whole turkey, necks, and giblets removed
- 4 garlic cloves, peeled and smashed
- ½ of medium onion, chopped
- 2 carrots, scrubbed and cut into thirds
- 2 celery stalks, cut into thirds
- 1 whole lemon, quartered

Preparation:
1. For the spice rub: in a bowl, mix all ingredients. Keep aside.
2. Rinse turkey well, and with a paper towel, pat dries completely.
3. Fold back the wings of the turkey.
4. Rub smashed garlic over outside of turkey evenly.
5. Rub inside and outside of turkey with spice rub generously.
6. Place lemon quarters in the cavity of the turkey.
7. Tie the legs of the turkey with kitchen twine.
8. In the pot of a Ninja Foodi, place the onion, carrots, celery, and 3 garlic cloves.
9. Arrange turkey over vegetables.
10. Close the Ninja Foodi with crisping lid and select "Slow Cook".
11. Set on "High" for 6-8 hours.
12. Press "Start/Stop" to begin cooking.
13. Now, close the Ninja Foodi with crisping lid and select "Broil" for 5 minutes.
14. Press "Start/Stop" to begin cooking.
15. Open the lid and place the turkey onto a platter for about 25-30 minutes before slicing.
16. Cut into desired sized pieces and serve alongside vegetables.
Nutrition Values Per Serving: Calories: 403, Fat: 18.6 g, Carbs: 2.2 g, Protein: 48.9 g

Chicken with Veggies

Prep time: 20 minutes
Cook time: 8 hours 40 minutes
Servings: 8
Ingredients:
* 2 pounds skinless, boneless chicken breast tenders
* 1 large onion, chopped
* 2 cups asparagus, trimmed and cut into 2-inch pieces
* 1 tablespoon fresh thyme, chopped
* 1 teaspoon garlic powder
* Salt and ground black pepper, as required
* 4 medium zucchinis, spiralized with blade C
* 1 cup sour cream
* 1 cup cheddar cheese, shredded

Preparation:
1. In the pot of Ninja Foodi, add the chicken, onion, asparagus, thyme, garlic powder, salt, and black pepper and mix well.
2. Close the Ninja Foodi with a crisping lid and select "Slow Cook".
3. Set on "LO" for 8 hours.
4. Press "Start/Stop" to begin cooking.
5. Open the lid and place the zucchini noodles over the chicken mixture and top with cheese and cream.
6. Close the Ninja Foodi with a crisping lid and select "Slow Cook".
7. Set on "LO" for 30-40 minutes.
8. Press "Start/Stop" to begin cooking.
9. Open the lid and stir the mixture well.
10. Serve hot.
Nutrition Values Per Serving: Calories: 292, Fat: 15 g, Carbs: 8.2 g, Protein: 32 g

Chicken Cauliflower Pilaf

Prep Time: 15 minutes
Cook time: 6 minutes
Servings: 10
Ingredients:
* 1 cup cauliflower rice
* 7 ounces chicken breasts, boneless
* 1 teaspoon salt
* 4 ounces mushrooms
* 1 tablespoon olive oil
* 1 white onion
* 1 tablespoon oregano
* 4 ounces raisins
* 5 ounces kale
* 7 ounces green beans
* 3 cups chicken stock
* 2 tablespoons oyster sauce

Preparation:
1. Slice the mushrooms and place them into the Ninja Foodi.
2. Chop the chicken breasts into medium-sized pieces and add them to the Ninja Foodi.
3. Peel the onion and dice it. Chop the kale and green beans.
4. Transfer the vegetables to the Ninja Foodi.
5. Top the mixture with olive oil, salt, oregano, raisins, and chicken stock.
6. Set the Ninja Foodi to "Pressure" mode and stir well.

7. Add the cauliflower rice and close the Ninja Foodi's lid.
8. Cook on "Pressure" mode for 6 minutes at High.
9. Once it is done, release the cooker's pressure then remove the Ninja Foodi's lid.
10. Let the pilaf rest and stir well before serving.
Nutrition Values Per Serving: Calories: 111, Fat: 3.2g, Carbs: 14.4g, Protein: 7.8g

Salsa Verde Dipped Chicken

Prep Time: 10 minutes
Cook time: 30 minutes
Servings: 6
Ingredients:
* 10 ounces Salsa Verde
* 1 tablespoon paprika
* 1 pound boneless chicken breasts
* 1 teaspoon salt
* 1 teaspoon ground coriander
* 1 teaspoon cilantro

Preparation:
1. Rub the boneless chicken breasts with paprika, salt, black pepper, and cilantro. Set the Ninja Foodi to "Pressure" mode.
2. Place the boneless chicken into the Ninja Foodi.
3. Sprinkle the meat with the salsa Verde and stir well.
4. Close the Ninja Foodi's lid and cook for 30 minutes.
5. Once it is done, release the pressure and transfer the chicken to the mixing bowl.
6. Shred the chicken well and serve.
Nutrition Values Per Serving: Calories: 222, Fat: 11.3g, Carbs: 21.02g, Protein: 9g

Italian Chicken Breasts

Prep Time: 10 minutes
Cook time: 25 minutes
Servings: 6
Ingredients:
* 13 ounces Italian-style salad dressing
* 1 teaspoon butter
* 1 pound chicken breast, skinless

Preparation:
1. Chop the chicken breasts roughly and place them in a suitable mixing bowl.
2. Sprinkle the chopped meat with the Italian-style salad dressing and mix well using your hands.
3. Let the chicken marinate breast for 1 hour in your refrigerator.
4. Set the Ninja Foodi to "Pressure" mode.
5. Add the butter into the Ninja Foodi.
6. Add marinated chicken breast and cook for 25 minutes.
7. Once it is done, remove the chicken from the Ninja Foodi and let it rest briefly.
8. Transfer the dish to a serving plate.
Nutrition Values Per Serving: Calories: 283, Fat: 20.6g, Carbs: 7.45g, Protein: 16g

Coconut Dipped Chicken Strips

Prep Time: 10 minutes
Cook time: 12 minutes
Servings: 8
Ingredients:
- ½ cup coconut
- 4 tablespoons butter
- 1 teaspoon salt
- ⅓ cup flour
- ½ teaspoon sugar
- ¼ teaspoon red chilli flakes
- 1 teaspoon onion powder
- 15 ounces boneless chicken breast

Preparation:
1. Cut the boneless chicken breast into the strips, sprinkle it with the salt and Chilli flakes, and stir.
2. Mix the coconut, flour, sugar, and onion powder in a suitable mixing bowl and stir well.
3. Set the Ninja Foodi to "Sauté" mode.
4. Add the butter into the Ninja Foodi and cook for 2 minutes.
5. Dip the chicken strips in the coconut mixture well and transfer the chicken strips into the Ninja Foodi.
6. Sauté the dish for 10 minutes on both sides.
7. When the chicken is golden brown, remove the chicken strips to a plate.
8. Let the dish rest briefly and serve.
Nutrition Values Per Serving: Calories: 197, Fat: 13.7g, Carbs: 2.3g, Protein: 16.6g

Crunchy Oregano Drumsticks

Prep time: 10 minutes
Cook time: 11 minutes
Servings: 8
Ingredients:
- 1 cup pork rind
- 1 tablespoon salt
- 1 tablespoon paprika
- 1 teaspoon ground black pepper
- 1 teaspoon cayenne pepper
- 1 teaspoon oregano
- ½ cup olive oil
- 1 tablespoon minced garlic
- 1 pound chicken drumsticks
- ½ cup cream
- 1 cup cream cheese

Preparation:
1. Combine the pork rind, salt, paprika, ground black pepper, cayenne pepper, oregano, and minced garlic in a mixing bowl and stir well.
2. Combine the cream and cream cheese together in separate mixing bowl.
3. Whisk the mixture until smooth. Pour the olive oil into the pressure cooker and preheat it at the "Sauté" mode for 3 minutes.
4. Dip the drumsticks in the cream cheese mixture and dip them in the pork rind mixture.
5. Transfer the chicken into the pressure cooker and cook for 8 minutes until golden brown.
6. When the drumsticks are cooked, remove them from the pressure cooker, and drain them on a paper towel to remove excess oil before serving.

Nutrition Values Per Serving: Calories 421, Fat 33.2, Carbs 2.5, Protein 29.4

Seasoned Whole Chicken

Prep Time: 15 minutes
Cook time: 30 minutes
Servings: 9
Ingredients:
- 2 pounds whole chicken, wash and cleaned
- 1 tablespoon salt
- 1 teaspoon black pepper
- 1 tablespoon olive oil
- 1 teaspoon butter
- 1 teaspoon fresh rosemary
- 1 lemon
- 1 tablespoon sugar
- 1 cup of water
- 1 teaspoon coriander, chopped
- ½ teaspoon cayenne pepper
- ¼ teaspoon turmeric

Preparation:
1. Mix the salt, black pepper, fresh rosemary, sugar, coriander, cayenne pepper, and turmeric in a suitable mixing bowl.
2. Rub the chicken with the spice mixture.
3. Sprinkle the chicken with olive oil. Set the Ninja Foodi to "Pressure" mode.
4. Pour the water into the Ninja Foodi and place the stuffed whole chicken.
5. Seal the lid and cook on Pressure mode at HI for 30 minutes.
6. Once it is done, release the cooker's pressure and open the Ninja Foodi's lid.
7. Remove the prepared chicken from the Ninja Foodi and let it rest.
8. Cut the cooked chicken into pieces and serve warm.
Nutrition Values Per Serving: Calories: 217, Fat: 9.5g, Carbs: 2.3g, Protein: 29.3g

Ninja Foodi Chicken & Carrot Stew

Prep Time: 10 minutes
Cook Time: 6 hours
Servings: 3
Ingredients:
- 2 (¼ pound) boneless chicken breasts, cubed
- ½ cup chopped onions
- ½ teaspoon dried thyme
- 1 garlic clove, minced
- 1½ cup cubed carrots
- ½ cup chopped tomatoes
- 1 cup chicken broth
- Salt and black pepper, to taste

Directions:
1. Add everything in the Ninja Foodi Multi-cooker and select "Slow Cook".
2. Close the pressure Lid and press the "Start/Stop" button.
3. Cook for about 6 hours at HIGH TEMP and take out.
4. Serve and enjoy!
Nutritional Values Per Serving: Calories: 226, Fat: 6.4g, Carbs: 16.6g, Protein: 25g

Chicken Noodle Soup

Prep Time: 15 minutes
Cook time: 29 minutes
Servings: 9
Ingredients:
- 6 ounces Shirataki noodles
- 8 cups water
- 1 carrot
- 1 tablespoon peanut oil
- 1 yellow onion
- ½ tablespoon salt
- 3 ounces celery stalk
- 1 teaspoon black pepper
- ½ lemon
- 1 teaspoon minced garlic
- 10 ounces chicken breast

Preparation:
1. Peel the carrot and onion and dice them.
2. Cut the chicken breast into halves.
3. Set the Ninja Foodi to "Pressure" mode.
4. Pour the peanut oil into the Ninja Foodi and preheat it for 1 minute.
5. Add the onion and carrot and stir well, cook it for 5 minutes, stirring constantly.
6. Add 4 cups of water and chicken breast.
7. Close the Ninja's lid and cook the dish on "Pressure" mode for 10 minutes.
8. Once it is done, remove the chicken from the Ninja Foodi and shred it.
9. Return the shredded chicken to the Ninja Foodi and close the Ninja's lid.
10. Cook the dish for 7 minutes. Add 4 cups of water and Shirataki noodles.
11. Close the Ninja's lid and cook the dish on "Pressure" mode for 7 minutes.
12. When the soup is done, transfer it from the Ninja Foodi to the serving bowls.
Nutrition Values Per Serving: Calories: 64, Fat: 2.3g, Carbs: 2.6g, Protein: 7.2g

Chicken Thigh Puttanesca

Prep Time: 15 minutes
Cook time: 25 minutes
Servings: 8
Ingredients:
- 1 ½ pounds chicken thighs
- ½ cup tomato paste
- 2 tablespoons capers
- 1 teaspoon salt
- ½ teaspoon black-eyed peas
- 3 garlic cloves
- 3 tablespoons olive oil
- 4 ounces black olives
- 1 tablespoon fresh basil, chopped
- ½ cup water

Preparation:
1. Set the Ninja Foodi to "Sauté" mode.
2. Pour the olive oil into the Ninja Foodi and preheat it for 1 minute.
3. Place the chicken thighs into the Ninja Foodi and sauté the chicken for 5 minutes.
4. Once the chicken thighs are golden, remove them from the Ninja Foodi and keep aside.
5. Put the tomato paste, capers, olives, black-eyed peas, and basil into the Ninja Foodi.

6. Peel the garlic and slice it. Add the sliced garlic to the Ninja Foodi mixture.
7. Add the salt and water. Stir the mixture well and sauté it for 3 minutes.
8. Add the chicken thighs and close the Ninja's lid.
9. Cook the dish on "Pressure" mode for 17 minutes.
10. Once it is done, open the Ninja Foodi's lid and transfer the dish to the serving bowl.
Nutrition Values Per Serving: Calories: 170, Fat: 8.8g, Carbs: 4.48g, Protein: 18g

Creamy Stuffed Chicken Breast

Prep Time: 10 minutes
Cook time: 20 minutes
Servings: 7
Ingredients:
- ⅓ cup basil
- 3 ounces dry tomatoes
- 1 pound chicken breast
- 1 tablespoon olive oil
- 3 ounces dill
- 1 teaspoon paprika
- ½ teaspoon ground ginger
- 1 teaspoon salt
- ½ teaspoon ground coriander
- ½ teaspoon cayenne pepper
- 2 tablespoons lemon juice
- ¼ cup sour cream

Preparation:
1. Wash the basil and chop it. Chop the dried tomatoes.
2. Mix the chopped ingredients in a suitable mixing bowl and sprinkle with the paprika and ground ginger and stir well.
3. Pound the prepared chicken breast with a mallet to flatten them.
4. Rub the chicken breast with the dill, salt, ground coriander, cayenne pepper, and lemon juice. Fill the chicken breast with the chopped basil mixture.
5. Set the Ninja Foodi to "Steam" mode. Spray the Ninja Foodi with olive oil. Spread the stuffed chicken breast with sour cream.
6. Close the chicken breasts with toothpicks and place them in the Ninja Foodi.
7. Close the Ninja Foodi's lid and cook for 20 minutes.
8. Once it is done, open the Ninja Foodi's lid and remove the chicken breast.
9. Remove the toothpicks, slice the stuffed chicken breast, and serve.
Nutrition Values Per Serving: Calories: 179, Fat: 9.4g, Carbs: 8.89g, Protein: 16g

Asian-Style Chicken Strips

Prep time: 10 minutes
Cook time: 30 minutes
Servings: 7
Ingredients:
- ½ cup soy sauce
- 1 tablespoon liquid stevia
- 1 tablespoon sesame seeds
- ½ cup chicken stock
- 1 tablespoon oregano
- 1 teaspoon cumin
- 1 pound boneless chicken breast
- 1 teaspoon butter

Preparation:
1. Cut the chicken breast into the strips and transfer the strips to the mixing bowl.
2. Combine the soy sauce and liquid stevia in a mixing bowl. Stir the mixture.
3. Add sesame seeds, chicken stock, oregano, cumin, and butter.
4. Whisk the mixture and combine it with the chicken strips. Let the chicken strips marinate for 10 minutes.
5. Set the pressure cooker to "Pressure" mode.
6. Transfer the chicken strips mixture to the pressure cooker. Close the lid and cook for 30 minutes.
7. When the dish is cooked, release the pressure and open the pressure cooker lid.
8. Transfer the chicken strips and soy sauce mixture to serving bowls.
Nutrition Values Per Serving: Calories 149, Fat 6.2, Carbs 2.3, Protein 20.3

Thai Chicken

Prep Time: 10 minutes
Cook time: 35 minutes
Servings: 8
Ingredients:
- 14 ounces boneless chicken breast
- 1 teaspoon black pepper
- 1 teaspoon paprika
- 1 teaspoon turmeric
- 3 tablespoons fish sauce
- ½ teaspoon curry
- 1 teaspoon salt
- 3 tablespoons butter
- ¼ cup fresh basil
- 1 teaspoon olive oil

Preparation:
1. Cut the boneless chicken breast into medium pieces.
2. Mix the black pepper, paprika, turmeric, curry, and salt in a suitable mixing bowl and stir well.
3. Toss the cut-up chicken pieces with the spice mixture and coat well.
4. Chop the basil and mix it with the butter in a small bowl.
5. Stir the mixture until smooth. Set the Ninja Foodi to "Sauté" mode.
6. Add the butter mixture into the Ninja Foodi. Melt it.
7. Transfer the chicken filets into the Ninja Foodi and sauté them for 10 minutes.
8. Add the olive oil and fish sauce.

9. Close the Ninja Foodi's lid and cook the dish on "Sear/Sauté" mode for 25 minutes.
10. Once cooked, remove the chicken from the Ninja Foodi.
11. Let the dish rest briefly and serve.
Nutrition Values Per Serving: Calories: 182, Fat: 12g, Carbs: 12.7g, Protein: 6g

Creamy Chicken Pancake

Prep Time: 20 minutes
Cook time: 15 minutes
Servings: 9
Ingredients:
- 1 cup flour
- 3 eggs
- 1 teaspoon salt
- 1 teaspoon psyllium husk powder
- ½ cup half and half
- ½ tablespoon baking soda
- 1 tablespoon apple cider vinegar
- 1 medium onion
- ½ teaspoon black pepper
- 7 ounces ground chicken
- 1 teaspoon paprika
- 1 tablespoon tomato paste
- 1 tablespoon butter
- 1 tablespoon olive oil
- 1 tablespoon sour cream

Preparation:
1. Beat the eggs in a suitable mixing bowl, add half and half and flour, and whisk until smooth batter forms.
2. Add the baking soda, salt, apple cider vinegar, and psyllium husk powder, and stir well.
3. Let the prepared batter rest for 10 minutes in the refrigerator.
4. Peel the onion and dice it. Mix the ground chicken with the black pepper, paprika, tomato paste, kosher salt, and sour cream in a suitable mixing bowl and stir well.
5. Set the Ninja Foodi to "Sauté" mode. Add the ground chicken mixture and sauté the meat for 10 minutes, stirring frequently.
6. Remove the chicken from the Ninja Foodi. Pour the sesame oil and begin to cook the pancakes.
7. Ladle a small amount of the batter into the Ninja Foodi.
8. Cook the chicken pancakes for 1 minute per side.
9. Place one pancake into the Ninja Foodi and spread it with the ground chicken.
10. Repeat the step until you form a pancake cake.
11. Close the Ninja's lid and cook the dish on "Pressure" mode for 10 minutes.
12. Once cooked, remove the cake from the Ninja Foodi and let it rest briefly.
13. Cut into slices and serve.
Nutrition Values Per Serving: Calories: 134, Fat: 9.4g, Carbs: 3.4g, Protein: 9.6g

Saucy Chicken Breast

Prep Time: 15 minutes
Cook time: 40 minutes
Servings: 8
Ingredients:
- 2 pounds chicken breasts
- 2 tablespoons ketchup
- ½ cup Sugar
- ⅓ cup soy sauce
- 1 teaspoon salt
- 2 ounces fresh rosemary
- 1 teaspoon ground white pepper
- ¼ cup garlic
- 2 tablespoons olive oil
- 1 white onion
- 4 tablespoons water
- 1 tablespoon flax meal
- ⅓ teaspoon red Chilli flakes
- 1 teaspoon oregano

Preparation:
1. Place the chicken breast into the Ninja Foodi. Set the Ninja Foodi to "Pressure" mode.
2. Mix the ketchup, sugar, soy sauce, salt, rosemary, and ground white pepper in a suitable mixing bowl and whisk until smooth.
3. Peel the garlic and white onion, and then slice the vegetables.
4. Mix the sliced vegetables with the chile flakes and oregano and stir.
5. Place sugar mixture into the Ninja Foodi. Mix well, close the Ninja's lid, and cook for 10 minutes.
6. Mix flax meal with water in a suitable mixing bowl.
7. Once it is done, release the cooker's pressure and open the lid.
8. Remove the chicken breast from the Ninja Foodi and chop it.
9. Pour the starch mixture into the Ninja Foodi and stir. Add the chicken and close the Ninja's lid.
10. Cook the chicken on "Sauté" mode for 30 minutes.
11. Once it is done, remove the dish from the Ninja Foodi, let it rest briefly, and serve.
Nutrition Values Per Serving: Calories: 295, Fat: 13.4g, Carbs: 9.5g, Protein: 34.6g

Duck Meat Tacos

Prep Time: 10 minutes
Cook time: 22 minutes
Servings: 7
Ingredients:
- 1 pound duck breast fillet
- 1 teaspoon salt
- 1 teaspoon Chilli powder
- 1 teaspoon onion powder
- 1 teaspoon oregano
- 1 teaspoon basil
- 1 cup lettuce
- 1 teaspoon black pepper
- 1 tablespoon tomato sauce
- 1 cup chicken stock
- 1 tablespoon olive oil
- 6 ounces Cheddar cheese
- 7 flour tortilla
- 1 teaspoon turmeric

Preparation:
1. Chop the duck fillet and transfer it to the blender.
2. Blend the mixture well. Set the Ninja Foodi to "Sauté" mode.
3. Place the blended duck fillet into the Ninja Foodi.
4. Sprinkle it with olive oil and stir well. Sauté the dish for 5 minutes.
5. Mix the salt, Chilli powder, onion powder, oregano, basil, black pepper, and turmeric in a suitable mixing bowl and stir.
6. Add tomato sauce. Sprinkle the blended duck fillet with the spice mixture.
7. Mix well and add chicken stock. Stir gently and close the Ninja's lid.
8. Cook the mixture at the "Pressure" mode for 17 minutes.
9. Wash the lettuce and chop it roughly. Grate the Cheddar cheese.
10. When the duck mixture is cooked, remove it from the Ninja Foodi and let it rest briefly.
11. Place the chopped lettuce in the tortillas.
12. Add the duck mixture to tortillas and top it with grated cheese.
13. Serve.
Nutrition Values Per Serving: Calories: 246, Fat: 12.9g, Carbs: 4.1g, Protein: 28.9g

Onions Stuffed with Chicken

Prep Time: 15 minutes
Cook time: 40 minutes
Servings: 5
Ingredients:
- 5 large white onions, chopped
- 1 pound ground chicken
- 1 cup cream
- 1 cup chicken stock
- 1 teaspoon salt
- 1 teaspoon oregano
- 1 teaspoon basil
- 1 egg
- 1 teaspoon turmeric
- 5 garlic cloves

Preparation:
1. Place the ground chicken in a suitable mixing bowl and sprinkle it with salt, oregano, basil, and turmeric.
2. Stir in egg and mix well evenly.
3. Set the Ninja Foodi to" Sear/Sauté" mode. Transfer the stuffed onions to the Ninja Foodi.
4. Add the chicken stock and cream. Close the Ninja's lid and cook for 40 minutes.
5. Once it is done, open the lid and let the onions sit for 2 minutes.
6. Transfer the stuffed onions to a serving plate and sprinkle them with the liquid from the Ninja Foodi.
7. Serve warm.
Nutrition Values Per Serving: Calories: 318, Fat: 19.3g, Carbs: 15.56g, Protein: 22g

Chicken Cutlets

Prep Time: 10 minutes
Cook time: 25 minutes
Servings: 8
Ingredients:
- 14 ounces ground chicken
- 1 teaspoon black pepper
- 1 teaspoon paprika
- 1 teaspoon cilantro
- 1 teaspoon oregano
- ½ teaspoon minced garlic
- 2 tablespoons starch
- 1 teaspoon red chile flakes
- 1 tablespoon oatmeal flour
- 1 egg

Preparation:
1. Place the ground chicken in a suitable mixing bowl.
2. Sprinkle it with black pepper, cilantro, and oregano.
3. Add paprika and minced garlic and mix using your hands.
4. Beat the egg in a separate bowl.
5. Add the starch and oatmeal flour to the egg and stir well until smooth.
6. Add the egg mixture to the ground meat.
7. Add the Chile flakes and mix well. Make the medium cutlets from the ground chicken mixture.
8. Set the Ninja Foodi to "Steam" mode.
9. Transfer the chicken cutlets to the Ninja Foodi trivet and place the trivet into the Ninja Foodi.
10. Close the Ninja's lid and cook the chicken cutlets on Steam mode for 25 minutes.
11. Once cooked, remove the food from the Ninja Foodi, let it rest, and serve.
Nutrition Values Per Serving: Calories: 96, Fat: 5.3g, Carbs: 1.89g, Protein: 10g

Savory Pulled Chicken

Prep Time: 10 minutes
Cook time: 22 minutes
Servings: 7
Ingredients
- 1 pound chicken breast, boneless
- 1 tablespoon Sugar
- 1 teaspoon black pepper
- 1 teaspoon olive oil
- 2 cups water
- 1 ounce bay leaf
- 1 tablespoon basil
- 1 tablespoon butter
- ½ cup cream
- 1 teaspoon salt
- 3 garlic cloves
- 1 teaspoon turmeric

Preparation:
1. Set the Ninja Foodi to "Pressure" mode.
2. Pour water into the Ninja Foodi and add the chicken breast.
3. Add the bay leaf. Close the Ninja's lid and cook for 12 minutes.
4. Once it is done, release the cooker's pressure and open the Ninja Foodi's lid.

5. Transfer the chicken breast to a mixing bowl and shred it.
6. Sprinkle the shredded chicken with sugar, black pepper, basil, butter, cream, salt, and turmeric and stir well.
7. Peel the garlic cloves and mince them.
8. Spray the Ninja Foodi with the olive oil inside and transfer the shredded chicken into a Ninja Foodi.
9. Cook the dish on "Sauté" mode for 10 minutes.
10. Once cooked, transfer it to a serving plate.
11. Devour!
Nutrition Values Per Serving: Calories: 122, Fat: 5.3g, Carbs: 4.4g, Protein: 14.4g

Chicken with Pomegranate Sauce

Prep Time: 10 minutes
Cook time: 29 minutes
Servings: 6
Ingredients:
- ½ cup pomegranate juice
- 2 tablespoons sugar
- 1 teaspoon cinnamon
- ¼ cup chicken stock
- 2 pounds chicken breast
- 1 teaspoon starch
- 1 teaspoon butter
- 1 tablespoon oregano
- 1 teaspoon turmeric
- ½ teaspoon red chili flakes

Preparation:
1. Set the Ninja Foodi to "Pressure" mode. Put the chicken breast into the Ninja Foodi and sprinkle it with oregano, butter, chicken stock, and chili flakes.
2. Stir the mixture and close the Ninja Foodi's lid. Cook the meat for 20 minutes.
3. Mix the pomegranate juice, sugar, cinnamon, starch, and turmeric and stir well until everything is dissolved.
4. Once it is done, open the Ninja Foodi's lid and remove the chicken.
5. Set the Ninja Foodi to "Sauté" mode.
6. Pour the pomegranate sauce into the Ninja Foodi and sauté it for 4 minutes.
7. Return the chicken back into the Ninja Foodi and stir the dish using a spoon.
8. Close the Ninja's lid and cook the chicken in "Pressure" mode for 5 minutes.
9. Once it is done, release the cooker's pressure then remove the Ninja Foodi's lid.
10. Transfer the juicy chicken to a serving plate.
11. Drizzle the pomegranate sauce on top.
Nutrition Values Per Serving: Calories: 198, Fat: 4.6g, Carbs: 4.7g, Protein: 32.2g

Herbed Chicken Wings

Prep Time: 10 minutes
Cook time: 20 minutes
Servings: 7
Ingredients:
- 4 tablespoons dry dill
- 1 cup Greek yogurt
- 1 teaspoon salt
- 1 teaspoon black pepper
- ½ teaspoon red chile flakes
- 1 teaspoon oregano
- 1 tablespoon olive oil
- 1 pound chicken wings
- 1 teaspoon lemon juice

Preparation:
1. Mix the yogurt, salt, black pepper, Chile flakes, oregano, and lemon juice in a suitable mixing bowl, blending until smooth.
2. Add 2 tbsp dill and stir well. Add the chicken wings and coat them with the yogurt mixture.
3. Let the chicken wings rest for 2 hours.
4. Set the Ninja Foodi to "Pressure" mode. Pour the olive oil into the Ninja Foodi.
5. Add the chicken wings. Sprinkle the chicken wings with the remaining dill.
6. Close the Ninja Foodi and cook for 20 minutes.
7. Once the wings are cooked, then remove them from the Ninja Foodi.
8. Let the wings rest briefly and serve.
Nutrition Values Per Serving: Calories: 122, Fat: 4.5g, Carbs: 2.77g, Protein: 17g

"Sauté" modeCreamy Pulled Chicken

Prep Time: 15 minutes
Cook time: 25 minutes
Servings: 7
Ingredients:
- 1 cup cream
- 1 cup chicken stock
- 1 tablespoon garlic sauce
- 1 tablespoon minced garlic
- 1 teaspoon nutmeg
- 1 teaspoon salt
- 12 ounces chicken breasts
- 1 tablespoon lemon juice

Preparation:
1. Mix the nutmeg and salt and stir well.
2. Sprinkle the chicken breasts with the salt mixture, coating them well.
3. Set the Ninja Foodi to "Pressure" mode.
4. Place the chicken into the Ninja Foodi.
5. Add chicken stock, minced garlic, and cream, stir well and close the Ninja's lid.
6. Cook on "Pressure" mode at HI for 25 minutes.
7. Once it is done, release the cooker's pressure and open the Ninja Foodi's lid.
8. Transfer the chicken to a mixing bowl.
9. Shred the meat using a fork. Add the garlic sauce, mix well, and serve.
Nutrition Values Per Serving: Calories: 169, Fat: 11.8g, Carbs: 3.32g, Protein: 12g

Mexican Chicken with Salsa

Prep Time: 13 minutes
Cook time: 15 minutes
Servings: 6
Ingredients:
- 1 cup salsa
- 1 teaspoon paprika
- 1 teaspoon salt
- 2 tablespoons minced garlic
- 15 ounces boneless chicken breast
- 1 teaspoon oregano

Preparation:
1. Mix the paprika, salt, minced garlic, and oregano in a suitable mixing bowl and stir.
2. Chop the boneless chicken breast and sprinkle it with the spice mixture.
3. Set the Ninja Foodi to "Pressure" mode.
4. Transfer the chicken mixture into the Ninja Foodi, add the salsa, and mix well using a wooden spoon.
5. Close the Ninja's lid and cook for 15 minutes.
6. Once it is done, release the cooker's pressure and open the Ninja Foodi's lid.
7. Transfer the cooked chicken with salsa to a serving bowl.
Nutrition Values Per Serving: Calories: 206, Fat: 10.3g, Carbs: 20.49g, Protein: 9g

Seasoned Chicken Strips

Prep Time: 10 minutes
Cook time: 8 minutes
Servings: 7
Ingredients:
- 1 cup flour
- 1 teaspoon kosher salt
- 1 teaspoon cayenne pepper
- ½ teaspoon cilantro
- ½ teaspoon oregano
- ½ teaspoon paprika
- ½ cup coconut milk
- 1 pound chicken fillet
- 3 tablespoons sesame oil
- 1 teaspoon turmeric

Preparation:
1. Place the flour in a suitable mixing bowl.
2. Add kosher salt, cayenne pepper, cilantro, oregano, paprika, and turmeric and mix well.
3. Pour the coconut milk into a separate bowl. Cut the chicken into strips.
4. Set the Ninja Foodi to "Sauté" mode. Pour the olive oil into the Ninja Foodi.
5. Dip the chicken strips in the coconut milk, then dip them in the flour mixture.
6. Repeat this step two more times.
7. Add the dipped chicken strips to the Ninja Foodi.
8. Sauté the chicken strips for 3 minutes on each side.
9. Transfer the chicken to a paper towel to drain any excess oil before serving.
10. Serve warm.
Nutrition Values Per Serving: Calories: 244, Fat: 18.1g, Carbs: 10.6g, Protein: 11.9g

BBQ Chicken Meatballs

Prep Time: 10 minutes
Cook time: 25 minutes
Servings: 8
Ingredients:
- ⅓ cup BBQ sauce
- 1 teaspoon salt
- 1 teaspoon sugar
- 3 tablespoons chives
- 12 ounces ground chicken
- 1 egg
- 1 tablespoon coconut flour
- 1 tablespoon olive oil
- 1 teaspoon oregano
- 1 red onion

Preparation:
1. Put the ground chicken in a suitable mixing bowl.
2. Sprinkle the ground meat with sugar, salt, chives, coconut flour, and oregano.
3. Peel the red onion, dice it, and add the onion to the ground chicken mixture.
4. Beat the egg in a suitable bowl and add it to the ground chicken.
5. Mix everything well using your hands until smooth.
6. Make small balls from the ground chicken.
7. Set the Ninja Foodi to "Sauté" mode. Pour the olive oil into the Ninja Foodi.
8. Put the chicken balls in the Ninja Foodi and sauté them for 5 minutes.
9. Stir them constantly to make all the sides of the chicken balls are brown.
10. Pour the barbecue sauce into the Ninja Foodi and close the Ninja's lid.
11. Cook the dish on "Sear/Sauté" mode for 20 minutes.
12. Once it is done, remove the dish from the Ninja Foodi and serve.
Nutrition Values Per Serving: Calories: 131, Fat: 5.7g, Carbs: 6.3g, Protein: 13.3g

Chicken Cheese Bowl

Prep Time: 15 minutes
Cook time: 30 minutes
Servings: 6
Ingredients:
- 7 ounces Feta cheese
- 10 ounces boneless chicken breast
- 1 teaspoon basil
- 1 tablespoon onion powder
- 1 teaspoon olive oil
- 1 tablespoon sesame oil
- 4 ounces green olives
- 2 cucumbers
- 1 cup water
- 1 teaspoon salt

Preparation:
1. Set the Ninja Foodi to "Pressure" mode.
2. Place the boneless chicken breast into the Ninja Foodi.
3. Add water, basil, and onion powder, stir well and close the Ninja's lid.
4. Cook on "Pressure" mode at High for 30 minutes.
5. Chop the Feta cheese roughly and sprinkle it with olive oil.
6. Slice the green olives. Chop the cucumbers into medium-sized cubes.
7. Mix the chopped cheese, sliced green olives, and cucumbers in a suitable mixing bowl.
8. Top the mixture with salt and sesame oil.
9. When the chicken is cooked, open the Ninja Foodi and remove it from the machine.
10. Allow the chicken to cool a little and chop roughly.
11. Return this chicken to the cheese mixture.
12. Mix well and serve.
Nutrition Values Per Serving: Calories: 279, Fat: 19.8g, Carbs: 15.37g, Protein: 11g

Chicken Dumplings

Prep Time: 10 minutes
Cook time: 25 minutes
Servings: 7
Ingredients:
- 1 teaspoon salt
- ¼ teaspoon sugar
- 1 cup flour
- ¼ cup whey
- 10 ounces boneless chicken breast
- 1 tablespoon olive oil
- 1 cup water
- 1 onion
- 1 teaspoon black pepper
- 1 teaspoon paprika

Preparation:
1. Mix salt, sugar, and flour in a suitable mixing bowl and stir.
2. Add the whey and mix well. Knead the dough.
3. Make a long log from the dough and cut it into small dumpling pieces.
4. Chop the chicken roughly and sprinkle it with the black pepper.
5. Place the chopped chicken into the Ninja Foodi.
6. Set the Ninja Foodi to "Pressure" mode.
7. Sprinkle the chopped chicken with olive oil and add water.
8. Close the Ninja Foodi's lid and cook for 15 minutes. Peel the onion and slice it.
9. Once it is done, release the cooker's pressure and open the Ninja Foodi's lid.
10. Remove the cooked chicken and shred it. Return the chicken back to the Ninja Foodi.
11. Add the dumplings and sliced onion. Sprinkle the dish with paprika.
12. Close the Ninja Foodi's lid and cook the dish on "Pressure" mode for 10 minutes.
13. Once it is done, remove the dish from the Ninja Foodi, let it rest briefly, and serve.
Nutrition Values Per Serving: Calories: 133, Fat: 7.1g, Carbs: 4.5g, Protein: 13.1g

Chicken Rissoles

Prep Time: 10 minutes
Cook time: 15 minutes
Servings: 8
Ingredients:
- 4 egg yolks
- 1 tablespoon turmeric
- 1 teaspoon salt
- 1 teaspoon dried parsley
- 1 tablespoon cream
- 12 ounces ground chicken
- 1 tablespoon almond oil
- 1 tablespoon sesame seeds
- 1 teaspoon minced garlic

Preparation:
1. Mix the turmeric, salt, dried parsley, and sesame seeds in a suitable mixing bowl.
2. Beat egg yolks in a mini bowl and pour in to the ground chicken in a large bowl.
3. Add the spice mixture and garlic and combine.
4. Make small rissoles from the ground chicken mixture. Set the Ninja Foodi to "Sauté" mode.
5. Pour the olive oil into the Ninja Foodi and add the chicken rissoles.
6. Sauté the chicken rissoles for 15 minutes, stirring frequently.
7. Once cooked, serve.
Nutrition Values Per Serving: Calories: 117, Fat: 8.4g, Carbs: 1.42g, Protein: 9g

Cheesy Chicken Fillets

Prep Time: 10 minutes
Cook time: 15 minutes
Servings: 7
Ingredients:
- 1 cup cream cheese
- 6 ounces Cheddar cheese
- 1 yellow onion
- 14 ounces boneless chicken breast
- 1 teaspoon olive oil
- 1 tablespoon black pepper
- 1 teaspoon red chile flakes
- 4 ounces apricot, pitted
- 3 tablespoons chicken stock

Preparation:
1. Cut the chicken breast into fillets and sprinkle the boneless chicken breasts with the black pepper, olive oil, and chile flakes.
2. Set the Ninja Foodi to "Sauté" mode. Transfer the chicken breasts into the Ninja Foodi and sauté for 5 minutes per side.
3. Meanwhile, grate the Cheddar cheese and mix it with the cream cheese.
4. Add chicken stock and mix well using a spoon.
5. Mix apricots with sliced onions in a bowl.
6. Once it is done, open the Ninja Foodi's lid.
7. Sprinkle the chicken with the onion mixture.
8. Add the Cheddar cheese mixture.
9. close the Ninja's lid and cook at the "Pressure" mode for 10 minutes.
10. Once it is done, release the cooker's pressure and open the Ninja Foodi's lid.
11. Transfer the chicken to the serving plates.

Nutrition Values Per Serving: Calories: 282, Fat: 18.1g, Carbs: 11.88g, Protein: 18g

Oregano Chicken Drumsticks

Prep Time: 5 minutes
Cook time: 18 minutes
Servings: 7
Ingredients:
- 1 pound chicken drumsticks
- 1 teaspoon salt
- 1 teaspoon paprika
- 1 teaspoon white pepper
- 1 cup water
- 1 teaspoon thyme
- ½ teaspoon oregano

Preparation:
1. Sprinkle the chicken drumsticks with salt, paprika, thyme, oregano, and white pepper and stir well.
2. Set the Ninja Foodi to "Pressure" mode at High.
3. Place the chicken drumsticks into the Ninja Foodi and add the water.
4. Close the Ninja's lid and cook for 18 minutes.
5. Once it is done, release the cooker's pressure and open the Ninja Foodi's lid.
6. Remove the drumsticks from the Ninja Foodi and transfer them to the serving platter.
Nutrition Values Per Serving: Calories: 112, Fat: 3.8g, Carbs: 0.5g, Protein: 17.9g

Ninja Foodi Turkey Stew

Prep Time: 20 minutes
Cook Time: 48 minutes
Servings: 6
Ingredients:
- 1½ pounds cooked turkey, chopped
- 1 cup pumpkin puree
- 2 tablespoons olive oil
- 2 cups chopped tomatoes
- 4 scallions, chopped
- 1½ cups water
- 2 teaspoons grated ginger
- Salt and black pepper, to taste

Directions:
1. Heat 1 tablespoon olive oil in a Ninja Foodi Multi-cooker and select "Sear/Sauté".
2. Press the "Start/Stop" button and sauté scallions and ginger in it for about 3 minutes. Take out and set aside.
3. Now, add remaining oil in the pot of Ninja Foodi Multi-cooker and cook turkey in it for about 3 minutes.
4. Stir in scallion mixture and cook for about 2 minutes.
5. Add in remaining ingredients and simmer for about 40 minutes.
6. Dish out and serve hot.
Nutritional Values Per Serving: Calories: 777, Fat: 25.8g, Carbs: 6.8g, Protein: 123g

Peanut Butter Duck

Prep Time: 10 minutes
Cook time: 25 minutes
Servings: 6
Ingredients:
- 4 tablespoons creamy peanut butter
- ½ cup fresh dill
- 1 teaspoon oregano
- 1 tablespoon lemon juice
- 1 teaspoon lime zest
- ¼ teaspoon cinnamon
- 1 teaspoon turmeric
- 1 teaspoon paprika
- ½ teaspoon cumin
- ½ teaspoon black pepper
- 1 cup chicken stock
- 1 tablespoon butter
- 1 pound duck breast
- ¼ cup red wine

Preparation:
1. Mix the chopped dill with the lime zest, cinnamon, turmeric, lemon juice, paprika, cumin, and black pepper and stir well.
2. Set the Ninja Foodi to "Pressure" mode.
3. Rub the duck with the spice mixture and place it into the Ninja Foodi.
4. Sprinkle the meat with oregano. Add the chicken stock, red wine, and butter.
5. Close the Ninja Foodi's lid and cook on "Pressure" mode for 18 minutes at High.
6. Once it is done, release the cooker's pressure then remove the Ninja Foodi's lid.
7. Set the Ninja Foodi to "Sauté" mode. Remove the dish from the Ninja Foodi.
8. Add the peanut butter into the Ninja Foodi and sauté it for 1 minute.
9. Add the duck and sauté the dish for 5 minutes.
10. Stir the duck a couple of times.
11. Once done, transfer the duck to a serving plate and let it rest briefly before serving.
Nutrition Values Per Serving: Calories: 198, Fat: 11.5g, Carbs: 4.74g, Protein: 19g

Chicken Broth with Fresh Herbs

Prep Time: 10 minutes
Cook time: 45 minutes
Servings: 13
Ingredients:
- 8 ounces drumsticks
- 8 ounces chicken wings
- ⅓ cup fresh thyme
- ¼ cup fresh dill
- ¼ cup fresh parsley
- 1 teaspoon black pepper
- 10 cups water
- 1 teaspoon salt
- 2 tablespoons fresh rosemary
- 1 garlic clove
- 1 onion

Preparation:
1. Wash the drumsticks and chicken wings carefully.
2. Chop them roughly and transfer the ingredients to the Ninja Foodi.

3. Set the Ninja Foodi to "Sauté" mode. Top the mixture with the salt and black pepper and stir well using your hands.
4. Wash the thyme, dill, and parsley and chop them. Put the chopped greens into the Ninja Foodi.
5. Add water and rosemary. Peel the onion and garlic.
6. Add the vegetables to the chicken mixture.
7. Close the Ninja Foodi's lid and cook the dish for 45 minutes.
8. Once it is done, discard the greens from the Ninja Foodi.
9. Remove the chicken from the Ninja Foodi.
10. Strain the chicken stock and serve it with the cooked chicken.
11. Serve warm.
Nutrition Values Per Serving: Calories: 35, Fat: 0.7g, Carbs: 3.06g, Protein: 4g

Spicy Pulled Duck

Prep Time: 10 minutes
Cook time: 27 minutes
Servings: 8
Ingredients:
- ⅓ cup red wine
- ½ cup chicken stock
- 1 teaspoon onion powder
- 14 ounces duck fillet
- 2 teaspoons cayenne pepper
- ¼ teaspoon minced garlic
- ⅓ cup fresh dill
- 1 teaspoon salt
- 1 teaspoon black pepper
- 1 tablespoon sour cream
- 1 tablespoon tomato puree

Preparation:
1. Mix the red wine and chicken stock in a suitable mixing bowl and stir.
2. Set the Ninja Foodi to "Sauté" mode.
3. Pour the chicken stock mixture into the Ninja Foodi and preheat it for 1 minute.
4. Mix the onion powder, cayenne pepper, salt, black pepper, and garlic in a suitable mixing bowl.
5. Stir the mixture and sprinkle the duck fillet with the spice mixture.
6. Place the duck fillet into the Ninja Foodi and close the Ninja's lid.
7. Cook the duck on "Pressure" mode for 25 minutes at High.
8. Once it is done, remove the dish from the Ninja Foodi and let it rest briefly.
9. Shred the duck using a fork. Leave a third of the liquid into the Ninja Foodi and return the shredded duck.
10. Add the tomato puree and sour cream. Chop the dill and sprinkle the dish with it.
11. Stir it gently and close the Ninja's lid.
12. Cook the dish on "Sauté" mode for 2 minutes.
13. Once it is done, transfer the hot dish to a serving plate and serve.
Nutrition Values Per Serving: Calories: 119, Fat: 7.9g, Carbs: 1.81g, Protein: 9g

Crispy Duck Cutlets

Prep Time: 10 minutes
Cook time: 20 minutes
Servings: 8
Ingredients:
- ¼ cup vermouth
- 1 pound ground duck
- 1 teaspoon salt
- 4 ounces keto bread
- ¼ cup cream
- 1 teaspoon paprika
- 1 teaspoon coconut flour
- 1 teaspoon white pepper

Preparation:
1. Mix the ground duck and vermouth in a suitable mixing bowl.
2. Chop the bread and mix it with the cream and stir well until smooth.
3. Use a blender, if necessary. Add the bread mixture to the ground duck.
4. Sprinkle the meat mixture with salt, paprika, and white pepper.
5. Add coconut flour and mix well using a spoon.
6. Make the medium cutlets from the duck mixture and transfer them to the trivet.
7. Set the Ninja Foodi to "Steam" mode.
8. Place the Ninja's trivet into the Ninja Foodi and close the Ninja's lid.
9. Cook the dish on Steam mode for 20 minutes.
10. Once it is done, remove the cutlets from the Ninja Foodi. Rest briefly and serve.
Nutrition Values Per Serving: Calories: 121, Fat: 5.4g, Carbs: 4.9g, Protein: 12.3g

Creamy Chicken Soup

Prep Time: 15 minutes
Cook time: 22 minutes
Servings: 8
Ingredients:
- 4 cups water
- 2 cups cream
- ⅓ cup half and half
- 1 tablespoon minced garlic
- 5 ounces mushrooms, chopped
- 1 onion
- 1 tablespoon olive oil
- ½ tablespoon salt
- 1 teaspoon fresh basil
- 1 teaspoon fresh dill
- 7 ounces chicken breast

Preparation:
1. Peel the onion. Set the Ninja Foodi to "Sauté" mode.
2. Transfer the onion and mushroom to the Ninja Foodi and add olive oil.
3. Sauté the vegetable mixture for 5 minutes, stirring constantly.
4. Add chicken and cream. Add the half and half and water.
5. Top the mixture with garlic, salt, dill, and basil, stir well, and close the Ninja's lid.
6. Cook the dish for 20 minutes in the "Pressure" mode.

7. Open the Ninja Foodi's lid and remove the chicken breast and shred it.
8. Blend the soup mixture using an immersion blender until smooth.
9. Add the shredded chicken and close the Ninja Foodi's lid.
10. Cook the soup at the "Pressure" mode for 2 minutes.
11. Ladle the cooked soup into serving bowls.
Nutrition Values Per Serving: Calories: 106, Fat: 6.9g, Carbs: 4.6g, Protein: 6.9g

Baked Chicken Bread

Prep Time: 15 minutes
Cook time: 40 minutes
Servings: 8
Ingredients:
- ½ tablespoon garam masala powder
- 8 ounces keto dough
- 1 teaspoon sesame seeds
- 1 egg yolk
- 1 teaspoon ground cilantro
- 1 teaspoon dill
- 10 ounces ground chicken
- ¼ cup fresh parsley
- 1 teaspoon olive oil
- 1 tablespoon black pepper
- 1 onion

Preparation:
1. Roll the dough using a rolling pin. Mix the ground chicken with the ground cilantro and black pepper and stir well.
2. Wash the parsley carefully and chop it. Add the parsley to the chicken mixture.
3. Peel the onion and dice it. Add the onion to the chicken mixture.
4. Mix the meat mixture using your hands. Set the Ninja Foodi to "Pressure" mode.
5. Place the ground meat mixture in the middle of the rolled dough.
6. Wrap the dough in the shape of the bread.
7. Spray the Ninja Foodi with the olive oil inside and put the chicken bread there.
8. Whisk the egg yolk and sprinkle the chicken bread with it.
9. Sprinkle the dish with sesame seeds.
10. Close the Ninja Foodi's lid and cook the dish for 40 minutes.
11. Once it is done, open the Ninja Foodi's lid and check to see if the dish is cooked using a toothpick.
12. Transfer the chicken bread to a serving plate and let it rest briefly.
13. Slice it and serve.
Nutrition Values Per Serving: Calories: 189, Fat: 5.3g, Carbs: 8.1g, Protein: 27.3g

Zesty Duck Legs

Prep Time: 10 minutes
Cook time: 25 minutes
Servings: 6
Ingredients:
- 1 pound duck legs
- ½ cup pomegranate juice
- ½ cup dill
- 1 teaspoon salt
- 1 teaspoon black pepper
- 1 teaspoon ground ginger
- 1 tablespoon olive oil
- ½ cup water
- 1 teaspoon brown sugar
- 1 tablespoon lime zest
- 2 teaspoons soy sauce
- ⅓ teaspoon peppercorn

Preparation:
1. Mix the black pepper, salt, lime zest, ground ginger, brown sugar, and peppercorn in a suitable mixing bowl and stir well.
2. Sprinkle the duck legs with the spice mixture and mix well using your hands.
3. Add the soy sauce, water, olive oil, and pomegranate juice.
4. Wash the dill and chop it. Sprinkle the duck legs mixture with the chopped dill.
5. Set the Ninja Foodi to "Pressure" mode at High.
6. Transfer the duck legs mixture into the Ninja Foodi and close the Ninja's lid.
7. Cook for 25 minutes. Once cooked, open the Ninja Foodi's lid and transfer the cooked duck legs to a serving dish.
8. Sprinkle the dish with the pomegranate sauce, if desired and serve
Nutrition Values Per Serving: Calories: 209, Fat: 11.4g, Carbs: 5.11g, Protein: 21g

Creamy Chicken Stew

Prep Time: 15 minutes
Cook time: 35 minutes
Servings: 8
Ingredients
- ½ cup tomato juice
- 1 tablespoon sugar
- 1 teaspoon salt
- 1 pound boneless chicken breast
- 1 tablespoon oregano
- 1 teaspoon cilantro
- 1 teaspoon fresh ginger, peeled and chopped
- 2 carrots, peeled and chopped
- 3 red onion, peeled and chopped
- 5 ounces shallot, chopped
- 1 tablespoon black pepper
- ½ cup cream
- 3 cups chicken stock
- 3 ounces scallions, chopped
- 2 tablespoons olive oil
- 3 ounces eggplants, peeled and chopped

Preparation:
1. Mix the tomato juice with the oregano, salt, black pepper, cilantro, and cream in a suitable mixing bowl and stir.
2. Set the Ninja Foodi to "Sauté" mode.

3. Add chopped vegetables to the Ninja Foodi and drizzle olive oil.
4. Sauté these vegetables for 5 minutes.
5. Add the tomato juice mixture and the rest of the ingredients to the pot.
6. Stir well using a spoon and close the Ninja Foodi's lid.
7. Cook chicken on "Pressure" mode for 30 minutes.
8. Release the pressure naturally, then remove the lid.
9. Serve warm.
Nutrition Values Per Serving: Calories: 205, Fat: 9g, Carbs: 13.7g, Protein: 18.4g

Sriracha Chicken Satay

Prep Time: 10 minutes
Cook time: 16 minutes
Servings: 8
Ingredients:
- 10 ounces boneless chicken thighs
- ½ cup sweet soy sauce
- ½ cup dark soy sauce
- 1 teaspoon lemongrass paste
- 1 tablespoon almond oil
- 1 teaspoon salt
- 1 tablespoon scallions
- ½ tablespoon sriracha

Preparation:
1. Chop the chicken thighs and sprinkle them with the lemongrass paste and salt and stir well.
2. Set the Ninja Foodi to "Pressure" mode. Place the chicken thighs into the Ninja Foodi and add the soy sauces.
3. Chop the scallions and add them into the Ninja Foodi.
4. Top the mixture with the sriracha and almond oil, stir well using a spoon and close the Ninja's lid.
5. Cook on "Pressure" mode for 16 minutes at high.
6. Once cooked, release the pressure and open the lid.
7. Transfer the cooked chicken satay to a serving plate and sprinkle it with the sauce from the Ninja Foodi.
8. Serve the dish hot.
Nutrition Values Per Serving: Calories: 85, Fat: 4.7g, Carbs: 1.98g, Protein: 9g

Baked Parmesan Chicken

Prep Time: 10 minutes
Cook time: 30 minutes
Servings: 8
Ingredients:
- 1 cup tomato, chopped
- 3 tablespoons butter
- 1 pound boneless chicken breast
- 1 teaspoon salt
- 1 teaspoon paprika
- 7 ounces Parmesan cheese
- ½ cup fresh basil
- 1 teaspoon cilantro
- 1 tablespoon sour cream

Preparation:
1. Grate the Parmesan cheese, mix it with the cilantro and paprika in a suitable mixing bowl, and stir.
2. Sprinkle the boneless chicken breast with the salt and place it into the Ninja Foodi.
3. Add the basil, butter, tomato, and sour cream.
4. Sprinkle the chicken with the grated cheese mixture and close the ninja's lid.
5. Cook the chicken on "Pressure" mode for 30 minutes at High.
6. Once it is done, release the cooker's pressure then remove the Ninja Foodi's lid.
7. Transfer the dish to a serving plate.
Nutrition Values Per Serving: Calories: 234, Fat: 14.2g, Carbs: 2g, Protein: 24.8g

Ninja Foodi Turkey & Beans Wrap

Prep Time: 10 minutes
Cook Time: 13 minutes
Servings: 3
Ingredients:
- ¼ pound lean ground turkey
- ¼ teaspoon ground cumin
- 3 butternut lettuce leaves
- ¼ teaspoon garlic powder
- 1½ tablespoons tomato sauce
- ¼ cup cooked black beans
- ¼ cup chopped onion
- 1½ tablespoons extra-virgin olive oil
- Salt and black pepper, to taste

Directions:
1. Add turkey, onion, tomato sauce, garlic powder, cumin, salt and pepper in a large bowl. Mix well.
2. Meanwhile, heat oil in a Ninja Foodi Multi-cooker and add turkey mixture in it.
3. Select "Pressure" and press the "Start/Stop" button at LO.
4. Cook for 10 minutes and stir in tomato sauce and beans.
5. Cook for about 3 minutes and take out.
6. Divide the mixture evenly on lettuce leaves and serve.
Nutritional Values Per Serving: Calories: 356, Fat: 28.7g, Carbs: 14.8g, Protein: 12.5g

Ninja Foodi Lime Chicken Soup

Prep Time: 10 minutes
Cook Time: 8 hours
Servings: 5
Ingredients:
- ¼ cup fresh lime juice
- 4 garlic cloves, minced
- ½ teaspoon oregano
- 1 onion, chopped
- 4 cups chicken broth
- 2 cups boneless chicken, cubed
- 1 tomato, chopped
- ½ teaspoon red chili powder
- ¾ cup chopped mushrooms
- ½ teaspoon ground cumin
- Salt and black pepper, to taste

Directions:
1. Add everything in the pot of Ninja Foodi Multi-cooker and select "Slow Cook".
2. Close the pressure Lid and press the "Start/Stop" button.
3. Cook for about 8 hours at LOW TEMP and open the lid.
4. Take out the chicken cubes and shred them properly.
5. Stir the shredded chicken in the Slow Cook and take out.
6. Serve and enjoy!
Nutritional Values Per Serving: Calories: 157, Fat: 5.4g, Carbs: 4.9g, Protein: 21g

Ninja Foodi Duck Stew

Prep Time: 10 minutes
Cook Time: 24 minutes
Servings: 3
Ingredients:
- 1 teaspoon canola oil
- ½ cup chopped carrot
- ¾ teaspoon minced garlic
- 1 cup beans, rinsed and drained
- ½ pound duck breasts, sliced
- ½ cup chopped celery
- ½ cup chopped onion
- ½ cup chicken broth
- 1 cup diced tomatoes
- Salt and pepper, to taste

Directions:
1. Heat oil inNinja Foodi Multi-cooker and select "Pressure".
2. Press the "Start/Stop" button and cook duck breasts in it for about 7 minutes.
3. Take out the duck and sauté celery, carrot, onion and garlic in the skillet for about 7 minutes.
4. Return duck in the pot of Ninja Foodi and stir in broth, beans and tomatoes.
5. Close the pressure Lid and cook for about 10 minutes.
6. Open the pressure Lid and take out.
7. Serve and enjoy!
Nutritional Values Per Serving: Calories: 159, Fat: 5g, Carbs: 9.4g, Protein: 19.2g

Ninja Foodi Chicken & Salsa Chili

Prep Time: 10 minutes
Cook Time: 8 hours 5 minutes
Servings: 4
Ingredients:
- 1 cup salsa
- ¾ cup water
- ½ jalapeno pepper, minced
- ½ teaspoon ground cumin
- 1 teaspoon chili powder
- ½ pound boneless chicken breast
- 1 garlic clove, minced
- ½ onion, chopped
- ½ avocado, chopped
- 1½ green bell peppers, chopped
- Salt and black pepper, to taste

Directions:
1. Add chicken, garlic, cumin, salsa, and water in a Ninja Foodi Multi-cooker and select "Slow Cook".
2. Close the pressure Lid and press the "Start/Stop" button.
3. Cook for about 6 hours on HIGH TEMP and open the lid.
4. Meanwhile, heat the non-stick skillet and cook onions, jalapeno pepper and bell pepper in it for about 5 minutes.
5. Now, take the chicken out of the Ninja Foodi Multi-cooker and shred it properly.
6. Place it back in the Slow Cook along with onion mixture, chili powder, avocado, salt and pepper. Mix well.
7. Cook for about 2 hours and take out.
8. Serve and enjoy!

Nutritional Values Per Serving: Calories: 239, Fat: 9.8g, Carbs: 20.7g, Protein: 19.9g

Ninja Foodi Cranberry Chicken

Prep Time: 20 minutes
Cook Time: 25 minutes
Servings: 6
Ingredients:
- 1½ pounds boneless chicken thighs
- 1 cup fresh cranberries
- ¼ cup chopped onion
- 2 tablespoons unsweetened applesauce
- 2 tablespoons fresh ginger, minced
- 2 tablespoons olive oil
- 1 cup chicken broth
- Salt and black pepper, to taste

Directions:
1. Heat oil in Ninja Foodi Multi-cooker and select "Pressure".
2. Press the "Start/Stop" button and add chicken, salt and pepper to it.
3. Cook for 5 minutes per side and take out the chicken. Set aside.
4. Sauté onions for about 3 minutes in the same pot and stir in broth.
5. Add cranberries after 5 minutes, followed by applesauce and cook for about 7 minutes.
6. Pour the cranberry mixture on the chicken and serve immediately.

Nutritional Values Per Serving: Calories: 308, Fat: 22.1g, Carbs: 4.1g, Protein: 21.1g

Bagel Chicken Tenders

Prep Time: 8 Minutes
Cook Time: 15-20 Minutes
Servings: 2
Ingredients:
- 6-8 chicken tenders
- ½ cup bread crumbs/ pork rind crumbs
- 2 tablespoons bagel seasoning
- 1 egg

Directions:
1. Start by washing the chicken breasts and cut them into tenders. You can also buy chicken tenderloins.
2. Now take two bowls and add eggs to one and bread crumb mixture to the other. Add bagel seasoning to the bread crumbs and mix it well.
3. Prepare one tender at a time by first coating it with an egg then rolling it in the crumb mixture.
4. Air Crisp it in Ninja Foodi Multi-Cooker by selecting Air Crisp Mode at 390° F for 20 minutes in a single layer.

Nutritional Values Per Serving: Calories: 433, Fat: 6.3g, Carbs: 15.9g, Protein: 44.3g

Creamy Chicken Zoodles

Prep Time: 10 minutes
Cook time: 27 minutes
Servings: 8
Ingredients:
- 5 ounces zoodles, cooked
- 1 pound boneless chicken breast
- 1 teaspoon cilantro
- 1 cup cream
- ⅓ cup chicken stock
- 1 teaspoon butter
- 1 teaspoon salt
- ½ cup cream cheese
- 1 teaspoon paprika
- 1 teaspoon garlic powder

Preparation:
1. Mix the cilantro, salt, paprika, and garlic powder in a suitable mixing bowl and stir well.
2. Sprinkle the boneless chicken breast with the spice mixture and mix well using your hands.
3. Set the Ninja Foodi to "Pressure" mode. Place the spiced chicken into the Ninja Foodi.
4. Add cream, chicken stock, and cream cheese. Stir the mixture and close the Ninja Foodi's lid.
5. Cook the dish for 25 minutes. Open the lid and transfer the chicken to a mixing bowl.
6. Shred it well using a fork. Transfer the shredded chicken into the Ninja Foodi.
7. Add cooked noodles, stir well, and close the Ninja's lid.
8. Cook the zucchini noodles on "Pressure" mode for 2 minutes at High.
9. Remove the cooked dish from the Ninja Foodi. Serve it warm.

Nutrition Values Per Serving: Calories: 186, Fat: 18.9g, Carbs: 2.2g, Protein: 18g

Glazed Chicken & Vegetables

Prep Time: 8-10 Minutes
Cook Time: 20-25 Minutes
Servings: 2
Ingredients:
- ½ pound chicken thighs boneless
- 2 tablespoons soya sauce
- 2 teaspoons Worcestershire sauce
- 2 tablespoons brown sugar
- 4 crushed garlic cloves
- 1 pound bag of frozen mixed vegetables
- 1 tablespoon vinegar optional
- 1 tablespoon olive oil
- Black pepper to taste

Directions:
1. Start by adding soya sauce, Worcestershire sauce, brown sugar and ginger garlic in a closable container or zip lock bag. Now add chicken in it and seal to coat it well with the marinade. Let it rest in the fridge for two to three hours.
2. Oil spray the Ninja Foodi Multi-Cooker Cook & Crisp Basket. Now put vegetables and chicken in the Ninja Foodi Multi-Cooker Cook & Crisp Basket.
3. Give a spray of olive oil again and sprinkle just a pinch of salt if preferred.
4. Air Crisp it for about 25 minutes at 390° F.
5. When the chicken reaches 165 °F internally, serve it!

Nutritional Values Per Serving: Calories: 397, Fat: 11.3g, Carbs: 25.5g, Protein: 27.4g

Ninja Foodi Spinach Chicken

Prep Time: 10 minutes
Cook Time: 10 minutes
Servings: 4
Ingredients:
- 1 pound chicken tenders
- 2 tablespoons sour cream
- 2 garlic cloves, minced
- 1¼ cups chopped spinach
- 2 tablespoons olive oil
- ¼ cup parmesan cheese, shredded
- Salt and black pepper, to taste

Directions:
1. Heat half of the oliveoil in a Ninja Foodi Multi-cooker and add chicken, salt and pepper in it.
2. Select "Pressure" and press the "Start/Stop" button.
3. Cook for about 2-minutes per side at Hi and take out the chicken. Set aside.
4. Add remaining oil in the pot of Ninja Foodi and sauté garlic in it for about 1 minute.
5. Add spinach, cream, and cheese in the skillet and cook for about 2 minutes.
6. Place chicken in the Ninja Foodi Multi-cooker's pot and simmer for about 5 minutes.
7. Take out and serve hot.

Serving Suggestions: Serve with onion rings on the top.
Variation Tip: Mozzarella cheese can also be used.
Nutritional Values Per Serving: Calories: 301, Fat: 17.1g, Carbs: 1.6g, Protein: 34.3g

Ninja Foodi Ground Turkey

Prep Time: 10 minutes
Cook Time: 8 minutes
Servings: 6
Ingredients:
- 1 tablespoon sesame oil
- 2 pounds lean ground turkey
- 1 onion, chopped
- ½ cup soy sauce
- ½ cup chicken broth
- 2 teaspoons ground ginger
- 3 garlic cloves, minced
- Salt and black pepper, to taste

Directions:
1. Add oil in a Ninja Foodi Multi-cooker and press the "Sear" button.
2. Press the "Start/Stop" button and sauté onion in it for about 3 minutes.
3. Add in garlic and turkey and mash the mixture with a fork.
4. Stir in chicken broth, soy sauce, salt and pepper and cook for about 5 minutes.
5. Take out and serve hot.

Nutritional Values Per Serving: Calories: 262, Fat: 13.3g, Carbs: 4.3g, Protein: 31.8g

Jalapeno Chicken Nachos

Prep Time: 8-9 Minutes
Cook Time: 8-9 Minutes
Servings: 2
Ingredients:
- 1 cup tortillas chips
- 1 pound minced chicken
- ¼ cup BBQ sauce
- Salt to taste
- ½ cup chicken broth
- ½ cup cheddar cheese
- ½ corn
- 2 tablespoons chopped olives
- ½ cup sliced jalapeno
- 1 coarsely cut onion
- Coriander to garnish

Directions:
1. Add the chicken, broth, and salt to a Ninja Foodi Multi-Cooker. For 8 minutes, Pressure Cook it on High and releases the pressure when finished quickly.
2. Stir in BBQ sauce after draining the liquid.
3. At 390° F, preheat the Ninja Foodi Multi-Cooker at Air Crisp Mode. Take Ninja Foodi Multi-Cooker Cook & Crisp Basket and align the parchment paper.
4. Place tortilla chips on the base. Now give a layer of shredder BBQ chicken and corn and top it off with cheddar cheese evenly.
5. For about 5 to 10 minutes place it in the Ninja Foodi Multi-Cooker and wait until cheese is melted. Then add olives, onions, jalapenos slice to the desired amount. Follow it by adding fresh coriander!

Nutritional Values Per Serving: Calories: 550, Fat: 25.5g, Carbs: 29.7g, Protein: 55g

Ninja Foodi Basil Pesto Chicken

Prep Time: 20 minutes
Cook Time: 30 minutes
Servings: 4
Ingredients:
- 4 boneless chicken breasts
- 3 garlic cloves, minced
- ½ cup pine nuts
- 2 cups fresh basil leaves
- ½ teaspoon red pepper flakes
- ½ cup olive oil
- Salt and black pepper, to taste

Directions:
1. Add olive oil, garlic, pine nuts, basil and red pepper flakes in a food processor. Pulse well.
2. Now, arrange chicken breasts in the pot of Ninja Foodi Multi-cooker and pour basil mixture on it.
3. Select "Bake" and close the Crisping Lid.
4. Press the "Start/Stop" button and bake for about 30 minutes at 375 degrees F.
5. Open the Crisping Lid and take out.
6. Serve and enjoy!
Nutritional Values Per Serving: Calories: 603, Fat: 47.3g, Carbs: 3.4g, Protein: 43.4g

Ninja Foodi Duck Fajita Platter

Prep Time: 10 minutes
Cook Time: 25 minutes
Servings: 4
Ingredients:
- 1 pound duck breasts, sliced
- ½ green bell pepper, chopped
- ½ red bell pepper, chopped
- 1 onion, sliced
- 2 tablespoons olive oil
- 1 teaspoon garlic powder
- 1 teaspoon ground cumin
- 2 teaspoons chili powder
- ½ teaspoon dried oregano
- Salt, to taste

Directions:
1. Add duck breasts, green bell pepper, red bell pepper and garlic powder in a large bowl. Mix well.
2. Add in chili powder, cumin, onion, olive oil, oregano and salt in the bowl. Toss to coat well.
3. Place the duck breasts in the pot of Ninja Foodi Multi-cooker and select "Bake".
4. Close the Crisping Lid and press the "Start/Stop" button.
5. Bake for about 25 minutes at 400 degrees F and open the lid.
6. Take out and serve hot.
Nutritional Values Per Serving: Calories: 237, Fat: 12g, Carbs: 6.7g, Protein: 26.1g

Ninja Foodi Barbeque Chicken Drumsticks

Prep Time: 10 minutes
Cook Time: 8 hours
Servings: 4
Ingredients:
- 12 chicken drumsticks
- 2 tablespoons red chili powder
- 1 teaspoon onion powder
- 1 teaspoon garlic powder
- 4 tablespoons honey
- 2 tablespoons apple cider vinegar
- 1 cup barbeque sauce
- 1 tablespoon paprika
- ½ tablespoon ground cumin
- Salt and black pepper, to taste

Directions:
1. Add everything except honey in a Ninja Foodi Multi-cooker and select "Slow Cook".
2. Close the pressure Lid and press the "Start/Stop" button.
3. Cook for about 8 hours at HIGH TEMP and open the lid.
4. Take out the drumsticks and pour honey on them.
5. Serve and enjoy!
Nutritional Values Per Serving: Calories: 416, Fat: 9.1g, Carbs: 44.4g, Protein: 39g

Chapter 5-Seafood and Fish Recipes

Cod Fish

Prep time: 30 minutes
Cook time: 10 minutes
Servings: 4
Ingredients:
- 4 cod fish fillets
- Salt and sugar to taste
- 1 teaspoon sesame oil
- 250 ml water
- 5 tablespoons light soy sauce
- 1 teaspoon dark soy sauce
- 3 tablespoons oil
- 5 slices ginger

Preparation:
1. Pat the cod fish fillets dry.
2. Season with the salt, sugar and sesame oil. Marinate for 15 minutes.
3. Set the Ninja Foodi to Air Crisp.
4. Put the fish on top of the basket. Cook at 350 degrees F for 3 minutes.
5. Flip and cook for 2 minutes. Take the fish out and set aside.
6. Put the rest of the ingredients in the pot.
7. Set it to sauté. Simmer and pour over the fish before serving.
Nutrition Values Per Serving: Calories 303, Fat 13.1g, Carbs 2.9g, Protein 41.5g

Pepper and Lemon Salmon Delight

Prep time: 5 minutes
Cook time: 6 minutes
Servings: 4
Ingredients:
- ¾ cup water
- Sprigs of parsley, basil, tarragon
- 1 pound salmon, skin on
- 3 teaspoons ghee
- ¾ teaspoon salt
- ½ teaspoon pepper
- ½ lemon, sliced
- 1 red bell pepper, julienned
- 1 carrot, julienned

Preparation:
1. Set your Ninja Foodi to Sauté mode and add water and herbs.
2. Place a steamer rack and add the salmon. Drizzle ghee on top of the salmon.
3. Season with pepper and salt. Cover lemon slices on top.
4. Lock up the lid and cook on HIGH pressure for 3 minutes.
5. Release the pressure naturally over 10 minutes.
6. Transfer the salmon to a platter. Add veggies to your pot and set the pot to Sauté mode.
7. Cook for 1-2 minutes. Serve the cooked vegetables with salmon. Enjoy!
Nutrition Values Per Serving: Calories: 464, Fat: 34g, Carbs: 3g, Protein: 34g

Amazing Panko Cod

Prep time: 5 minutes
Cook time: 15 minutes
Servings: 6
Ingredients:
- 2 uncooked cod fillets, 6 ounces each
- 3 teaspoons kosher salt
- ¾ cup panko bread crumbs
- 2 tablespoons butter, melted
- ¼ cup fresh parsley, minced
- 1 lemon. Zested and juiced

Preparation:
1. Preheat your Ninja Foodi at 390 degrees F and place cook & crisp basket inside.
2. Season cod with salt.
3. Take a bowl and add bread crumbs, parsley, lemon juice, zest, butter, and mix well.
4. Coat fillets with the bread crumbs mixture and place fillets in your cook & crisp basket.
5. Lock Crisping Lid and cook on Air Crisp mode for 15 minutes at 360 degrees F.
6. Serve and enjoy!
Nutrition Values Per Serving: Calories: 554, Fat: 24g, Carbs: 5g, Protein: 37g

Salmon and Kale Delight

Prep time: 10 minutes
Cook time: 5 minutes
Servings: 4
Ingredients:
- 1 lemon, juiced
- 2 salmon fillets
- ¼ cup extra virgin olive oil
- 1 teaspoon Dijon mustard
- 4 cups kale, thinly sliced, ribs removed
- 1 teaspoon salt
- 1 avocado, diced
- 1 cup pomegranate seeds
- 1 cup walnuts, toasted
- 1 cup goat parmesan cheese, shredded

Preparation:
1. Season salmon with salt and keep it on the side. Place a trivet in your Ninja Foodi.
2. Place salmon over the trivet. Lock lid and cook on HIGH pressure for 15 minutes.
3. Release pressure naturally over 10 minutes. Transfer salmon to a serving platter.
4. Take a bowl and add kale, season with salt.
5. Take another bowl and make the dressing by adding lemon juice, Dijon mustard, olive oil, and red wine vinegar.
6. Season kale with dressing and add diced avocado, pomegranate seeds, walnuts and cheese.
7. Toss and serve with the fish. Enjoy!
Nutrition Values Per Serving: Calories: 234, Fat: 14g, Carbs: 12g, Protein: 16g

Lemon Garlic Shrimp

Prep time: 40 minutes
Cook time: 10 minutes
Servings: 4
Ingredients:
- 1 pound shrimp, peeled and deveined
- 1 tablespoon olive oil
- 4 cloves garlic, minced
- 1 tablespoon lemon juice
- Salt to taste

Preparation:
1. Mix the olive oil, salt, lemon juice and garlic. Toss shrimp in the mixture.
2. Marinate for 15 minutes. Place the shrimp in the Ninja Foodi basket.
3. Seal the crisping lid. Select the air crisp setting.
4. Cook at 350 degrees F for 8 minutes. Flip and cook for 2 more minutes.

Nutrition Values Per Serving: Calories 170, Fat 5.5g, Carbs 2.8g, Protein 26.1g

Garlic and Lemon Prawn Delight

Prep time: 5 minutes
Cook time: 10 minutes
Servings: 4
Ingredients:
- 2 tablespoons olive oil
- 1 pound prawns
- 2 tablespoons garlic, minced
- ⅔ cup fish stock
- 1 tablespoon butter
- 2 tablespoons lemon juice
- 1 tablespoon lemon zest
- Salt and pepper to taste

Preparation:
1. Set your Ninja Foodi to Sauté mode and add butter and oil, let it heat up.
2. Stir in remaining ingredients. Lock lid and cook on LOW pressure for 5 minutes.
3. Quick release pressure. Serve and enjoy!

Nutrition Values Per Serving: Calories: 236, Fat: 12g, Carbs: 2g, Protein: 27g

Air Fried Scallops

Prep time: 5 minutes
Cook time: 5 minutes
Servings: 4
Ingredients:
- 12 scallops
- 3 tablespoons olive oil
- Salt and pepper to taste

Preparation:
1. Gently rub scallops with salt, pepper, and oil.
2. Transfer to your Ninja Foodi's insert, and place the insert in your Foodi.
3. Lock Crisping Lid and cook for 4 minutes at 390 degrees F.
4. Half through, make sure to give them a nice flip and keep cooking. Serve warm and enjoy!

Nutrition Values Per Serving: Calories: 372, Fat: 11g, Carbs: 0.9g, Protein: 63g

Packets of Lemon and Dill Cod

Prep time: 10 minutes
Cook time: 5-10 minutes
Servings: 4
Ingredients:
- 2 tilapia cod fillets
- Salt, pepper and garlic powder to taste
- 2 sprigs fresh dill
- 4 slices lemon
- 2 tablespoons butter

Preparation:
1. Lay out 2 large squares of parchment paper.
2. Place fillet in center of each parchment square and season with salt, pepper and garlic powder.
3. On each fillet, place 1 sprig of dill, 2 lemon slices, 1 tablespoon of butter.
4. Place trivet at the bottom of your Ninja Foodi. Add 1 cup of water into the pot.
5. Close parchment paper around fillets and fold to make a nice seal.
6. Place both packets in your pot. Lock lid and cook on HIGH pressure for 5 minutes.
7. Quick release pressure. Serve and enjoy!

Nutrition Values Per Serving: Calories: 259, Fat: 11g, Carbs: 8g, Protein: 20g

Spicy Catfish

Prep time: 10 minutes
Cook time: 13 minutes
Servings: 2
Ingredients:
- 2 tablespoons almond flour
- 1 teaspoon red chili powder
- ½ teaspoon paprika
- ½ teaspoon garlic powder
- Salt, as required
- 2 (6 ounces) catfish fillets
- 1 tablespoon olive oil

Preparation:
1. Arrange the greased cook & crisp basket in the pot of Ninja Foodi.
2. Close the Ninja Foodi with crisping lid and select "Air Crisp".
3. Set the temperature to 400 degrees F for 5 minutes.
4. Press "Start/Stop" to begin preheating.
5. In a bowl, mix together the flour, paprika, garlic powder and salt.
6. Add the catfish fillets and coat with the mixture evenly.
7. Now, coat each fillet with oil.
8. After preheating, open the lid.
9. Place the catfish fillets into the cook & crisp basket.
10. Close the Ninja Foodi with crisping lid and select "Air Crisp".
11. Set the temperature to 400 degrees F for 13 minutes.
12. Press "Start/Stop" to begin cooking.
13. Flip the fish fillets once halfway through.
14. Open the lid and serve hot.

Nutrition Values Per Serving: Calories: 458, Fat: 34.2 g, Carbs: 7.5 g, Protein: 32.8 g

Buttery Scallops

Prep time: 10 minutes
Cook time: 5 minutes
Servings: 4
Ingredients:
- 4 garlic cloves, minced
- 4 tablespoons rosemary, chopped
- 2 pounds sea scallops
- 12 cups butter
- Salt and pepper to taste

Preparation:
1. Set your Ninja Foodi to Sauté mode and add butter, rosemary, and garlic.
2. Saute for 1 minute.
3. Add scallops, salt, and pepper.
4. Saute for 2 minutes.
5. Lock Crisping lid and Air Crisp for 3 minutes at 350 degrees F
6. Serve and enjoy!
Nutrition Values Per Serving: Calories: 279, Fat: 16g, Carbs: 5 g, Protein: 25 g

Sweet Tuna Patties

Prep time: 30 minutes
Cook time: 15 minutes
Servings: 2
Ingredients:
- 2 cans tuna flakes
- ½ tablespoon almond flour
- 1 teaspoon dried dill
- 1 tablespoon mayo
- ½ teaspoon onion powder
- 1 teaspoon garlic powder
- Salt and pepper to taste
- 1 tablespoon lemon juice

Preparation:
1. Mix all the ingredients in a bowl. Form patties. Set the tuna patties on the Ninja Foodi basket. Seal the crisping lid. Set it to air crisp.
2. Cook at 400 degrees F for 10 minutes. Flip and cook for 5 more minutes.
Nutrition Values Per Serving: Calories 141, Fat 6.4g, Carbs 5.2g, Protein 17g

Breathtaking Cod Fillets

Prep time: 10 minutes
Cook time: 5-10 minutes
Servings: 4
Ingredients:
- 1 pound frounceen cod fish fillets
- 2 garlic cloves, halved
- 1 cup chicken broth
- ½ cup packed parsley
- 2 tablespoons oregano
- 2 tablespoons almonds, sliced ½ teaspoon paprika

Preparation:
1. Take the fish out of the freezer and let it defrost.
2. Take a food processor and stir in garlic, oregano, parsley, paprika, 1 tablespoon of almond and process. Set your Ninja Foodi to "Sauté" mode and add olive oil, let it heat up.

3. Add remaining almonds and toast, transfer to a towel. Pour broth in a pot and add herb mixture.
4. Cut fish into 4 pieces and place in a cook & crisp basket, transfer cook & crisp basket to the pot.
5. Lock lid and cook on HIGH pressure for 3 minutes. Quick release pressure once has done.
6. Serve steamed fish by pouring over the sauce. Enjoy!
Nutrition Values Per Serving: Calories: 246, Fat: 10g, Carbs: 8g, Protein: 15g

Glazed Haddock

Prep time: 15 minutes
Cook time: 11 minutes
Servings: 4
Ingredients:
- 1 garlic clove, minced
- ¼ teaspoon fresh ginger, grated finely
- ½ cup low-sodium soy sauce
- ¼ cup fresh lime juice
- ½ cup chicken broth
- ¼ cup sugar
- ¼ teaspoon red pepper flakes, crushed
- 1 pound haddock steak

Preparation:
1. Select "Sear/Sauté" setting of Ninja Foodi and place all ingredients except haddock steak.
2. Press "Start/Stop" to begin and cook for about 3-4 minutes, stirring continuously.
3. Press "Start/Stop" to stop cooking and transfer the mixture into a bowl.
4. Set aside to cool.
5. In a bowl, reserve half of the marinade.
6. In a resealable bag, add the remaining marinade and haddock steak.
7. Seal the bag and shake to coat well.
8. Refrigerate for about 30 minutes.
9. Arrange the greased cook & crisp basket in the pot of Ninja Foodi.
10. Close the Ninja Foodi with crisping lid and select "Air Crisp".
11. Set the temperature to 390 degrees F for 5 minutes.
12. Press "Start/Stop" to begin preheating.
13. After preheating, open the lid.
14. Place the haddock steak into the cook & crisp basket.
15. Close the Ninja Foodi with crisping lid and select "Air Crisp".
16. Set the temperature to 390 degrees F for 11 minutes.
17. Press "Start/Stop" to begin cooking.
18. Open the lid and transfer the haddock steak onto a serving platter.
19. Immediately coat the haddock steaks with the remaining glaze.
20. Serve immediately.
Nutrition Values Per Serving: Calories: 192, Fat: 1.2 g, Carbs: 15.1 g, Protein: 3.2 g

Awesome Cherry Tomato Mackerel

Prep time: 5 minutes
Cook time: 7 minutes
Servings: 4
Ingredients:
- 4 Mackerel fillets
- ¼ teaspoon onion powder
- ¼ teaspoon lemon powder
- ¼ teaspoon garlic powder
- ½ teaspoon salt
- 2 cups cherry tomatoes
- 3 tablespoons melted butter
- 1 and ½ cups water
- 1 tablespoon black olives

Preparation:
1. Grease baking dish and arrange cherry tomatoes at the bottom of the dish.
2. Top with fillets sprinkle all spices. Drizzle melted butter over.
3. Add water to your Ninja Foodi.
4. Lower rack in Ninja Foodi and place baking dish on top of the rack.
5. Lock lid and cook on LOW pressure for 7 minutes. Quick release pressure. Serve and enjoy!
Nutrition Values Per Serving: Calories: 325, Fat: 24g, Carbs: 2g, Protein: 21g

Parmesan Tilapia

Prep time: 10 minutes
Cook time: 4 hours
Servings: 4
Ingredients:
- ½ cup Parmesan cheese, grated
- ¼ cup mayonnaise
- ¼ cup fresh lemon juice
- Salt and ground black pepper, as required
- 4 (4-ounce) tilapia fillets
- 2 tablespoons fresh cilantro, chopped

Preparation:
1. In a bowl, mix together all ingredients except tilapia fillets and cilantro.
2. Coat the fillets with mayonnaise mixture evenly.
3. Place the filets over a large piece of foil.
4. Wrap the foil around fillets to seal them.
5. Arrange the foil packet in the bottom of Ninja Foodi.
6. Close the Ninja Foodi with crisping lid and select "Slow Cook".
7. Set on "Low" for 3-4 hours.
8. Press "Start/Stop" to begin cooking.
9. Open the lid and transfer the foil parcel onto a platter.
10. Carefully open the parcel and serve hot with the garnishing of cilantro.
Nutrition Values Per Serving: Calories: 190, Fat: 8.5 g, Carbs: 3.9 g, Protein: 25.4 g

Fresh Steamed Salmon

Prep time: 5 minutes

Cook time: 5 minutes
Servings: 4
Ingredients:
- 2 salmon fillets
- ¼ cup onion, chopped
- 2 stalks green onion stalks, chopped
- 1 whole egg
- Almond meal
- Salt and pepper to taste
- 2 tablespoons olive oil

Preparation:
1. Add a cup of water to your Ninja Foodi and place a steamer rack on top.
2. Place the fish. Season the fish with salt and pepper and lock up the lid.
3. Cook on HIGH pressure for 3 minutes. Once done, quick release the pressure.
4. Remove the fish and allow it to cool.
5. Break the fillets into a bowl and add egg, yellow and green onions.
6. Add ½ a cup of almond meal and mix with your hand. Divide the mixture into patties.
7. Take a large skillet and place it over medium heat. Add oil and cook the patties. Enjoy!
Nutrition Values Per Serving: Calories: 238, Fat: 15g, Carbs: 1g, Protein: 23g

Hearty Cod Fillets

Prep time: 10 minutes
Cook time: 5-10 minutes
Servings: 4
Ingredients:
- 1 pound frozen codfish fillets
- 2 garlic cloves, halved
- 1 cup chicken broth
- ½ cup packed parsley
- 2 tablespoons oregano
- 2 tablespoons almonds, sliced
- ½ teaspoon paprika

Preparation:
1. Take the fish out of the freezer and let it defrost.
2. Take a food processor and stir in garlic, oregano, parsley, paprika, 1 tablespoon of almond and process.
3. Set your Ninja Foodi to "Sauté" mode and add olive oil, let it heat up.
4. Add remaining almonds and toast, transfer to a towel.
5. Pour broth in a pot and add the herb mixture.
6. Cut fish into 4 pieces and place in a cook & crisp basket, transfer cook & crisp basket to the pot.
7. Lock lid and cook on HIGH Pressure for 3 minutes.
8. Quick release pressure once has done.
9. Serve steamed fish by pouring over the sauce.
10. Enjoy!
Nutrition Values Per Serving: Calories: 246, Fat: 10g, Carbs: 8 g, Protein: 15 g

Ranch Warm Fillets

Prep time: 5 minutes
Cook time: 13 minutes
Servings: 4
Ingredients:
- ¼ cup panko
- ½ packet ranch dressing mix powder
- 1 and ¼ tablespoons vegetable oil
- 1 egg beaten
- 2 tilapia fillets
- A garnish of herbs and chilies

Preparation:
1. Preheat your Ninja Foodi with the cook & crisp basket inside at 350 degrees F.
2. Take a bowl and mix in ranch dressing and panko.
3. Beat eggs in a shallow bowl and keep it on the side.
4. Dip fillets in the eggs, then in the panko mix.
5. Place fillets in your Ninja Foodi's insert and transfer insert to Ninja Foodi.
6. Lock Crisping Lid and Air Crisp for 13 minutes at 350 degrees F.
7. Garnish with chilies and herbs. Enjoy!
Nutrition Values Per Serving: Calories: 301, Fat: 12g, Carbs: 1.5g, Protein: 28g

Salmon in Dill Sauce

Prep time: 10 minutes
Cook time: 2 hours
Servings: 6
Ingredients:
- 2 cups water
- 1 cup chicken broth
- 2 tablespoons fresh lemon juice
- ¼ cup fresh dill, chopped
- ½ teaspoon lemon zest, grated
- 6 (4-ounce) salmon fillets
- Salt and ground black pepper, as required

Preparation:
1. In the pot of Ninja Foodi, mix together the water, broth, lemon juice, lemon juice, dill and lemon zest.
2. Arrange the salmon fillets on top, skin side down and sprinkle with salt and black pepper.
3. Close the Ninja Foodi with crisping lid and select "Slow Cook".
4. Set on "Low" for 1-2 hours.
5. Press "Start/Stop" to begin cooking.
6. Open the lid and serve hot.
Nutrition Values Per Serving: Calories: 164, Fat: 7.4 g, Carbs: 1.6 g, Protein: 23.3 g

Buttered Salmon

Prep time: 10 minutes
Cook time: 10 minutes
Servings: 2
Ingredients:
- 2 (6-ounce) salmon fillets
- Salt and ground black pepper, as required
- 1 tablespoon butter, melted
Preparation:

1. Arrange the greased cook & crisp basket in the pot of Ninja Foodi.
2. Close the Ninja Foodi with crisping lid and select "Air Crisp".
3. Set the temperature to 360 degrees F for 5 minutes.
4. Press "Start/Stop" to begin preheating.
5. Season each salmon fillet with salt and black pepper and then coat with the melted butter.
6. After preheating, open the lid.
7. Arrange the salmon fillets into the prepared cook & crisp basket in a single layer.
8. Close the Ninja Foodi with crisping lid and select "Air Crisp".
9. Set the temperature to 360 degrees F for 10 minutes.
10. Press "Start/Stop" to begin cooking.
11. Open the lid and serve hot.
Nutrition Values Per Serving: Calories: 276, Fat: 16.3 g, Carbs: 0 g, Protein: 33.1 g

Scallops with Spinach

Prep time: 15 minutes
Cook time: 10 minutes
Servings: 3
Ingredients:
- 1 (10-ounce) package frozen spinach, thawed and drained
- 12 sea scallops
- Olive oil cooking spray
- Salt and ground black pepper, as required
- ¾ cup heavy whipping cream
- 1 tablespoon tomato paste
- 1 teaspoon garlic, minced
- 1 tablespoon fresh basil, chopped

Preparation:
1. Arrange the greased cook & crisp basket in the pot of Ninja Foodi.
2. Close the Ninja Foodi with crisping lid and select "Air Crisp".
3. Set the temperature to 350 degrees F for 5 minutes.
4. Press "Start/Stop" to begin preheating.
5. In the bottom of a 7-inch heatproof pan, place the spinach.
6. Spray each scallop with cooking spray and then sprinkle with a little salt and black pepper.
7. Arrange scallops on top of the spinach in a single layer.
8. In a bowl, add the cream, tomato paste, garlic, basil, salt and black pepper and mix well.
9. Place the cream mixture over the spinach and scallops evenly.
10. After preheating, open the lid.
11. Place the pan into cook & crisp basket.
12. Close the Ninja Foodi with crisping lid and select "Air Crisp".
13. Set the temperature to 350 degrees F for 10 minutes.
14. Press "Start/Stop" to begin cooking.
15. Open the lid and serve hot.
Nutrition Values Per Serving: Calories: 237, Fat: 12.4 g, Carbs: 8.4 g, Protein: 23.8 g

Awesome Sock-Eye Salmon

Prep time: 5 minutes
Cook time: 7 minutes
Servings: 4
Ingredients:
- 4 sockeye salmon fillets
- 1 teaspoon Dijon mustard
- ¼ teaspoon garlic, minced
- ¼ teaspoon onion powder
- ¼ teaspoon lemon pepper
- ½ teaspoon garlic powder
- ¼ teaspoon salt
- 2 tablespoons olive oil
- 1 and ½ cups water

Preparation:
1. Take a bowl and add mustard, lemon juice, onion powder, lemon pepper, garlic powder, salt, and olive oil. Brush spice mix over salmon.
2. Add water to the cooking pot. Place rack and place salmon fillets on rack.
3. Lock lid and cook on LOW pressure for 7 minutes.
4. Quick release pressure. Serve and enjoy!
Nutrition Values Per Serving: Calories: 353, Fat: 25g, Carbs: 0.6g, Protein: 40g

Cod Parcel

Prep time: 15 minutes
Cook time: 8 minutes
Servings: 2
Ingredients:
- 2 (4-ounce) cod fillets
- ½ teaspoon garlic powder
- Salt and ground black pepper, as required
- 2 fresh dill sprigs
- 4 lemon slices
- 2 tablespoons butter

Preparation:
1. Arrange 2 large parchment squares onto a smooth surface.
2. Place 1 fillet in the center of each parchment square and sprinkle with garlic powder, salt and black pepper.
3. Top each fillet with 1 dill sprig, 2 lemon slices and 1 tablespoon of butter.
4. Fold each parchment paper around the fillets to seal.
5. In the pot of Ninja Foodi, place 1 cup of water.
6. Arrange the "Reversible Rack" in the pot of Ninja Foodi.
7. Place the fish parcels over the "Reversible Rack".
8. Close the Ninja Foodi with the pressure lid and place the pressure valve to "Seal" position.
9. Select "Pressure" and set to "High" for 8 minutes.
10. Press "Start/Stop" to begin cooking.
11. Switch the valve to "Vent" and do a "Quick" release.
12. Open the lid and transfer the fish parcels onto serving plates.
13. Carefully unwrap the parcels and serve.
Nutrition Values Per Serving: Calories: 227, Fat: 12.9 g, Carbs: 10.3 g, Protein: 21.8 g

Simple Salmon Stew

Prep time: 10-60 minutes
Cook time: 5-10 minutes
Servings: 4
Ingredients:
- 1 cup fish broth
- Salt and pepper to taste
- 1 medium onion, chopped
- 1-2 pounds salmon fillets, cubed
- 1 tablespoon butter

Preparation:
1. Take a large-sized bowl and add shrimp, alongside listed ingredients.
2. Let them sit for 30-50 minutes.
3. Take your inner pot and grease it well, add butter and transfer the marinated shrimp to the pot.
4. Lock lid and cook on Bake/Roast mode for 15 minutes at 355 degrees F.
5. Open the lid, serve, and enjoy!
Nutrition Values Per Serving: Calories: 173, Fat: 8g, Carbs: 0.1 g, Protein: 23 g

Shrimp Scampi

Prep time: 15 minutes
Cook time: 7 minutes
Servings: 3
Ingredients:
- 4 tablespoons salted butter
- 1 tablespoon fresh lemon juice
- 1 tablespoon garlic, minced
- 2 teaspoons red pepper flakes, crushed
- 1 pound shrimp, peeled and deveined
- 2 tablespoons fresh basil, chopped
- 1 tablespoon fresh chives, chopped
- 2 tablespoons chicken broth

Preparation:
1. Arrange a 7-inch round baking pan in the cook & crisp basket.
2. Now, arrange the cook & crisp basket in the pot of Ninja Foodi.
3. Close the Ninja Foodi with crisping lid and select "Air Crisp".
4. Set the temperature to 325 degrees F for 5 minutes.
5. Press "Start/Stop" to begin preheating.
6. After preheating, open the lid and carefully remove the pan from Ninja Foodi.
7. In the heated pan, place butter, lemon juice, garlic, and red pepper flakes and mix well.
8. Place the pan in the cook & crisp basket.
9. Close the Ninja Foodi with crisping lid and select "Air Crisp".
10. Set the temperature to 325 degrees F for 7 minutes. Press "Start/Stop" to begin cooking.
11. Press "Start/Stop" to begin cooking.
12. After 2 minutes of cooking, stir in the shrimp, basil, chives and broth.
13. Open the lid and place the pan onto a wire rack for about 1 minute.
14. Stir the mixture and serve hot.
Nutrition Values Per Serving: Calories: 245, Fat: 15.7 g, Carbs: 3.1 g, Protein: 26.4 g

Seafood & Tomato Stew

Prep time: 10 minutes
Cook time: 4 hours 50 minutes
Servings: 8
Ingredients:
- 2 tablespoons olive oil
- 1 pound tomatoes, chopped
- 1 large yellow onion, chopped finely
- 2 garlic cloves, minced
- 2 teaspoons curry powder
- 6 sprigs fresh parsley
- Salt and ground black pepper, as required
- 1½ cups chicken broth
- 1½ pounds salmon, cut into cubes
- 1½ pounds shrimp, peeled and deveined

Preparation:
1. In the pot of Ninja Foodi, add all ingredients except seafood and mix well.
2. Close the Ninja Foodi with crisping lid and select "Slow Cook".
3. Set on "High" for 4 hours.
4. Press "Start/Stop" to begin cooking.
5. Open the lid and stir in the seafood.
6. Now, set on "Low" for 50 minutes.
7. Press "Start/Stop" to begin cooking.
8. Open the lid and serve hot.
Nutrition Values Per Serving: Calories: 272, Fat: 10.7 g, Carbs: 6 g, Protein: 37.6 g

Shrimp Zoodles

Prep time: 5 minutes
Cook time: 7 minutes
Servings: 4
Ingredients:
- 4 cups zoodles
- 1 tablespoon basil, chopped
- 2 tablespoons Ghee
- 1 cup vegetable stock
- 2 garlic cloves, minced
- 2 tablespoons olive oil
- ½ lemon
- ½ teaspoon paprika

Preparation:
1. Set your Ninja Foodi to Sauté mode and add ghee, let it heat up.
2. Add olive oil as well.
3. Add garlic and cook for 1 minute.
4. Add lemon juice, shrimp and cook for 1 minute.
5. Stir in rest of the ingredients and lock lid, cook on LOW Pressure for 5 minutes.
6. Quick release Pressure and serve.
7. Enjoy!
Nutrition Values Per Serving: Calories: 227, Fat: 6g, Carbs: 5g, Protein: 27g

Tuna Bake

Prep Time: 3 minutes
Cook time: 10 minutes
Servings: 2
Ingredients:
- 1 can cream-of-mushroom soup
- 1 ½ cups water
- 1 ¼ cups macaroni pasta
- 1 can tuna
- ½ cup frozen peas
- ½ teaspoon salt
- 1 teaspoon pepper
- ½ cup shredded cheddar cheese

Preparation:
1. Mix soup and water in Ninja Foodi.
2. Add remaining ingredients except for cheese. Stir.
3. Close Ninja Foodi, set to Pressure mode at high, and set the time to 4 minutes.
4. Once done cooking, do a quick release.
5. Remove the pressure lid.
6. Stir in cheese and roast for 5 minutes.
7. Serve and enjoy.
Nutrition Values Per Serving: Calories: 378, Fat 14.1g, Carbs: 34.0g, Protein: 28.0g

Limed Haddock Fish

Prep Time: 15 minutes
Cook time: 25 minutes
Servings: 4
Ingredients:
- 1 garlic clove, minced
- ¼ teaspoon fresh ginger, grated finely
- ½ cup low-sodium soy sauce
- ¼ cup fresh lime juice
- ½ cup chicken broth
- ¼ cup sugar
- ¼ teaspoon red pepper flakes, crushed
- 1 pound haddock steak

Preparation:
1. Select "Sear/Sauté" mode of Ninja Foodi and place all ingredients except haddock steak.
2. Press "Start/Stop" to begin and cook for about 3-4 minutes, stirring continuously.
3. In a suitable bowl, reserve half of the marinade.
4. In a resealable bag, add the remaining marinade and haddock steak.
5. Seal the haddock's ziplock bag and shake it well to coat.
6. Refrigerate for about 30 minutes.
7. Arrange the greased cook & crisp basket into the Ninja Foodi's pot of Ninja Foodi.
8. Close the Ninja Foodi with a crisping lid and select "Air Crisp" mode.
9. Set the temperature to 390 degrees F for almost 5 minutes.
10. Press "Start/Stop" to begin preheating.
11. After preheating, open the lid.
12. Place the haddock steak into the cook & crisp Basket.
13. Close the Ninja Foodi with a crisping lid and select "Air Crisp" mode.
14. Set the temperature to 390 degrees F for almost 11 minutes.
15. Hit the "Start/Stop" button to initiate cooking.
16. Open the lid and transfer the haddock steak onto a serving platter.
17. Immediately coat the haddock steaks with the remaining glaze.
18. Serve immediately.
Nutrition Values Per Serving: Calories: 192, Fat: 1.2g, Carbs: 15.1g, Protein: 3.2g

Buttered Crab Legs

Prep time: 15 minutes
Cook time: 4 minutes
Servings: 2
Ingredients:
* 1½ pounds frozen crab legs
* Salt, as required
* 2 tablespoons butter, melted

Preparation:
1. In the pot of Ninja Foodi, place 1 cup of water and 1 teaspoon of salt.
2. Arrange the "Reversible Rack" in the pot of Ninja Foodi.
3. Place the crab legs over the "Reversible Rack "and sprinkle with salt.
4. Close the Ninja Foodi with the pressure lid and place the pressure valve to "Seal" position.
5. Select "Pressure" and set to "High" for 4 minutes.
6. Press "Start/Stop" to begin cooking.
7. Switch the valve to "Vent" and do a "Quick" release.
8. Open the lid and transfer crab legs onto a serving platter.
9. Drizzle with butter and serve.
Nutrition Values Per Serving: Calories: 445, Fat: 16.7 g, Carbs: 0 g, Protein: 65.4 g

New Orleans Seafood Gumbo

Prep Time: 5 minutes
Cook time: 20 minutes
Servings: 2
Ingredients:
* 1 sea bass filet patted dry and cut into 2" chunks
* 1 tablespoon ghee or avocado oil
* 1 tablespoon Cajun seasoning
* 1 small yellow onion diced
* 1 small bell pepper diced
* 1 celery rib diced
* 2 Roma tomatoes diced
* 1 tablespoon tomato paste
* 1 bay leaf
* ½ cup bone broth
* ¾ pound medium to large raw shrimp deveined
* Sea salt
* Black pepper

Preparation:
1. Set the Ninja Foodi to Sauté mode and heat the oil.
2. Season fish chunks with pepper, salt, and half of Cajun seasoning.
3. When the oil is hot, sear fish chunks for 3 minutes per side and transfer to a plate.
4. Stir in remaining Cajun seasoning, celery, and onions. Sauté for 2 minutes.
5. Stir in bone broth, bay leaves, tomato paste, and diced tomatoes. Mix well. Add back fish.
6. Close Ninja Foodi, set to Pressure mode at HI, and set the time to 5 minutes.
7. Once done cooking, do a quick release.
8. Stir in shrimps, cover and cook 5 minutes in the residual heat.
9. Serve and enjoy.

Nutrition Values Per Serving: Calories: 357, Fat 12.6g, Carbs: 14.8g, Protein: 45.9g

Tomato Dipped Tilapia

Prep Time: 2 minutes
Cook time: 4 minutes
Servings: 2
Ingredients:
* 2 tilapia fillets
* Salt and black pepper
* 2 Roma tomatoes, diced
* 2 minced garlic cloves
* ¼ cup chopped basil, fresh
* 1 tablespoon olive oil
* ¼ teaspoon salt
* ⅛ teaspoon pepper
* 1 tablespoon Balsamic vinegar

Preparation:
1. Add a cup of water to Ninja Foodi, place cook & crisp basket, and add tilapia in the basket. Season with pepper and salt.
2. Close Ninja Foodi, set to Steam mode and set the time to 2 minutes.
3. Mix black pepper, olive oil, salt, basil, garlic, and tomatoes, then mix well.
4. Once done cooking, do a quick release.
5. Serve and enjoy with the basil-tomato dressing.
Nutrition Values Per Serving: Calories: 196, Fat 12.0g, Carbs: 2.0g, Protein: 20.0g,

Sweet Mahi-Mahi

Prep Time: 4 minutes
Cook time: 10 minutes
Servings: 2
Ingredients:
* 2 6-ounce mahi-mahi fillets
* Salt
* Black pepper, to taste
* 1-2 cloves garlic, minced or crushed
* 1" piece ginger, finely grated
* ½ lime, juiced
* 2 tablespoons honey
* 1 tablespoon nana mi togarashi
* 2 tablespoons sriracha
* 1 tablespoon orange juice

Preparation:
1. In a heatproof dish that fits inside the Ninja Foodi, mix well orange juice, sriracha, Nanami togarashi, honey-lime juice, ginger, and garlic.
2. Season mahi-mahi with pepper and salt.
3. Place in a bowl of sauce and cover well in the sauce. Seal dish securely with foil.
4. Add a cup of water in Ninja Foodi, place trivet, and add a dish of mahi-mahi on a trivet.
5. Close Ninja Foodi, set to Steam mode and set the time to 10 minutes.
6. Once done cooking, do a quick release.
7. Serve and enjoy.
Nutrition Values Per Serving: Calories: 200, Fat 0.8g, Carbs: 20.1g, Protein: 28.1g

Salmon Bake

Prep Time: 5 minutes
Cook time: 20 minutes
Servings: 2
Ingredients:
- 1 cup chicken broth
- 1 cup milk
- 1 salmon filet
- 2 tablespoons olive oil
- Ground pepper to taste
- 1 teaspoon minced garlic
- 1 cup frozen vegetables
- ½ can cream-of-celery soup
- ¼ teaspoon dill
- ¼ teaspoon cilantro
- 1 teaspoon Italian spice
- 1 teaspoon poultry seasoning
- 1 tablespoon ground parmesan

Preparation:
1. Set the Ninja Foodi to Sauté mode and add oil to heat.
2. Place the salmon in the heated oil and cook for 2 minutes per side.
3. Stir in garlic, cook for 30 seconds then add broth and cook for 3 minutes.
4. Add the spices, milk, vegetables, noodles and stir.
5. Add the cream of celery soup on top and stir well.
6. Cover the pressure lid. Set the Ninja Foodi to Pressure mode at HI and cook for 8 minutes.
7. Once done cooking, do a quick release.
8. Serve and enjoy with a sprinkle of parmesan.

Nutrition Values Per Serving: Calories: 616, Fat 32.6g, Carbs: 28.7g, Protein: 51.8g

Creamy Salmon

Prep Time: 3 minutes
Cook time: 10 minutes
Servings: 2
Ingredients:
- 2 frozen salmon filets
- ½ cup water
- 1 ½ teaspoons minced garlic
- ¼ cup heavy cream
- 1 cup parmesan cheese grated
- 1 tablespoon chopped fresh chives
- 1 tablespoon chopped fresh parsley
- 1 tablespoon fresh dill
- 1 teaspoon fresh lemon juice
- Salt and black pepper, to taste

Preparation:
1. Add water and trivet to the pot. Place fillets on top of the trivet.
2. Close Ninja Foodi, set to Pressure mode at HI, and set the time to 4 minutes.
3. Once done cooking, do a quick release.
4. Transfer salmon to a serving plate. And remove trivet.
5. Press Start/Stop and then set the Ninja Foodi to sauté mode.
6. Stir in heavy cream once the water begins to boil. Boil for 3 minutes.
7. Stir in lemon juice, parmesan cheese, dill, parsley, and chives.
8. Season with pepper and salt to taste.

9. Serve and enjoy.
Nutrition Values Per Serving: Calories: 423, Fat 25.0g, Carbs: 6.4g, Protein: 43.1g,

Sea Bass Curry

Prep Time: 2 minutes
Cook time: 3 minutes
Servings: 2
Ingredients:
- 1 can coconut milk
- Juice, 1 lime
- 1 tablespoon red curry paste
- 1 teaspoon fish sauce
- 1 teaspoon coconut aminos
- 1 teaspoon honey
- 2 teaspoons sriracha
- 2 cloves garlic, minced
- 1 teaspoon ground turmeric
- 1 teaspoon ground ginger
- ½ teaspoon of sea salt
- ½ teaspoon white pepper
- 1 pound sea bass, cut into 1" cubes
- ¼ cup chopped fresh cilantro
- 2 lime wedges

Preparation:
1. Mix black pepper, ginger, salt, garlic, sriracha, turmeric, honey, red curry paste, coconut aminos, fish sauce, lime juice, and coconut milk in a suitable bowl.
2. Place fish in the pot and pour coconut milk mixture over it.
3. Close the Ninja Foodi, set to Pressure mode at HI, and cook for 3 minutes.
4. Once done cooking, do a quick release.
5. Serve and enjoy with equal amounts of lime wedge and cilantro.

Nutrition Values Per Serving: Calories: 749, Fat 50.0g Carbs: 16.6g, Protein: 58.0g

Ninja Foodi Broiled Mahi-Mahi

Prep Time: 10 minutes
Cook Time: 10 minutes
Servings: 2
Ingredients:
- ½ pound mahi-mahi fillets
- ½ tablespoon olive oil
- 2 tablespoon fresh orange juice
- ½ teaspoon dried thyme
- ½ teaspoon cayenne pepper
- Salt and black pepper, to taste

Directions:
1. Add everything except mahi-mahi fillets in a large bowl and mix well.
2. Stir in mahi-mahi and toss to coat well.
3. Set aside the mixture for about half an hour and remove the fillets from the bowl.
4. Place them in Ninja Foodi Multi-cooker and press the "Broil" button.
5. Close the Crisping Lid and press the "Start/Stop" button.
6. Broil for about 10 minutes and open the lid.
7. Dish out and serve hot.

Nutritional Values Per Serving: Calories: 130, Fat: 3.6g, Carbs: 2.1g, Protein: 21.3g

Fish Coconut Curry

Prep Time: 5 minutes
Cook time: 15 minutes
Servings: 2
Ingredients:
- 1 pound fish steaks or fillets, rinsed and cut into bite-size pieces
- 1 tomato, chopped
- 1 green chile, julienned
- 1 small onion, julienned
- 2 garlic cloves, squeezed
- ½ tablespoon grated ginger
- 2 bay laurel leaves
- 1 teaspoon ground coriander
- 1 teaspoon ground cumin
- ½ teaspoon ground turmeric
- ½ teaspoon Chilli powder
- ½ teaspoon ground fenugreek
- 1 cup unsweetened coconut milk
- Salt to taste

Preparation:
1. Set the Ninja Foodi to Sauté mode and heat the oil.
2. Add garlic, sauté for a minute. Stir in ginger and onions.
3. Sauté for 5 minutes. Stir in bay leaves, fenugreek, Chilli powder, turmeric, cumin, and coriander.
4. Sauté for 1 minute, then pour in coconut milk to deglaze the pot.
5. Stir in tomatoes and green chilies. Mix well.
6. Add fish and mix well.
7. Cover the pressure lid. Set the Ninja Foodi to Pressure mode at LO and cook for 5 minutes.
8. Once done cooking, do a quick release.
9. Serve and enjoy.
Nutrition Values Per Serving: Calories: 434, Fat 29.8g, Carbs: 11.7g, Protein: 29.7g

Mixed Seafood Stew

Prep Time: 5 minutes
Cook time: 35 minutes
Servings: 2
Ingredients:
- 1 tablespoon vegetable oil
- ½ 14.5-ounce can fire-roasted tomatoes
- ½ cup diced onion
- ½ cup chopped carrots
- ½ cup water
- ½ cup white wine or broth
- 1 bay leaf
- ½ tablespoon tomato paste
- 1 tablespoon minced garlic
- 1 teaspoon fennel seeds toasted and ground
- ½ teaspoon dried oregano
- 1 teaspoon salt
- 1 teaspoon red pepper flakes
- 2 cups mixed seafood
- 1 tablespoon fresh lemon juice

Preparation:
1. Set the Ninja Foodi to Sauté mode and heat oil.
2. Once hot, stir in onion and garlic. Sauté for 5 minutes.

3. Stir in tomatoes, bay leaves, tomato paste, oregano, salt, and pepper flakes. Cook for 5 minutes.
4. Stir in bell pepper, water, wine, and fennel seeds. Mix well.
5. Close Ninja Foodi, set to Pressure mode at HI, and set the time to 15 minutes.
6. Once done cooking, do a quick release.
7. Stir in defrosted mixed seafood.
8. Cover and let it cook for 10 minutes in the residual heat.
9. Serve and enjoy with a dash of lemon juice.
Nutrition Values Per Serving: Calories: 202, Fat 10.0g, Carbs: 10.0g, Protein: 18.0g

Salmon Pasta

Prep Time: 5 minutes
Cook time: 10 minutes
Servings: 2
Ingredients:
- 4 ounces dry pasta
- 1 cup water
- 3 ounces smoked salmon, broken in bite-sized pieces
- ¼ lemon
- Salt and black pepper
- ½ teaspoon grated lemon zest
- ½ teaspoon lemon juice
- 2 tablespoons heavy cream
- 1 tablespoon walnuts
- 1 clove garlic
- 1 cup packed baby spinach
- 1 ½ tablespoons olive oil
- ¼ cup grated parmesan + more for serving/garnish
- Kosher Salt and black pepper, to taste
- 1 teaspoon grated lemon zest
- ¼ cup heavy cream

Preparation:
1. Make the sauce in a blender by pulsing garlic and walnuts until chopped.
2. Add ¼ teaspoon pepper, ¼ teaspoon salt, ½ cup parmesan, oil, and ⅔ of spinach. Puree until smooth.
3. Add butter, water, and pasta in Ninja Foodi.
4. Cover and seal the pressure lid.
5. Close Ninja Foodi, set to Pressure mode at HI, and set the time to 4 minutes.
6. Once done cooking, do a quick release.
7. Press Star/Stop to stop and then set to Sauté mode.
8. Stir in remaining parmesan, remaining spinach, sauce, lemon juice, lemon zest, heavy cream, and smoked salmon. Mix well and sauté for 5 minutes.
9. Serve and enjoy.
Nutrition Values Per Serving: Calories: 465, Fat 29.0g, Carbs: 31.0g, Protein: 20.1g

Ninja Foodi Squid Rings

Prep Time: 10 minutes
Cook Time: 13 minutes
Servings: 6
Ingredients:
- ½ onion, sliced
- 2 pounds squid, cut into rings
- 2 teaspoons extra-virgin olive oil
- 2 eggs, beaten
- Salt and black pepper, to taste

Directions:
1. Add oil and onion in a Ninja Foodi Multi-cooker and select "Pressure".
2. Press the "Start/Stop" button and sauté for about 5 minutes.
3. Add in squid rings, salt and pepper. Toss to coat well.
4. Simmer for about 5-minutes and stir in eggs.
5. Close the pressure Lid and cook for about 3 minutes at HIGH pressure.
6. Take out, serve and enjoy!
Nutritional Values Per Serving: Calories: 177, Fat: 5.1g, Carbs: 5.6g, Protein: 25.5g

Ninja Foodi Stir-Fried Shrimp

Prep Time: 5 minutes
Cook Time: 6 minutes
Servings: 6
Ingredients:
- 2 pounds shrimp, peeled and deveined
- 8 tablespoons tamari
- 8 garlic cloves, minced
- 2 tablespoons olive oil
- Salt and black pepper, to taste

Directions:
1. Add oil in Ninja Foodi Multi-cooker and sauté garlic in it for about 1 minute.
2. Stir in shrimp, salt, tamari and black pepper and close the pressure Lid.
3. Select "Pressure" and press the "Start/Stop" button.
4. Cook for about 5 minutes at HIGH pressure and open the lid.
5. Take out, serve and enjoy!
Nutritional Values Per Serving: Calories: 240, Fat: 7.3g, Carbs: 5g, Protein: 37.2g

Ninja Foodi Rosemary Scallops

Prep Time: 10 minutes
Cook Time: 8 minutes
Servings: 6
Ingredients:
- 2 pounds sea scallops
- 4 tablespoons fresh rosemary, chopped
- 4 tablespoons extra-virgin olive oil
- 4 garlic cloves, minced
- Salt and black pepper, to taste

Directions:
1. Add olive oil, rosemary and garlic in the pot of Ninja Foodi Multi-cooker, sauté for about 2 minutes and select "Sear".
2. Stir in scallops, salt and pepper and close the pressure Lid.

3. Press the "Start/Stop" button and cook for about 3 minutes on each side.
4. Open the lid and take out.
5. Serve and enjoy!
Nutritional Values Per Serving: Calories: 223, Fat: 10.8g, Carbs: 5.7g, Protein: 25.6g

Shrimp Scampi Linguini

Prep Time: 5 Minutes
Cook Time: 3 Minutes
Servings: 8
Ingredients:
- 1 pound linguini
- 1 pound (31 to 40) shrimp
- Salt and pepper (to taste)
- 3 tablespoons olive oil
- 3 tablespoons butter (salted)
- 2 tablespoons garlic (minced)
- 1 cup dry white wine
- 1 cup chicken broth
- ¼ teaspoon red pepper flakes
- 1 lemon (juice of the lemon)
- ¼ cup parmesan cheese (shredded)

Directions:
1. Turn Ninja Foodi Multi-Cooker on Sauté on High.
2. Pour in olive oil.
3. Add butter and stir.
4. Add shrimp, season with salt and pepper and then stir.
5. Add garlic and juice of one lemon. Be careful not to get the lemon seeds in the pot.
6. Pour in white wine and chicken broth.
7. Add red pepper flakes and stir.
8. Break linguine in half and add in layers, criss crossing each layer so the pasta does not stick to itself.
9. Once all pasta has been added to the Ninja Foodi Multi-Cooker Pot, press pasta into liquid as much as possible, without stirring. **Do not stir** once you have added the pasta. If you do, your pasta may burn to the bottom of the pan.
10. Put Pressure Lid on Ninja Foodi Multi-Cooker and move valve to Seal position.
11. Change Ninja Foodi Multi-Cooker to Pressure Cook setting on High for 3 minutes and push start.
12. When timer beeps, quick release pressure by moving valve to Vent position. Turn Ninja Foodi Multi-Cooker off.
13. Open Ninja Foodi Multi-Cooker Pressure Lid and stir shrimp and pasta until its well-combined. Don't panic if your pasta is not 100% cooked. It will continue to cook after you add in the parmesan cheese.
14. Add parmesan cheese and stir.
15. Close the Ninja Foodi Multi-Cooker Lid (**do not turn on**) and let the pasta and sauce continue to combine for about 5 minutes. Stir and Enjoy!!!
Nutritional Values Per Serving: Calories: 396, Fat: 12g, Carbohydrates 45g, Protein: 21g

Ninja Foodi Parsley Baked Salmon

Prep Time: 10 minutes
Cook Time: 20 minutes
Servings: 3
Ingredients:
- 1 pound salmon fillets
- ¾ tablespoon olive oil
- 1½ tablespoons fresh parsley, minced
- ¼ teaspoon ginger powder
- Salt and black pepper, to taste

Directions:
1. Place salmon fillets in Ninja Foodi Multi-cooker and top them with olive oil, parsley, ginger powder, salt and pepper.
2. Press the "Bake" button and close the Crisping Lid.
3. Press the "Start/Stop" button and bake for 20 minutes at 400 degrees F.
4. Open the lid and take out.
5. Serve and enjoy!

Nutritional Values Per Serving: Calories: 233, Fat: 12.9g, Carbs: 0.6g, Protein: 29.6g

Lobster Tail

Prep Time: 4 Minutes
Cook Time: 6 Minutes
Servings: 2
Ingredients:
- 4 lobster tails
- 4 tablespoons butter (unsalted)
- 2 crushed garlic cloves
- 1 tablespoon mixed dried herbs
- 1 teaspoon Slash parsley
- Salt and pepper to taste

Directions:
1. Preheat the Ninja Foodi Multi-Cooker at 375° F for the Bake function by setting the Bake Mode for 5 minutes.
2. Meanwhile, cut the lobster using kitchen scissors then cut the center of the tail until you reach the fins. Do not cut them. Use your fingers to bring the meat up to the top by pulling apart the tail and closing the shell.
3. It should create a butterfly with the meat when you're cutting it so that it can easily be moved to the top of the shell.
4. Melt the butter, add garlic and parsley and mix well in a small bowl. Now drench the lobster tails in a butter mixture.
5. Now place the lobster tail in the Ninja Foodi Multi-Cooker Cook & Crisp Basket very carefully, and spray olive oil generously.
6. For 5 minutes cook the lobsters, or until the internal temperature of the meat reaches at least 145° F. Lift the lid of the Ninja Foodi Multi-Cooker once it's done.
7. Take out the golden lobsters and serve!

Nutritional Values Per Serving: Calories: 565, Fat: 36g, Carbs: 0.2g, Protein: 46.3g

Salmon with Soy Sauce

Prep Time: 3 minutes
Cook time: 15 minutes
Servings: 2
Ingredients:
- 1 pound salmon
- 1 tablespoon dark soy sauce
- 2 teaspoons minced ginger
- 1 teaspoon minced garlic
- 1 teaspoon salt
- 1 ½ teaspoons ground pepper
- 2 tablespoons low sugar marmalade

Preparation:
1. In a heatproof pan that fits inside your Ninja Foodi, add salmon.
2. Mix all the sauce ingredients and pour over the salmon. Allow marinating for 15-30 minutes. Cover pan with foil securely.
3. Put 2 cups of water in Ninja Foodi and add the trivet.
4. Place the pan of salmon on the trivet.
5. Cover the pressure lid. Set to Pressure mode at LO, and cook for 5 minutes.
6. Once done cooking, do a quick release.
7. Serve and enjoy.

Nutrition Values Per Serving: Calories: 177, Fat 5.0g, Carbs: 8.8g, Protein: 24.0g

Ninja Foodi Asparagus Scallops

Prep Time: 10 minutes
Cook Time: 10 minutes
Servings: 8
Ingredients:
- 1½ pounds scallops
- 2 tablespoons coconut oil
- 2 teaspoons lemon zest, finely grated
- ¼ cup shallots, chopped
- 1½ pounds asparagus, chopped
- 2 garlic cloves, minced
- 2 tablespoons fresh lemon juice
- 2 tablespoons fresh rosemary, chopped
- Salt and black pepper, to taste

Directions:
1. Add oil in Ninja Foodi Multi-cooker and sauté shallots in it for about 2 minutes.
2. Select "Sear" and press the "Start/Stop" button.
3. Add in garlic and rosemary and Sauté for about 1 minute.
4. Stir in asparagus and lemon zest and cook for about 2 minutes.
5. Add in scallops, lemon juice, salt and pepper and cook for about 5 minutes.
6. Take out and serve hot.

Nutritional Values Per Serving: Calories: 375, Fat: 6.3g, Carbs: 21.3g, Protein: 59.5g

Ninja Foodi Roasted Tilapia

Prep Time: 10 minutes
Cook Time: 6 minutes
Servings: 2
Ingredients:
- ½ pound tilapia
- ½ tablespoon fresh lime juice
- ¼ tablespoon red pepper flakes
- ½ tablespoon olive oil
- ½ teaspoon black pepper
- Salt, to taste

Directions:
1. Add everything except tilapia fillets in a large bowl. Mix well
2. Add in tilapia, toss to coat well and set aside for about half an hour.
3. Place marinated tilapia fillets the pot of Ninja Foodi Multi-cooker and select "Roast".
4. Close the Crisping Lid and press the "Start/Stop" button.
5. Roast for about 3-minutes per side and open the lid.
6. Take out, serve and enjoy!
Nutritional Values Per Serving: Calories: 130, Fat: 4.7g, Carbs: 1.6g, Protein: 21.3g

Ninja Foodi Ginger Cod

Prep Time: 10 minutes
Cook Time: 20 minutes
Servings: 2
Ingredients:
- ½ pound cod fillets
- 1 tablespoon fresh lime juice
- ½ tablespoon fresh ginger, minced
- 1 tablespoon coconut aminos
- Salt and black pepper, to taste

Directions:
1. Add lime juice, fresh ginger, coconut aminos, salt and pepper in a bowl. Mix well.
2. Add cod fillets in the mixture and toss to coat well.
3. Place them in the pot of Ninja Foodi Multi-cooker and press the "Bake" button.
4. Close the Crisping Lid and press the "Start/Stop" button.
5. Bake for about 20-minutes at 325 degrees F and open the lid.
6. Take out, serve and enjoy!
Nutritional Values Per Serving: Calories: 109, Fat: 1.1g, Carbs: 4.3g, Protein: 20.5g

Ninja Foodi Salmon with Sweet Potatoes

Prep Time: 10 minutes
Cook Time: 9 hours
Servings: 3
Ingredients:
- ½ pound salmon fillets, cubed
- ¾ cup chicken broth
- ¼ teaspoon ground nutmeg
- 2 sweet potatoes, sliced thinly
- ½ onion, chopped
- Salt and black pepper, to taste

Directions:
1. Place half of the sweetpotatoes in the bottom of the Ninja Foodi Multi-cooker and season them with salt and pepper.
2. Place salmon fillets and onion on the top and sprinkle ground nutmeg on it.
3. Then, top with remaining sweet potato slices and close the pressure Lid.
4. Select "Slow Cook" and press the "Start/Stop" button.
5. Cook for about 9 hours at LOW TEMP and open the lid.
6. Take out, serve and enjoy!
Nutritional Values Per Serving: Calories: 236, Fat: 5.3g, Carbs: 29.9g, Protein: 17.6g

Ninja Foodi Ginger Salmon

Prep Time: 10 minutes
Cook Time: 18 minutes
Servings: 3
Ingredients:
- ¼ pound salmon fillets
- ½ teaspoon fresh ginger, minced
- ½ tablespoon sesame seeds
- ½ tablespoon coconut aminos
- ½ tablespoon fresh lime juice
- Salt and black pepper, to taste

Directions:
1. Add all the ingredients to a large bowl and mix well.
2. Dredge salmon fillets in the mixture and transfer them to the pot of Ninja Foodi Multi-cooker.
3. Press the "Bake" button and close the Crisping Lid.
4. Press the "Start/Stop" button and bake for about 18 minutes at 325 degrees F.
5. Open the Crisping Lid and take out.
6. Serve and enjoy!
Nutritional Values Per Serving: Calories: 64, Fat: 3.1g, Carbs: 1.7g, Protein: 7.7g

Instant Catfish Fillet

Prep Time: 4-5 Minutes
Cook Time: 15-20 Minutes
Servings: 1
Ingredients:
- 3-4 Catfish fillets
- ½ cup fish fry
- Olive oil spray

Directions:
1. Now evenly coat each catfish fillet with fish fry.
2. Place it in at Air Crisp Mode of Ninja Foodi Multi-Cooker and give it an oil spray. Let it cook for 10 minutes at 390° F.
3. Flip the catfish, give another oil spray and cook for another 10 minutes and serve it!
Nutritional Values Per Serving: Calories: 266, Fat: 3.4g, Carbs: 28g, Protein: 27g

Ninja Foodi Salmon

Prep Time: 5-6 Minutes
Cook Time: 4-5 Minutes
Servings: 4
Ingredients:
- 2 salmon fillets
- 1 cup water
- Juice from 1 lemon, about ½ cup
- Lemon slices
- 4-5 sprigs of fresh dill (or rosemary)
- Salt and pepper to taste

Directions:
1. Pour water and lemon juice into the Ninja Foodi Multi-Cooker.
2. Add lemon slices and dill.
3. Add the fillets.
4. Add the lemon slices on top of the salmon.
5. Sprinkle with salt and pepper.
6. Secure the Ninja Foodi Multi-Cooker Pressure Lid.
7. Make sure the valve is set to Seal, use the manual settings and cook on High Pressure for 4 minutes. Add an additional minute if the fillet is frozen.
8. Once done, release the valve to Vent (quick release) and then open the lid.
9. Serve the salmon immediately or store in fridge.

Nutritional Values Per Serving: Calories: 273, Fat: 14g, Carbs: 10g, Protein: 25g

Butter Lime Salmon

Prep Time: 5-6 Minutes
Cook Time: 4-5 Minutes
Servings: 1
Ingredients
- 2 salmon fillets
- 4 tablespoons lemon juice
- ½ teaspoon lemon zest
- 1 teaspoon rosemary
- 2 fresh dill stalks
- Salt and pepper to taste

Directions:
1. Into the instant pot of Ninja Foodi Multi-Cooker, pour water and lemon juice.
2. Then add lemon zest and dill into it.
3. Into the Ninja Foodi Multi-Cooker Pot, add a wire rack at the lowest setting.
4. Now place salmon fillets on the rack, it is suggested to cut them if they don't fit well in it.
5. Season it by sprinkling salt and pepper on it. Sprinkle rosemary on both sides.
6. Secure the Ninja Foodi Multi-Cooker Pressure Lid.
7. Make sure to set the valve on the Seal. Cook on High Pressure for 4 minutes. For the frozen fillet add another minute to the Cook Time:. Release the valve on the Vent and then open its lid once done fully. And it's ready to be served instantly or it can also be stored in the freezer!

Nutritional Values Per Serving: Calories: 405, Fat: 15.1g, Carbs: 26g, Protein: 41.7g

Cool Indian Palak Paneer

Prep time: 10 minutes
Cook time: 5 minutes
Servings: 4
Ingredients
- 2 teaspoons olive oil
- 5 garlic cloves, chopped
- 1 tablespoon fresh ginger, chopped
- 1 large yellow onion, chopped
- ½ jalapeno chile, chopped
- 1 pound fresh spinach
- 2 tomatoes, chopped
- 2 teaspoons ground cumin
- ½ teaspoon cayenne
- 2 teaspoons Garam masala
- 1 teaspoon ground turmeric
- 1 teaspoon salt
- ½ cup water
- 1 and ½ cups paneer cubes
- ½ cup heavy whip cream

Preparation:
1. Preheat your Ninja Foodi using Sauté mode on HIGH heat, once the pot is hot, add oil and let it shimmer.
2. Add garlic, ginger and chile, sauté for 2-3 minutes.
3. Add onion, spinach, tomatoes, cumin, cayenne, garam masala, turmeric, salt and water.
4. Lock lid and cook on Pressure mode at HI for 2 minutes.
5. Release pressure naturally over 10 minutes.
6. Use an immersion blender to puree the mixture to your desired consistency.
7. Gently stir in paneer and top with a drizzle of cream. Enjoy!
Nutrition Values Per Serving: Calories: 185, Fat: 14g, Carbs: 7g, Protein: 7g

Offbeat Cauliflower and Cheddar Soup

Prep time: 10 minutes
Cook time: 5 minutes
Servings:8
Ingredients
- ¼ cup butter
- ½ sweet onion, chopped
- 1 head cauliflower, chopped
- 4 cups herbed vegetable stock
- ½ teaspoon ground nutmeg
- 1 cup heavy whip cream
- Salt and pepper as needed
- 1 cup cheddar cheese, shredded

Preparation:
1. Set your Ninja Foodi to Sauté mode and add butter , let it heat up and melt.
2. Add onion and cauliflower, sauté for 10 minutes until tender and lightly browned.
3. Add vegetable stock and nutmeg, bring to a boil.
4. Lock lid and cook on Pressure mode at HI for 5 minutes, quick release pressure once done.

5. Remove pot and from Ninja Foodi and stir in heavy cream, puree using immersion blender.
6. Season with more salt and pepper and serve with a topping of cheddar.
7. Enjoy!
Nutrition Values Per Serving: Calories: 227, Fat: 21g, Carbs: 4g, Protein: 8g

Groovy Broccoli Florets

Prep time: 10 minutes
Cook time: 6 minutes
Servings: 4
Ingredients
- 4 tablespoons butter, melted
- Salt and pepper to taste
- 2 pounds broccoli florets
- 1 cup whipping cream

Preparation:
1. Place a cook & crisp basket in your Ninja Foodi (bottom part) and add water.
2. Place florets on top of the basket and lock lid.
3. Cook on Pressure mode at HI for 5 minutes.
4. Quick release pressure.
5. Transfer florets from the cook & crisp basket to the pot.
6. Add salt, pepper, butter and stir.
7. Lock crisping lid and cook on Air Crisp mode for 360 degrees F.
8. Serve and enjoy!
Nutrition Values Per Serving: Calories: 178, Fat: 14g, Carbs: 8g, Protein: 5g

Awesome Veggie Hash

Prep time: 10 minutes
Cook time: 15 minutes
Servings: 4
Ingredients
- 1 cup cauliflower, chopped
- 1 teaspoon mustard
- ½ cup dark leaf kale, chopped
- 1 tablespoon lemon juice
- ½ cup spinach, chopped
- ½ teaspoon salt
- 2 garlic cloves
- ½ teaspoon pepper
- 6 whole eggs
- 3 teaspoons coconut oil

Preparation:
1. Set your Ninja Foodi to Sauté mode and add coconut oil, add garlic, cook until fragrant.
2. Add chopped cauliflower and cook for 5 minutes.
3. Stir in all ingredients except eggs, cook for 2 minutes.
4. Stir in eggs, lock lid and cook on Pressure mode at HI for 2 minutes.
5. Quick release pressure.
6. Enjoy!
Nutrition Values Per Serving: Calories: 480, Fat: 35g, Carbs: 8g, Protein: 22g

Complete Cauliflower Zoodles

Prep time: 10 minutes
Cook time: 8 minutes
Servings: 6
Ingredients
- 2 tablespoons butter
- 2 cloves garlic
- 7-8 cauliflower florets
- 1 cup vegetable broth
- 2 teaspoons salt
- 2 cups spinach, coarsely chopped
- 2 green onions, chopped
- 1 pound zoodles (Spiralized Zucchini)

Garnish
- Chopped sun-dried tomatoes
- Balsamic vinegar
- Gorgonzola cheese

Preparation:
1. Set your Ninja Foodi to Sauté mode and add butter, allow the butter to melt.
2. Add garlic cloves and sauté for 2 minutes.
3. Add cauliflower, broth, salt and lock up the lid and cook on Pressure mode at HI for 6 minutes.
4. Prepare the zoodles.
5. Perform a naturally release over 10 minutes.
6. Use an immersion blender to blend the mixture in the pot to a puree.
7. Pour the sauce over the zoodles.
8. Serve with a garnish of cheese, sun-dried tomatoes and a drizzle of balsamic vinegar.
9. Enjoy!
Nutrition Values Per Serving: Calories: 78, Fat: 5g, Carbs 0.6g, Protein:8g

Ginger and Butternut Bisque Yum

Prep time: 10 minutes
Cook time: 8 minutes
Servings: 6
Ingredients
- 1 cup diced yellow onion
- 4 minced cloves of garlic
- 2 teaspoons peeled and chopped ginger
- 1 cup chopped carrot
- 1 green apple chopped
- 1 peeled and chopped butternut squash
- 1 teaspoon salt
- 2 cups water
- ¼ cup finely chopped parsley
- Black pepper

Preparation:
1. Prepare the ingredients accordingly and keep them on the side.
2. Set your Ninja Foodie to Sauté mode and add onions, cook until transparent.
3. Add just a splash of water.
4. Add garlic, carrot, ginger, apple, squash, and salt.
5. Give it a nice stir.
6. Add water and lock up the lid.
7. Cook on Pressure mode at HI for 5 minutes.
8. Naturally, release the pressure.
9. Allow it to cool for 15 minutes.

10. Blend the soup in batches, or you may use an immersion blender as well to blend in the pot until it is creamy.
11. Add parsley and season with some black pepper.
12. Serve and enjoy!
Nutrition Values Per Serving: Calories: 116, Fat: 5g, Carbs: 14g, Protein: 3g

Cheese Dredged Cauliflower Delight

Prep time: 5 minutes
Cook time: 30 minutes
Servings: 6
Ingredients
- 1 tablespoon Keto-Friendly mustard
- 1 head cauliflower
- 1 teaspoon avocado mayonnaise
- ½ cup parmesan cheese, grated
- ¼ cup butter, cut into small pieces

Preparation:
1. Set your Ninja Foodi to Sauté mode and add butter, let it melt.
2. Add cauliflower and sauté for 3 minutes.
3. Add remaining ingredients and lock lid.
4. Cook on Pressure mode at HI for 30 minutes.
5. Release pressure naturally over 10 minutes.
6. Serve and enjoy!
Nutrition Values Per Serving: Calories: 155, Fat: 13g, Carbs: 2g, Protein: 7g

Vegetable Platter

Prep time: 5 minutes
Cook time: 3 hours 5 minutes
Serving: 6
Ingredients:
- 1 cup grape tomatoes
- 2 cups okra
- 1 cup mushrooms
- 2 cups yellow bell peppers
- 1 and ½ cups red onions
- 2 and ½ cups zucchini
- ½ cup olive oil
- ½ cup balsamic vinegar
- 1 tablespoon fresh thyme, chopped
- 2 tablespoons fresh basil, chopped

Preparation:
1. Slice and chop okra, onions, tomatoes, zucchini, mushrooms.
2. Add veggies to a large container and mix.
3. Take another dish and add oil and vinegar, mix in thyme and basil.
4. Toss the veggies into Ninja Foodi and pour marinade. Stir well.
5. Close lid and cook on 3 hours on Slow Cook mode (HIGH), making sure to stir after every hour.
Nutrition Values Per Serving: Calories: 233, Fat: 18g, Carbs: 14g, Protein: 3g

Garlic and Swiss Chard Garlic

Prep time: 10 minutes
Cook time: 4 minutes
Servings: 4
Ingredients
- 2 tablespoons ghee
- 3 tablespoons lemon juice
- ½ cup chicken stock
- 4 bacon slices, chopped
- 1 bunch Swiss chard, chopped
- ½ teaspoon garlic paste
- Salt and pepper to taste

Preparation:
1. Set your Ninja Foodi to Sauté mode and add bacon, stir well and cook for a few minutes.
2. Add ghee, lemon juice, garlic paste, and stir.
3. Add Swiss chard, salt, pepper, and stock.
4. Lock lid and cook on Pressure mode at HI for 3 minutes.
5. Quick release pressure and serve.
6. Enjoy!
Nutrition Values Per Serving: Calories: 160, Fat: 8g, Carbs: 6g, Protein: 4g

Powerful Medi-Cheese Spinach

Prep time: 5 minutes
Cook time: 15 minutes
Servings: 4
Ingredients
- 4 tablespoons butter
- 2 pounds spinach, chopped and boiled
- Salt and pepper to taste
- ⅔ cup Kalamata olives, halved and pitted
- 1 and ½ cups feta cheese, grated
- 4 teaspoons fresh lemon zest, grated

Preparation:
1. Take a bowl and mix spinach, butter, salt, pepper and transfer the mixture to your cook &crisp basket of the Ninja Foodi.
2. Transfer basket to your Foodi and lock Crisping lid.
3. Cook for 15 minutes on Air Crisp mode on 340 degrees F.
4. Serve by stirring in olives, lemon zest and feta.
5. Enjoy!
Nutrition Values Per Serving: Calories: 274, Fat: 18g, Carbs: 6g, Protein: 10g

Thyme and Carrot Dish with Dill

Prep time: 5 minutes
Cook time: 5 minutes
Servings: 4
Ingredients
- ½ cup water
- 1 pound baby carrots
- 3 tablespoons stevia
- 1 tablespoon thyme, chopped
- 1 tablespoon dill, chopped
- Salt and pepper to taste
- 2 tablespoons ghee

Preparation:

1. Add trivet to your Ninja Foodi, add carrots and add water.
2. Lock lid and cook on Pressure mode at HI for 3 minutes.
3. Quick release pressure.
4. Drain and transfer to a bowl.
5. Set your Ninja Foodi to Sauté mode and add ghee, let it melt.
6. Add stevia, thyme dill, and carrots.
7. Stir well for a few minutes.
8. Serve and enjoy!
Nutrition Values Per Serving: Calories: 162, Fat: 4g, Carbs: 8g, Protein: 3g

Delicious Mushroom Stroganoff

Prep time: 5 minutes
Cook time: 10 minutes
Servings: 6
Ingredients
- ¼ cup unsalted butter, cubed
- 1 pound cremini mushrooms, halved
- 1 large onion, halved
- 4 garlic cloves, minced
- 2 cups vegetable broth
- ½ teaspoon salt
- ¼ teaspoon fresh black pepper
- 1 and ½ cups sour cream
- ¼ cup fresh flat-leaf parsley, chopped
- 1 cup grated parmesan cheese

Preparation:
1. Add butter, mushrooms, onion, garlic, vegetable broth, salt, pepper and paprika.
2. Gently stir and lock lid.
3. Cook onPressure mode at HI for 5 minutes.
4. Release pressure naturally over 10 minutes.
5. Serve by stirring in sour cream and with a garnish of parsley and parmesan cheese.
6. Enjoy!
Nutrition Values Per Serving: Calories: 453, Fat: 37g, Carbs: 11g, Protein: 19g

Chives and Radishes Platter

Prep time: 10 minutes
Cook time: 7 minutes
Servings: 4
Ingredients
- 2 cups radishes, quartered
- ½ cup chicken stock
- Salt and pepper to taste
- 2 tablespoons melted ghee
- 1 tablespoon chives, chopped
- 1 tablespoon lemon zest, grated

Preparation:
1. Add radishes, stock, salt, pepper, zest to your Ninja Foodi and stir.
2. Lock lid and cook on Pressure mod at HI for 7 minutes.
3. Quick release pressure.
4. Add melted ghee, toss well.
5. Sprinkle chives and enjoy!
Nutrition Values Per Serving: Calories: 102, Fat: 4g, Carbs: 6g, Protein: 5g

Everyday Use Veggie-Stock

Prep time: 10 minutes
Cook time: 100 minutes
Servings: 2
Ingredients
- 1 onion, quartered
- 2 large carrots, peeled and cut into 1 inch pieces
- 1 tablespoon olive oil
- 12 ounces mushrooms, sliced
- ¼ teaspoon salt
- 3 and ½ cups water

Preparation:
1. Take cook and crisp basket out of the inner pot, close crisping lid and let it preheat for 3 minutes at 400 degrees F on Bake/Roast settings.
2. While the pot heats up, add onion, carrot chunks in the Cook and Crisp basket and drizzle vegetable oil, toss well.
3. Place basket back into the inner pot, close crisping lid and cook for 15 minutes at 400 degrees F on Bake/Roast mode.
4. Make sure to shake the basket halfway through.
5. Remove basket from pot and add onions, carrots, mushrooms, water and season with salt.
6. Lock pressure lid and seal the valves, cook on Pressure mode at HI for 60 minutes.
7. Release the pressure naturally over 10 minutes.
8. Line a colander with cheesecloth and place it over a large bowl, pour vegetables and stock into the colander.
9. Strain the stock and discard veggies.
10. Enjoy and use as needed!
Nutrition Values Per Serving: Calories: 45, Fat: 4g, Carbs: 3g, Protein: 0g

Spicy Green Beans

Prep time: 10 minutes
Cook time: 15 minutes
Servings: 8
Ingredients:
- 12 ounces green beans
- 1 teaspoon garlic powder
- 1 teaspoon onion powder
- 4 garlic cloves
- 2 tablespoons olive oil
- 1 teaspoon cayenne pepper
- 1 jalapeno pepper
- 1 teaspoon butter
- ½ teaspoon salt
- 1 cup water

Preparation:
1. Wash the green beans and cut each into two equal parts.
2. Toss the green beans in a suitable mixing bowl.
3. Sprinkle the vegetables with onion powder, cayenne pepper, and salt and stir.
4. Remove all the seeds from the jalapeno and chop finely.
5. Add the chopped jalapeno to the green bean's mixture.

6. Peel the garlic and slice it. Mix the sliced garlic with olive oil.
7. Blend the mixture and transfer it to the Ninja Foodi.
8. Add the water and stir. Put the green beans in the Ninja Foodi and close the Ninja's lid.
9. Set the Ninja Foodi mode to "Sauté", and cook the vegetables for 15 minutes.
10. Once cooked, you should have firm but not crunchy green beans.
11. Remove the green beans from the Ninja Foodi and discard the liquid before serving.
Nutrition Values Per Serving: Calories: 49, Fat: 4.1g, Carbs: 3g, Protein: 1g

Lemon Artichokes

Prep time: 10 minutes
Cook time: 5 hours
Servings: 4
Ingredients:
- 5 large artichokes
- 1 teaspoon sea salt
- 2 stalks celery, sliced
- 2 large carrots, cut into matchsticks
- Juice from ½ a lemon
- ¼ teaspoon black pepper
- 1 teaspoon dried thyme
- 1 tablespoon dried rosemary
- Lemon wedges for garnish

Preparation:
1. Remove the stalk from your artichokes and remove the tough outer shell.
2. Transfer the chokes to your Ninja Foodi and add 2 cups of boiling water.
3. Add celery, lemon juice, salt, carrots, black pepper, thyme, rosemary.
4. Cook on Slow Cook mode (HIGH) for 4-5 hours.
5. Serve the artichokes with lemon wedges. Serve and enjoy!
Nutrition Values Per Serving: Calories: 205, Fat: 2g, Carbs: 12g, Protein: 34g

Special Lunch-Worthy Green Beans

Prep time: 5 minutes
Cook time: 10 minutes
Servings: 4
Ingredients
- 2-3 pounds fresh green beans
- 2 tablespoons butter
- 1 garlic clove, minced
- Salt and pepper to taste
- 1 and ½ cups water

Preparation:
1. Add all listed ingredients to your Ninja Foodi pot.
2. Lock lid and cook on Pressure mode at HI for 5 minutes.
3. Release pressure quickly and serve.
4. Enjoy!
Nutrition Values Per Serving: Calories: 87, Fat: 6g, Carbs: 7g, Protein: 3g

Sweet Tomato Salsa

Prep time: 10 minutes
Cook time: 8 minutes
Servings: 6
Ingredients:
- 2 cups tomatoes, chopped
- 1 teaspoon sugar
- ⅓ cup fresh cilantro
- 2 white onions, chopped
- 1 teaspoon black pepper
- 1 teaspoon cayenne pepper
- ½ jalapeno pepper, chopped
- 1 teaspoon olive oil
- 1 tablespoon minced garlic
- ⅓ cup green olives
- 1 teaspoon paprika
- ⅓ cup basil
- 1 tablespoon sugar

Preparation:
1. Transfer the vegetables to the Ninja Foodi and sprinkle them with olive oil.
2. Close the Ninja's lid and cook the ingredients on the "Steam" mode for 8 minutes.
3. Meanwhile, wash the tomatoes and chop them.
4. Place the chopped tomatoes in the bowl. Chop the cilantro.
5. Add the chopped cilantro, black pepper, Chili pepper, and minced garlic in the chopped tomatoes.
6. Add green olives, chop them or leave them whole as desired.
7. Chop the basil and add it to the salsa mixture. Add paprika and olive oil.
8. Once cooked, transfer the veggies from the Ninja Foodi to a plate.
9. Chop the vegetables and add them to the salsa mixture. Sprinkle the dish with sugar.
10. Mix well and serve.
Nutrition Values Per Serving: Calories: 41, Fat: 1.1g, Carbs: 7.7g, Protein: 1.2g

Zucchini Pesto Meal

Prep time: 10 minutes
Cook time: 10 minutes
Servings: 4
Ingredients:
- 1 tablespoon olive oil
- 1 onion, chopped
- 2 and ½ pounds roughly chopped zucchini
- ½ cup water
- 1 and ½ teaspoons salt
- 1 bunch basil leaves
- 2 garlic cloves, minced
- 1 tablespoon extra-virgin olive oil
- Zucchini for making zoodles

Preparation:
1. Set the Ninja Foodi to Sauté mode and add olive oil.
2. Once the oil is hot, add onion and sauté for 4 minutes.
3. Add zucchini, water, and salt. Lock up the lid and cook on HIGH pressure for 3 minutes.
4. Release the pressure naturally. Add basil, garlic, and leaves.

5. Use an immersion blender to blend everything well until you have a sauce-like consistency.
6. Take the extra zucchini and pass them through a Spiralizer to get noodle like shapes.
7. Toss the Zoodles with sauce and enjoy!
Nutrition Values Per Serving: Calories: 71, Fat: 4g, Carbs: 6g, Protein: 3g

Red Cabbage

Prep time: 10 minutes
Cook time: 10 minutes
Serving: 6
Ingredients:
- 6 cups red cabbage, chopped
- 1 tablespoon apple cider vinegar
- ½ cup Keto-Friendly applesauce
- 1 cup water
- 3 garlic cloves, minced
- 1 small onion, chopped
- 1 tablespoon olive oil
- Salt and pepper to taste

Preparation:
1. Add olive oil to Ninja Foodi.
2. Set it to Sauté mode and let it heat up, add onion and garlic and sauté for 2 minutes.
3. Add remaining ingredients and stir. Lock lid and cook on HIGH pressure for 10 minutes.
4. Quick release pressure. Stir well and serve. Enjoy!
Nutrition Values Per Serving: Calories: 81, Fat: 6g, Carbs: 4g, Protein: 2g

Garlic and Ginger Red Cabbage Platter

Prep time: 10 minutes
Cook time: 8 minutes
Serving: 6
Ingredients:
- 2 tablespoons coconut oil
- 1 tablespoon butter
- 3 garlic cloves, crushed
- 2 teaspoons fresh ginger, grated
- 8 cups red cabbage, shredded
- 1 teaspoon salt
- ½ teaspoon pepper
- ⅓ cup water

Preparation:
1. Set your Ninja Foodi to Sauté mode and add coconut oil and butter, allow to heat up.
2. Add garlic and ginger and mix. Add cabbage, pepper, salt, and water.
3. Mix well and lock up the lid, cook on HIGH pressure for 5 minutes.
4. Perform a quick release and mix. Serve and enjoy!
Nutrition Values Per Serving: Calories: 96, Fat: 6g, Carbs: 9g, Protein: 1.8g

Very Rich and Creamy Asparagus Soup

Prep time: 10 minutes
Cook time: 5-10 minutes
Servings: 4
Ingredients:
* 1 tablespoon olive oil
* 3 green onions, sliced crosswise into ¼-inch pieces
* 1 pound asparagus, tough ends removed, cut into 1 inch pieces
* 4 cups vegetable stock
* 1 tablespoon unsalted butter
* 1 tablespoon almond flour
* 2 teaspoons salt
* 1 teaspoon white pepper
* ½ cup heavy cream

Preparation:
1. Set your Ninja Foodi to "Sauté" mode and add oil, let it heat up.
2. Add green onions and sauté for a few minutes, add asparagus and stock.
3. Lock lid and cook on HIGH pressure for 5 minutes.
4. Take a small saucepan and place it over low heat, add butter, flour and stir until the mixture foams and turns into a golden beige, this is your blond roux.
5. Remove from heat. Release pressure naturally over 10 minutes.
6. Open the lid and add roux, salt, and pepper to the soup.
7. Use an immersion blender to puree the soup.
8. Taste and season accordingly, swirl in cream and enjoy!
Nutrition Values Per Serving: Calories: 192, Fat: 14g, Carbs: 8g, Protein: 6g

Parsley Carrot Fries

Prep time: 10 minutes
Cook time: 18 minutes
Servings: 2
Ingredients:
* 2 carrots, peeled
* 1 teaspoon salt
* 1 tablespoon olive oil
* 1 teaspoon dried parsley

Preparation:
1. Cut the carrots into the fries and sprinkle with the salt and dried parsley.
2. Mix well and transfer them into the Ninja Foodi.
3. Close the Ninja's lid and cook the fries on the "Air Crisp" mode for 18 minutes at 385 degrees F.
4. Once done, remove the Ninja's lid and toss well.
5. Serve.
Nutrition Values Per Serving: Calories: 85, Fat: 7g, Carbs: 6g, Protein: 0.5g

Vegetable Salad with Cheese

Prep time: 10 minutes
Cook time: 15 minutes
Servings: 7
Ingredients:
* 2 medium carrots
* 7 ounces turnips
* 1 tablespoon olive oil
* 1 red onion
* 4 garlic cloves
* 5 ounces feta cheese
* 1 teaspoon butter
* 1 teaspoon onion powder
* 1 tablespoon salt
* 1 teaspoon black pepper
* 1 red sweet bell pepper

Preparation:
1. Put all the vegetables in the Ninja Foodi and cook them on "Steam" mode for 15 minutes.
2. Chop the cooked vegetables into small pieces.
3. Mix them in a suitable mixing bowl. Add butter and stir.
4. Top the mixture with onion powder, salt, black pepper.
5. Add feta cheese and add rest of the components to the salad.
6. Mix well and serve.
Nutrition Values Per Serving: Calories: 107, Fat: 6.9g, Carbs: 8.2g, Protein: 3.8g

Creative Coconut Cabbage

Prep time: 10 minutes
Cook time: 7 minutes
Servings: 4
Ingredients:
* 2 tablespoons lemon juice
* ⅓ medium carrot, sliced
* ½ ounces, yellow onion, sliced
* ½ cup cabbage, shredded
* 1 teaspoon turmeric powder
* 1 ounce dry coconut
* ½ tablespoon mustard powder
* ½ teaspoon mild curry powder
* 1 large garlic cloves, diced
* 1 and ½ teaspoons salt
* ⅓ cup water
* 3 tablespoons olive oil
* 3 large whole eggs
* 3 large egg yolks

Preparation:
1. Set your Ninja Foodi to Sauté mode and add oil, stir in onions, salt and cook for 4 minutes.
2. Stir in spices, garlic and sauté for 30 seconds.
3. Stir in rest of the ingredients, lock lid and cook on HIGH pressure for 3 minutes.
4. Naturally, release pressure over 10 minutes.
5. Serve and enjoy!
Nutrition Values Per Serving: Calories: 400, Fat: 34g, Carbs: 10g, Protein: 14g

Eggplant Turnip Casserole

Prep time: 10 minutes
Cook time: 20 minutes
Servings: 8
Ingredients:
- 3 eggplants, chopped
- 1 white onion, chopped
- 1 bell pepper, chopped
- 1 turnip, chopped
- 1 teaspoon salt
- 1 teaspoon black pepper
- 1 teaspoon cayenne pepper
- ½ teaspoon white pepper
- 1 cup cream
- 5 ounces Parmesan, grated

Preparation:
1. Mix white onion, bell pepper, and turnip.
2. Add salt, black pepper, cayenne pepper, and white pepper.
3. In the cooker place, eggplants. Then add the layers of onion mixture.
4. Add cheese and cream. Close and seal the lid.
5. Cook the casserole for 10 minutes on "Pressure" cooking mode.
6. Then make quick pressure release, then serve warm.
Nutrition Values Per Serving: Calories: 144, Fat: 6g, Carbs: 17.3g, Protein: 8.5g

Herbed Radish

Prep time: 10 minutes
Cook time: 8 minutes
Servings: 5
Ingredients:
- 3 cups radish, trimmed
- 1 tablespoon olive oil
- 1 tablespoon butter
- 1 teaspoon salt
- 1 teaspoon dried dill

Preparation:
1. Cut the radishes into halves and place them into the mixing bowl.
2. Sprinkle them with olive oil, salt, and dried dill.
3. Give a good shake to the vegetables.
4. After this, transfer them to the Ninja Foodi and add butter.
5. Close the Ninja's lid and set Air Crisp mode.
6. Cook the radishes for 8 minutes at 375 degrees F.
7. Stir the radish once cooked half way through.
8. Transfer the radishes to the serving plates and serve them hot.
Nutrition Values Per Serving: Calories: 56, Fat: 5.2g, Carbs: 2.5g, Protein: 0.5g

Well Dressed Brussels

Prep time: 10 minutes
Cook time: 4-5 hours
Servings: 4
Ingredients:

- 2 pounds Brussels, halved
- 2 red onions, sliced
- 2 tablespoons apple cider vinegar
- 1 tablespoon extra-virgin olive oil
- 1 teaspoon ground cinnamon
- ½ cup pecans, chopped

Preparation:
1. Add Brussels and onions to Ninja Foodi. Take a small bowl and add cinnamon, vinegar, olive oil.
2. Pour mixture over sprouts and toss.
3. Place lid and cook on Slow Cook mode (LOW) for 4-5 hours. Enjoy!
Nutrition Values Per Serving: Calories: 176, Fat: 10g, Carbs: 14g, Protein: 4g

Creamy Asparagus Mash

Prep time: 6 minutes
Cook time: 6 minutes
Servings: 1
Ingredients:
- ½ cup asparagus
- ½ cup water
- 1 tablespoon heavy cream
- 1 tablespoon fresh basil, chopped
- ½ teaspoon salt
- ¾ teaspoon lemon juice

Preparation:
1. Put asparagus in the Ninja Foodi. Add water and salt.
2. Close and seal the lid. Cook the vegetables on "Pressure" cooking mode for 6 minutes.
3. Open the lid and drain half of the liquid. Add fresh basil.
4. Using the hand blender, blend the mixture until smooth.
5. Then add lemon juice and heavy cream. Stir the mash and transfer it into the serving bowls.
Nutrition Values Per Serving: Calories: 67, Fat: 5.7g, Carbs: 3.2g, Protein: 1.9g

Rosemary Dredged Green Beans

Prep time: 5 minutes
Cook time: 3 hours
Servings: 4
Ingredients:
- 1 pound green beans
- 1 tablespoon rosemary, minced
- 1 teaspoon fresh thyme, minced
- 2 tablespoons lemon juice
- 2 tablespoons water

Preparation:
1. Add listed ingredients to Ninja Foodi.
2. Lock lid and cook on Slow Cook Mode(LOW) for 3 hours. Unlock lid and stir. Enjoy!
Nutrition Values Per Serving: Calories: 40, Fat: 0g, Carbs: 9g, Protein: 2g

Crisping lidAwesome Butternut Squash Soup

Prep time: 10 minutes
Cook time: 16 minutes
Servings: 4
Ingredients
• 1 and ½ pounds butternut squash, baked, peeled and cubed
• ½ cup green onions, chopped
• 3 tablespoons butter
• ½ cup carrots, peeled and chopped
• ½ cup celery, chopped
• 29 ounces vegetable stock
• 1 garlic clove, peeled and minced
• ½ teaspoon Italian seasoning
• 15 ounces canned tomatoes, diced
• Salt and pepper to taste
• ⅛ teaspoon red pepper flakes
• ⅛ teaspoon nutmeg, grated
• 1 and ½ cups half and half
Preparation:
1. Set your Ninja Foodi to "Sauté" mode and add butter, let it melt.
2. Add celery, carrots, onion and stir cook for 3 minutes.
3. Add garlic, stir cook for 1 minute.
4. Add squash, tomatoes, stock, Italian seasoning, salt, pepper, pepper flakes and nutmeg, stir.
5. Lock lid and cook on Pressure mode at H1 for 10 minutes.
6. Release pressure naturally over 10 minutes.
7. Use an immersion blender to puree the mix.
8. Set the food to Sauté mode on LOW and add half and half, stir cook for 1-2 minutes until thickened.
9. Divide and serve with a sprinkle of green onions on top.
10. Enjoy!
Nutrition Values Per Serving: Calories: 250, Fat: 22g, Carbs: 8g, Protein: 3g

Beet Borscht

Prep time: 5 minutes
Cook time: 45 minutes
Serving: 6
Ingredients:
• 8 cups beets
• ½ cup celery, diced
• ½ cup carrots, diced
• 2 garlic cloves, diced
• 1 medium onion, diced
• 3 cups cabbage, shredded
• 6 cups beef stock
• 1 bay leaf
• 1 tablespoon salt
• ½ tablespoon thyme
• ¼ cup fresh dill, chopped
• ½ cup coconut yogurt
Preparation:
1. Add the washed beets to a steamer in the Ninja Foodi.
2. Add 1 cup of water. Steam for 7 minutes.
3. Perform a quick release and drop into an ice bath.

4. Carefully peel off the skin and dice the beets.
5. Transfer the diced beets, celery, carrots, onion, garlic, cabbage, stock, bay leaf, thyme and salt to your Ninja Foodi. Lock up the lid and set the pot to Slow Cook mode, cook for 45 minutes.
6. Release the pressure naturally. Transfer to bowls and top with a dollop of dairy-free yogurt.
7. Enjoy with a garnish of fresh dill!
Nutrition Values Per Serving: Calories: 625, Fat: 46g, Carbs:19g, Protein:90g

Slow-Cooked Brussels

Prep time: 5 minutes
Cook time: 4 hours
Servings: 4
Ingredients:
• 1 pound Brussels sprouts, bottom trimmed and cut
• 1 tablespoon olive oil
• 1½ tablespoon Dijon mustard
• ¼ cup water
• Salt and pepper as needed
• ½ teaspoon dried tarragon
Preparation:
1. Add Brussels, salt, water, pepper, mustard to Ninja Foodi.
2. Add dried tarragon and stir.
3. Lock lid and cook on Slow Cook mode (LOW) for 5 hours until the Brussels are tender.
4. Stir well and add Dijon over Brussels. Stir and enjoy!
Nutrition Values Per Serving: Calories: 83, Fat: 4g, Carbs: 11g, Protein: 4g

Cheesy Dumplings

Prep Time: 10 minutes
Cook time: 15 minutes
Servings: 6
Ingredients:
• 1 cup cottage cheese
• ½ cup flour
• 1 teaspoon baking soda
• 1 teaspoon salt
• 2 tablespoons Sugar
• 4 tablespoons coconut milk
• 1 teaspoon basil
• 3 eggs
Preparation:
1. Blend the cottage cheese in a blender, add eggs and continue blending until smooth.
2. Transfer the mixture to the bowl and add baking soda and flour.
3. Top the mixture with salt, sugar, coconut milk, and basil. Knead the dough.
4. Make the small logs from the dough.
5. Set the Ninja Foodi mode to "Steam", transfer the dough logs to the Ninja Foodi, and close the Ninja's lid.
6. Cook for 15 minutes. Once it is done, remove the dumplings from the Ninja Foodi.
7. Serve immediately.
Nutrition Values Per Serving: Calories: 102, Fat: 6.5g, Carbs: 2.6g, Protein: 8.7g

Green Pepper Tomato Salsa

Prep Time: 7 minutes
Cook time: 10 minutes
Servings: 5
Ingredients:
- 1 cup tomatoes
- 1 teaspoon cumin
- 1 teaspoon ground coriander
- 1 tablespoon cilantro
- ½ cup fresh parsley
- 1 lime
- 1 sweet green pepper
- 1 red onion
- 1 teaspoon garlic powder
- 1 teaspoon olive oil
- 5 garlic cloves

Preparation:
1. Remove the seeds from the sweet green pepper and cut it in half.
2. Peel the onion and garlic cloves. Place the vegetables in the Ninja Foodi and sprinkle them with ½ teaspoon of olive oil.
3. Close the Ninja's lid, and set the Ninja Foodi to "Sauté" mode for 10 minutes.
4. Meanwhile, chop the tomatoes and parsley.
5. Peel the lime and squeeze the juice from it.
6. Mix the lime juice with the chopped parsley, cilantro, ground coriander, and garlic powder and stir well.
7. Sprinkle the chopped tomatoes with the lime mixture.
8. Remove the vegetables from the Ninja Foodi.
9. Rough chop the bell pepper and onions and add the ingredients to the tomato mixture.
10. Mix well and serve.
Nutrition Values Per Serving: Calories: 38, Fat: 1.2g, Carbs: 6.86g, Protein: 1g

Buttered Green Peas

Prep Time: 10 minutes
Cook time: 17 minutes
Servings: 5
Ingredients:
- 2 cups green peas
- ½ cup fresh mint
- 1 tablespoon dried mint
- 1 cup water
- 1 teaspoon salt
- 1 tablespoon butter
- ½ teaspoon peppercorn
- 1 teaspoon olive oil

Preparation:
1. Wash the mint and chop it. Transfer the chopped mint to the Ninja Foodi.
2. Add water and close the Ninja Foodi's lid.
3. Cook the mixture on the "Pressure" mode for 7 minutes.
4. Strain the mint leaves from the water and discard them.
5. Add green peas, dried mint, salt, peppercorn to the liquid into the Ninja Foodi's pot, and close the Ninja's lid.
6. Cook the dish in the "Pressure" mode for 10 minutes.
7. Rinse the cooked green peas in a colander.

8. Put the peas in the serving bowl and add butter and olive oil.
9. Stir the cooked dish gently until the butter is dissolved.
Nutrition Values Per Serving: Calories: 97, Fat: 4.6g, Carbs: 11.48g, Protein: 3g

Caramelized Onion

Prep time: 10 minutes
Cook time: 30-35 minutes
Serving: 6
Ingredients:
- 7 tablespoons unsalted butter
- 3 large onions sliced
- 2 tablespoons water
- 1 teaspoon salt

Preparation:
1. Set your Ninja Foodi to Sauté mode and add set temperature to medium heat, preheat the inner pot for 5 minutes. Add butter and let it melt, add onions, water, and stir.
2. Lock lid and cook on HIGH pressure for 30 minutes. Quick release the pressure.
3. Remove lid and set the pot to Sauté mode, let it sear in medium-high heat for 15 minutes until all liquid is gone. Serve and enjoy!
Nutrition Values Per Serving: Calories: 283, Fat: 19g, Carbs: 18g, Protein: 10g

Parmesan Tomatoes

Prep Time: 7 minutes
Cook time: 7 minutes
Servings: 5
Ingredients:
- 10 ounces big tomatoes
- 7 ounces Parmesan cheese
- ½ teaspoon paprika
- 3 tablespoons olive oil
- 1 tablespoon basil
- 1 teaspoon cilantro
- 1 teaspoon onion powder

Preparation:
1. Wash the tomatoes and slice them into thick slices.
2. Spray the Ninja Foodi with olive oil inside.
3. Transfer the tomato slices to the Ninja Foodi.
4. Mix the paprika, basil, and cilantro and mix well.
5. Grate the Parmesan cheese and sprinkle the tomato slices with the cheese and spice mixture.
6. Close the Ninja Foodi's lid and cook on the "Sauté" mode for 7 minutes.
7. Once it is done, open the Ninja Foodi's lid and let the tomatoes rest briefly.
8. Transfer the dish to the serving plate.
Nutrition Values Per Serving: Calories: 250, Fat: 19.3g, Carbs: 7.85g, Protein: 12g

Turmeric Cauliflower Rice

Prep Time: 10 minutes
Cook time: 5 minutes
Servings: 2
Ingredients:
- 1 cup cauliflower
- 1 tablespoon turmeric
- ½ teaspoon onion powder
- ½ teaspoon garlic powder
- 1 teaspoon dried dill
- ½ teaspoon salt
- 1 teaspoon butter
- 2 pecans, chopped
- ½ cup water

Preparation:
1. Chop the cauliflower roughly and place it in the food processor.
2. Pulse it 3-4 time or until you get cauliflower rice.
3. After this, transfer the vegetables to the cooker.
4. Add onion powder, garlic powder, dried dill, and salt.
5. Then add chopped pecans and water.
6. Stir the mixture gently with the help of the spoon and close the Ninja's lid.
7. Cook it on "Pressure" cooking mode for 5 minutes.
8. Then use quick pressure release and open the lid.
9. Drain the water using the colander.
10. Transfer the cauliflower rice to the big bowl, add turmeric and butter.
11. Mix the mixture well. Serve it warm.
Nutrition Values Per Serving: Calories: 145, Fat: 12.3g, Carbs: 8.1g, Protein: 3.1g

Turmeric Turnip Fries

Prep Time: 15 minutes
Cook time: 14 minutes
Servings: 5
Ingredients:
- 1 pound turnips, peeled
- 1 tablespoon avocado oil
- 1 teaspoon dried oregano
- 1 teaspoon onion powder
- ½ teaspoon salt
- 1 teaspoon turmeric

Preparation:
1. Cut the turnips into the fries and sprinkle them with the dried oregano, avocado oil, onion powder, and turmeric.
2. Mix the turnip and let it soak the spices for 5-10 minutes.
3. After this, place them in the cook & crisp basket and close the Ninja's lid.
4. Set Air Crisp mode at 390 degrees F and cook the fries for 14 minutes.
5. Stir the turnips fries twice during the cooking.
6. When the meal gets a light brown color, it is cooked.
7. Transfer it to the serving plates and sprinkle it with salt.
Nutrition Values Per Serving: Calories: 34, Fat: 0.4g, Carbs: 7g, Protein: 0.9g

Soft Cloud Bread

Prep Time: 15 minutes
Cook time: 7 minutes
Servings: 4
Ingredients:
- 1 egg
- ¾ teaspoon cream of tartar
- 1 tablespoon cream cheese
- ¾ teaspoon onion powder
- ¾ teaspoon dried cilantro

Preparation:
1. Separate egg white from egg yolk and place them into the separated bowls.
2. Whisk the egg white with the cream of tartar until the strong peaks.
3. After this, whisk the cream cheese with the egg white until fluffy.
4. Add onion powder and dried cilantro. Stir gently.
5. After this, carefully add egg white and stir it.
6. Scoop the mixture into the Ninja cooker to get small "clouds" and lower the crisp lid.
7. Cook the bread for 7 minutes at 360 degrees F or until it is light brown.
8. Allow it to cool then serve.
Nutrition Values Per Serving: Calories: 27, Fat: 0.2g, Carbs: 0.9g, Protein: 1.6g

Bok Choy with Mustard Sauce

Prep Time: 10 minutes
Cook time: 12 minutes
Servings: 7
Ingredients:
- 1 pound bok choy
- 1 cup water
- ⅓ cup soy sauce
- 1 teaspoon salt
- 1 teaspoon red Chilli flakes
- 5 tablespoons mustard
- ⅓ cup cream
- 1 teaspoon cumin seeds
- 1 teaspoon black pepper
- 1 tablespoon butter
- ¼ cup garlic clove

Preparation:
1. Wash the bok choy and chop it into pieces.
2. Mix water, soy sauce, salt, Chilli flakes, cumin seeds, and black pepper together.
3. Blend the mixture. Peel the garlic clove and cut into thin slices.
4. Add the butter in the Ninja Foodi and sliced garlic.
5. Set the Ninja Foodi to "Sauté" mode and sauté for 1 minute.
6. Add the cream, soy sauce mixture, and bok choy. Close the Ninja's lid.
7. Set the pot to "Sauté" mode and cook for 10 minutes.
8. Drain the water from the Ninja Foodi and sprinkle the bok choy with the mustard, stirring well.
9. Cook until tender about 2 minutes, then transfer the dish to the serving plate.
10. Enjoy.
Nutrition Values Per Serving: Calories: 83, Fat: 4.8g, Carbs: 7.4g, Protein: 4.2g

Cheesy Zucchini

Prep Time: 10 minutes
Cook time: 10 minutes
Servings: 6
Ingredients:
- 1 pound yellow zucchini
- 3 tablespoons minced garlic
- ½ cup coconut flour
- 3 tablespoons olive oil
- 3 eggs
- ¼ cup coconut milk
- 7 ounces Romano cheese
- 1 teaspoon salt

Preparation:
1. Wash the zucchini and slice them. Mix the minced garlic and salt and stir the mixture.
2. Mix the minced garlic mixture and zucchini slices and mix well.
3. Add the eggs to the suitable mixing bowl and whisk the mixture.
4. Add coconut milk and coconut flour. Stir it carefully until combined.
5. Grate the Romano cheese and add it to the egg mixture and mix.
6. Pour the olive oil in the Ninja Foodi and pre-heat it.
7. Dip the sliced zucchini into the egg mixture.
8. Transfer the dipped zucchini to the Ninja Foodi and cook the dish in the "Sauté" mode for 2 minutes on each side.
9. Once cooked, remove it from the Ninja Foodi, drain any excess fat using a paper towel, and serve.

Nutrition Values Per Serving: Calories: 301, Fat: 21.6g, Carbs: 12.5g, Protein: 16g

Seasoned Deviled Eggs

Prep Time: 15 minutes
Cook time: 5 minutes
Servings: 7
Ingredients:
- 1 tablespoon mustard
- ¼ cup cream
- 1 teaspoon salt
- 8 eggs
- 1 teaspoon mayonnaise
- ¼ cup dill
- 1 teaspoon ground white pepper
- 1 teaspoon minced garlic

Preparation:
1. Put the eggs in the Ninja Foodi and add water.
2. Cook the eggs at high pressure for 5 minutes.
3. Remove the eggs from the Ninja Foodi and chill.
4. Peel the eggs and cut them in half. Remove the egg yolks and mash them.
5. Add the mustard, cream, salt, mayonnaise, ground white pepper, and minced garlic to the mashed egg yolks.
6. Chop the dill and sprinkle the egg yolk mixture with the dill. Mix well until smooth.
7. Transfer this egg yolk mixture to a pastry bag fill the egg whites with the yolk mixture.
8. Serve immediately.

Nutrition Values Per Serving: Calories: 170, Fat: 12.8g, Carbs: 2.42g, Protein: 11g

Black Peas Pickled Garlic

Prep Time: 10 minutes
Cook time: 9 minutes
Servings: 12
Ingredients:
- 2 cups garlic
- 1 tablespoon salt
- 1 tablespoon olive oil
- 1 teaspoon fennel seeds
- ¼ teaspoon black peas
- 3 cups water
- 5 tablespoons apple cider vinegar
- 1 teaspoon lemon juice
- 1 teaspoon lemon zest
- 1 tablespoon stevia
- 1 teaspoon red Chilli flakes

Preparation:
1. Place the salt, olive oil. Fennel seeds, black peas, lemon juice, lemon zest, stevia, and Chilli flakes in the Ninja Foodi.
2. Add water and stir it. Preheat the liquid on the "Pressure" mode for 5 minutes.
3. Meanwhile, peel the garlic. Put the garlic into the preheated liquid.
4. Add apple cider vinegar and stir the mixture.
5. Close the Ninja Foodi's lid and cook the garlic on the "Pressure" mode for 4 minutes.
6. Open the Ninja Foodi's lid and leave the garlic in the liquid for 7 minutes.
7. Transfer the garlic to the liquid into a glass jar, such as a Mason jar.
8. Seal the jar tightly and keep it in your refrigerator for at least 1 day before serving.

Nutrition Values Per Serving: Calories: 46, Fat: 1.3g, Carbs: 7.7g, Protein: 1.5g

Saucy Kale

Prep Time: 5 minutes
Cook Time: 15 minutes
Servings: 4
Ingredients:
- 1-pound kale, torn
- 2 leeks, sliced
- 2 tablespoons balsamic vinegar
- 1 tablespoon parsley, chopped
- Black pepper and salt to the taste
- 2 shallots, chopped
- ½ cup tomato sauce

Directions:
1. In your Ninja Foodi, combine the kale with the leeks and the other ingredients.
2. Put the Ninja Foodi's lid on and cook on High for 15 minutes.
3. Release the pressure quickly for 5 minutes, divide the mix between plates and serve.

Nutritional Values Per Serving: Calories: 100, Fat: 2g, Carbs: 3.4g, Protein: 4g

Butternut Squash Fries

Prep Time: 10 minutes
Cook time: 15 minutes
Servings: 5
Ingredients:
- 1 pound butternut squash
- 1 teaspoon salt
- ¼ cup water
- 2 tablespoons turmeric
- 3 tablespoons peanut oil

Preparation:
1. Wash the butternut squash and peel it. Cut the butternut squash into strips.
2. Sprinkle the cubes with salt, turmeric, and peanut oil.
3. Stir the mixture well. Place the butternut squash strips into the Ninja Foodi and set it to "Sauté" mode.
4. Sauté the vegetables for 10 minutes. Stir the mixture frequently.
5. Add water and close the Ninja Foodi's lid.
6. Cook the dish on "Pressure" mode for 5 minutes.
7. Once it is done, the butternut squash cubes should be tender but not mushy.
8. Transfer the dish to the serving plate and rest briefly before serving.
Nutrition Values Per Serving: Calories: 124, Fat: 8.3g, Carbs: 13.13g, Protein: 1g

Italian Potatoes

Prep Time: 6 Minutes
Cook Time: 10-12 Minutes
Servings: 4
Ingredients:
- 4 potatoes
- 1 tablespoon olive oil
- 2 lemons
- ½ teaspoon salt
- 1 tablespoon Italian Seasoning
- 1 teaspoon mixed herbs

Directions:
1. Wash off the potatoes and cut them into wedges.
2. In the Ninja Foodi Multi-Cooker, set the inner pot and then pour in half a cup of water. Now add the Ninja Foodi Multi-Cooker Cook & Crisp Basket into the inner pot and dump in wedges to it.
3. Preheat Ninja Foodi Multi-Cooker, Pressure Cook on Low temperature setting for 20 minutes.
4. Pressure Cook potatoes at High temperature for 4 minutes.
5. Meanwhile, prepare your seasoning mixture by combining Italian seasoning, lemon juice, herbs, salt, and olive oil in a mixing bowl and put its side.
6. Once the potatoes are cooked, release the pressure by setting the valve to vent. After the pressure has been released remove the lid, take one tablespoon of olive oil, and spread evenly on the potatoes.
7. Now for an additional three to 5 minutes, cook wedges in the Ninja Foodi Multi-Cooker,

until the desired crispiness is achieved. Sprinkle some more seasoning and serve!
Nutrition Information per Serving: Calories: 70, Fat: 4.1g, Carbs: 11g, Protein: 1.2g

Zucchini Noodles

Prep Time: 10 minutes
Cook time: 10 minutes
Servings: 6
Ingredients:
- 2 medium green zucchinis
- 1 tablespoon wine vinegar
- 1 teaspoon white pepper
- ½ teaspoon cilantro
- ¼ teaspoon nutmeg
- 1 cup chicken stock
- 1 garlic clove

Preparation:
1. Wash the zucchini and use a spiralizer to make the zucchini noodles.
2. Peel the garlic and chop it.
3. Mix the cilantro, chopped garlic clove, nutmeg, and white pepper in a suitable mixing bowl.
4. Sprinkle the zucchini noodles with the spice mixture.
5. Pour the chicken stock in the Ninja Foodi and sauté the liquid.
6. Add the zucchini noodles and wine vinegar and stir the mixture gently.
7. Cook for 3 minutes on the "Sauté" mode.
8. Remove the zucchini noodles from the Ninja Foodi and serve.
Nutrition Values Per Serving: Calories: 28, Fat: 0.7g, Carbs: 3.94g, Protein: 2g

Cabbage with Carrots

Prep Time: 5 minutes
Cook Time: 20 minutes
Servings: 4
Ingredients:
- 1 Napa cabbage, shredded
- 2 carrots, sliced
- 2 tablespoons olive oil
- 1 red onion, chopped
- Black pepper and salt to the taste
- 2 tablespoons sweet paprika
- ½ cup tomato sauce

Directions:
1. Set the Foodi on Sauté mode, stir in the oil, heat it up, add the onion and sauté for 5 minutes.
2. Add the carrots, the cabbage and the other ingredients, toss.
3. Put the Ninja Foodi's lid on and cook on High for 15 minutes.
4. Release the pressure quickly for 5 minutes, divide everything between plates and serve.
Nutritional Values Per Serving: Calories: 140, Fat: 3.4g, Carbs: 1.2g, Protein: 3.5 g

Marinated Olives

Prep Time: 10 minutes
Cook time: 17 minutes
Servings: 7
Ingredients:
- 3 cups olives
- 1 tablespoon red Chilli flakes
- 1 teaspoon cilantro
- ⅓ cup olive oil
- 4 tablespoons apple cider vinegar
- 3 tablespoons minced garlic
- ⅓ cup water
- 3 garlic cloves
- 1 ounce bay leaf
- ¼ cup water
- 1 teaspoon clove
- 4 tablespoons lime juice

Preparation:
1. Mix the Chilli flakes, cilantro, apple cider vinegar, minced garlic, bay leaf, water, and lime juice in a suitable mixing bowl.
2. Add the chopped garlic to the Chilli flake mixture and sprinkle it with the garlic.
3. Add water and place the mixture in the Ninja Foodi.
4. Close the Ninja Foodi's lid and cook it in the "Pressure" mode for 10 minutes.
5. Once it is done, remove the mixture from the Ninja Foodi and transfer it to a sealed container.
6. Add olive oil and olives then cook on Sauté mode for 7 minutes.
7. Serve.

Nutrition Values Per Serving: Calories: 186, Fat: 16.9g, Carbs: 10.57g, Protein: 1g

Ninja Foodi Cauliflower Fried Rice

Prep Time: 10 minutes
Cook Time: 15 minutes
Servings: 4
Ingredients:
- 4 cups riced cauliflower
- ¼ cup diced green onion
- ½ teaspoon garlic powder
- ½ teaspoon ground ginger
- 2 tablespoons low-sodium soy sauce
- 1 egg, beaten
- ½ cup peas
- ¼ cup shredded carrots
- 2 tablespoons olive oil

Directions:
1. Add olive oil in Ninja Foodi Multi-cooker. Select to sauté mode.
2. Press the "Start/Stop" button and sauté peas, carrot and onion in it.
3. Add in egg, garlic powder, and ginger. Stir properly.
4. Stir in cauliflower rice and close the pressure Lid.
5. Cook for about 5 minutes and open the lid.
6. Add in soy sauce and mix well.
7. Take out, serve and enjoy!

Nutritional Values Per Serving: Calories: 130, Fat: 8.2g, Carbs: 9.8g, Protein: 5.1g

Zucchinis Spinach Fry

Prep Time: 5 minutes
Cook Time: 17 minutes
Servings: 4
Ingredients:
- 2 zucchinis, sliced
- 1-pound baby spinach
- ½ cup tomato sauce
- Black pepper and salt
- 1 tablespoon avocado oil
- 1 red onion, chopped
- 1 tablespoon sweet paprika
- ½ teaspoon garlic powder
- ½ teaspoon chilli powder

Directions:
1. Set the Foodi on Sauté, stir in the oil, heat it up, add the onion and sauté for 2 minutes.
2. Add the zucchinis, spinach, and the other ingredients Put the Ninja Foodi's lid on and cook on High for 15 minutes.
3. Release the pressure quickly for 5 minutes, divide everything between plates and serve.

Nutritional Values Per Serving: Calories: 130, Fat: 5.5g, Carbs: 3.3g, Protein: 1g

Broccoli Cauliflower

Prep Time: 10 minutes
Cook Time: 15 minutes
Servings: 4
Ingredients:
- 2 cups broccoli florets
- 1 cup cauliflower florets
- 2 tablespoons lime juice
- 1 tablespoon avocado oil
- ⅓ cup tomato sauce
- 2 teaspoons ginger, grated
- 2 teaspoons garlic, minced
- 1 tablespoon chives, chopped

Directions:
1. Set the Foodi on Sauté mode, stir in the oil, heat it up, add the garlic and the ginger and sauté for 2 minutes.
2. Stir in the broccoli, cauliflower and the rest of the ingredients.
3. Put the Ninja Foodi's lid on and cook on High for 13 minutes.
4. naturally Release the pressure for 10 minutes, divide everything between plates and serve.

Nutritional Values Per Serving: Calories: 118, Fat: 1.5g, Carbs: 4.3g, Protein: 6g

Eggplant with Kale

Prep Time: 5 minutes
Cook Time: 15 minutes
Servings: 4
Ingredients:
- Juice of 1 lime
- 1-pound eggplant, roughly cubed
- 1 cup kale, torn
- A pinch of black pepper and salt
- ½ teaspoon chilli powder
- ½ cup chicken stock
- 3 tablespoons olive oil

Directions:
1. Set the Foodi on Sauté mode, stir in the oil, heat it up, add the eggplant and sauté for 2 minutes.
2. Stir in the kale and the rest of the ingredients.
3. Put the Ninja Foodi's lid on and cook on and cook on High for 13 minutes.
4. Release the pressure quickly for 5 minutes, divide the mix between plates and serve.
Nutritional Values Per Serving: Calories: 110, Fat: 3g, Carbs: 4.3g, Protein: 1.1g

Leeks and Carrots

Prep Time: 5 minutes
Cook Time: 15 minutes
Servings: 4
Ingredients:
- 2 leeks, roughly sliced
- 2 carrots, sliced
- 1 teaspoon ginger powder
- 1 teaspoon garlic powder
- ½ cup chicken stock
- Black pepper and salt to the taste
- 2 tablespoons lemon juice
- 2 tablespoons olive oil
- ½ tablespoon balsamic vinegar

Directions:
1. In your Ninja Foodi, combine the leeks with the carrots and the other ingredients.
2. Put the Ninja Foodi's lid on and cook on High for 15 minutes.
3. Release the pressure quickly for 5 minutes, divide the mix between plates and serve.
Nutritional Values Per Serving: Calories: 133, Fat: 3.4g, Carbs: 5g, Protein: 2.1g

Creamy Kale

Prep Time: 5 minutes
Cook Time: 15 minutes
Servings: 4
Ingredients:
- 1 tablespoon lemon juice
- 2 tablespoons balsamic vinegar
- 1-pound kale, torn
- 1 tablespoon ginger, grated
- 1 garlic clove, minced
- 2 tablespoons olive oil
- 1 cup heavy cream
- A pinch of black pepper and salt
- 2 tablespoons chives, chopped

Directions:
1. Set the Foodi on Sauté mode, stir in the oil, heat it up, add the garlic and the ginger and sauté for 2 minutes.
2. Stir in the kale, lemon juice and the other ingredients.
3. Put the Ninja Foodi's lid on and cook on High for 13 minutes.
4. Release the pressure quickly for 5 minutes, divide between plates and serve.
Nutritional Values Per Serving: Calories: 130, Fat: 2g, Carbs: 3.4g, Protein: 2g

Pomegranate Radish Mix

Prep Time: 5 minutes
Cook Time: 8 minutes
Servings: 4
Ingredients:
- 1-pound radishes, roughly cubed
- Black pepper and salt to the taste
- 2 garlic cloves, minced
- ½ cup chicken stock
- 2 tablespoons pomegranate juice
- ¼ cup pomegranate seeds

Directions:
1. In your Ninja Foodi, combine the radishes with the stock and the other ingredients.
2. Put the Ninja Foodi's lid on and cook on High for 8 minutes.
3. Release the pressure quickly for 5 minutes, divide everything between plates and serve.
Nutritional Values Per Serving: Calories: 133, Fat: 2.3g, Carbs: 2.4g, Protein: 2g

Bell Peppers Mix

Prep Time: 5 minutes
Cook Time: 16 minutes
Servings: 4
Ingredients:
- 1-pound red bell peppers, cut into wedges
- ½ teaspoon curry powder
- ½ cup tomato sauce
- Black pepper and salt to the taste
- 1 tablespoon olive oil
- 2 garlic cloves, minced
- 1 tablespoon parsley, chopped

Directions:
1. Put the reversible rack in the Foodi, add the baking pan inside and grease it with the oil.
2. Add the peppers, curry powder and the other ingredients except for the parsley, toss a bit and
3. Cook on Baking mode at 380 degrees F for 16 minutes.
4. Divide cooked peppers between plates and serve with the parsley sprinkled on top.
Nutritional Values Per Serving: Calories: 150, Fat: 3.5g, Carbs: 3.1g, Protein: 1.2g

Minty Radishes

Prep Time: 5 minutes
Cook Time: 15 minutes
Servings: 4
Ingredients:
- 1-pound radishes, halved
- black pepper and salt
- 2 tablespoons balsamic vinegar
- 2 tablespoons mint, chopped
- 2 tablespoons olive oil

Directions:
1. In your Ninja Foodi's basket, combine the radishes with the vinegar and the other ingredients, and
2. Cook on Air Crisp at 380 degrees F for 15 minutes.
3. Divide the radishes between plates and serve.
Nutritional Values Per Serving: Calories: 170, Fat: 4.5g, Carbs: 7.4g, Protein: 4.6g

Okra Stew

Prep Time: 5 minutes
Cook Time: 12 minutes
Servings: 4
Ingredients:
- 1-pound okra, trimmed
- 2 leeks, sliced
- Black pepper and salt to the taste
- 1 cup tomato sauce
- ¼ cup pine nuts, toasted
- 1 tablespoon cilantro, chopped

Directions:
1. In your Ninja Foodi, mix the okra with the leeks and the other ingredients except the cilantro,
2. Put the Ninja Foodi's lid on and cook on High for 12 minutes.
3. Release the pressure quickly for 5 minutes, divide the okra mix into bowls and serve with the cilantro sprinkled on top.
Nutritional Values Per Serving: Calories: 146, Fat: 3g, Carbs: 4g, Protein: 3g

Beets and Carrots

Prep Time: 5 minutes
Cook Time: 20 minutes
Servings: 4
Ingredients:
- 1-pound beets, peeled and roughly cubed
- 1-pound baby carrots, peeled
- Black pepper and salt to the taste
- 2 tablespoons olive oil
- 1 tablespoon chives, minced

Directions:
1. In a suitable, mix the beets with the carrots and the other ingredients and toss.
2. Put the beets and carrots in the Foodi's basket.
3. Cook on Air Crisp at 390 degrees F for 20 minutes, divide between plates and serve.
Nutritional Values Per Serving: Calories: 150, Fat: 4.5g, Carbs: 7.3g, Protein: 3.6g

Blackberry Cake

Prep time: 8 minutes
Cook time: 25 minutes
Servings: 4
Ingredients:
- 4 tablespoons butter
- 3 tablespoons Erythritol
- 2 eggs, whisked
- ½ teaspoon vanilla extract
- 1 ounce blackberries
- 1 cup almond flour
- ½ teaspoon baking powder

Preparation:
1. Combine together all the liquid ingredients.
2. Then add baking powder, almond flour, and Erythritol.
3. Stir the mixture until smooth.
4. Add blackberries and stir the batter gently with the help of the spoon.
5. Take the non-sticky springform pan and transfer the batter inside.
6. Place the springform pan in the pot and lower the crisping lid.
7. Cook the cake for 20 minutes at 365 degrees F.
8. When the time is over – check the doneness of the cake with the help of the toothpick and cook for 5 minutes more if needed.
9. Chill it little and serve!
Nutrition Values Per Serving: Calories 173, Fat 16.7, Carbs 2.2, Protein 4.2

Lava Cups

Prep time: 6 minutes
Cook time: 8 minutes
Servings: 2
Ingredients:
- 2 eggs, whisked
- 3 tablespoons flax meal
- 2 teaspoons cocoa powder
- ½ teaspoon baking powder
- 2 tablespoons heavy cream
- Cooking spray

Preparation:
1. Spray the cake cups with the cooking spray inside.
2. Mix up together all the remaining ingredients and pour the mixture into the prepared cups.
3. Cover the cups with foil and place in Ninja Foodi.
4. Set the Bake mode 355 degrees F.
5. Close the lid and cook the dessert for 8 minutes.
6. Serve the cooked lava cups hot!
Nutrition Values Per Serving: Calories 165, Fat 13.9, Carbs 5.3, Protein 8.4

Keto Brownie

Prep time: 10 minutes
Cook time: 32 minutes
Servings: 6
Ingredients:
- 3 tablespoons Truvia
- 1 ounce sugar-free chocolate chips
- 2 eggs, whisked
- ½ teaspoon vanilla extract
- 3 tablespoon butter, melted
- 1 tablespoon almond flour

Preparation:
1. Whisk together the melted butter, almond flour, vanilla extract, and Truvia.
2. Melt the chocolate chips and add them in the butter mixture.
3. Add eggs and stir until smooth.
4. Pour the batter into Ninja Foodi basket (Bake mode) and cook at 360 degrees F for 32 minutes.
5. Then check if the brownie cooked and chill well.
6. Cut it into the Servings: and serve!
Nutrition Values Per Serving: Calories 99, Fat 8.8, Carbs 5.9, Protein 2.4

Vanilla Creme Brulee

Prep time: 20 minutes
Cook time: 10 minutes
Servings: 3
Ingredients:
- 1 cup heavy cream
- 4 egg yolks
- 3 tablespoons Truvia
- ½ teaspoon vanilla extract

Preparation:
1. Whisk together the egg yolks and 2 tablespoons of Truvia.
2. Add heavy cream and stir until homogenous.
3. Place the mixture into the ramekins and cover them with the foil.
4. Make the small holes on the top of the foil with the help of the toothpick.
5. Pour ½ cup of water in Ninja Foodi basket and insert trivet.
6. Place the ramekins on the trivet and close the pressure cooker lid.
7. Cook the dessert on Pressure mode at HI for 10 minutes.
8. Then make the quick pressure release for 5 minutes.
9. Let the dessert chill for 10 minutes.
10. Remove the foil from the ramekins and sprinkle the surface of creme brulee with Truvia.
11. Use the hand torch to caramelize the surface.
12. Serve it!
Nutrition Values Per Serving: Calories 212, Fat 20.8, Carbs 6.7, Protein 4.4

Ginger Cookies

Prep time: 10 minutes
Cook time: 14 minutes
Servings: 7
Ingredients:
- 1 cup almond flour
- 3 tablespoons butter
- 1 egg
- ½ teaspoon baking powder
- 3 tablespoons Erythritol
- 1 teaspoon ground ginger
- ½ teaspoon ground cinnamon
- 3 tablespoons heavy cream

Preparation:
1. Beat the egg in the bowl and whisk it gently.
2. Add baking powder, Erythritol, ground ginger, ground cinnamon, heavy cream, and flour.
3. Stir gently and add butter.
4. Knead the non-sticky dough.
5. Roll up the dough with the help of the rolling pin and make the cookies with the help of the cutter.
6. Place the cookies in the basket in one layer and close the lid.
7. Set the Bake mode and cook the cookies for 14 minutes at 350 degrees F.
8. When the cookies are cooked – let them chill well and serve!
Nutrition Values Per Serving: Calories 172, Fat 15.6, Carbs 4.1, Protein 4.4

Chip Cookies

Prep time: 10 minutes
Cook time: 9 minutes
Servings: 8
Ingredients:
- 1 ounce sugar-free chocolate chips
- 3 tablespoons butter
- 1 cup almond flour
- 1 egg, whisked
- 2 tablespoons Erythritol

Preparation:
1. Mix up together the almond flour and the whisked egg.
2. Add butter and Erythritol, and mix up the mixture until homogenous.
3. Add chocolate chips and knead the homogenous dough.
4. Make 8 small balls from the dough and transfer them on the rack of Ninja Foodi.
5. Close the crisping lid and set Bake mode.
6. Cook the chip cookies for 9 minutes at 360 degrees F.
7. Chill the cookies and serve!
Nutrition Values Per Serving: Calories 145, Fat 12.3, Carbs 8.4, Protein 3.9

Cinnamon Bites

Prep time: 10 minutes
Cook time: 12 minutes
Servings: 5
Ingredients:
- 1 teaspoon ground cinnamon

- 1 cup almond flour
- ½ teaspoon baking powder
- 1 teaspoon olive oil
- ¼ cup almond milk
- 1 teaspoon butter
- ½ teaspoon vanilla extract
- 1 cup water, for cooking

Preparation:
1. Combine together all the dry ingredients.
2. Then add butter and almond milk in the dry ingredients.
3. Add vanilla extract and olive oil and knead the smooth and non-sticky dough.
4. Make the medium balls from the dough and place them in the silicone molds.
5. Pour water in Ninja Foodi basket.
6. Place the molds on the rack in Ninja Foodi.
7. Close the lid and seal it.
8. Set Pressure mode at HI.
9. Cook the cinnamon bites for 10 minutes.
10. Then make natural pressure release for 10 minutes.
11. Then remove the liquid from the basket and lower the crisping lid.
12. Set Air Crisp and cook the bites for 2 minutes more.
13. Serve!
Nutrition Values Per Serving: Calories 180, Fat 15.2, Carbs 6.1, Protein 5.1

Keto Brownie Batter

Prep time: 10 minutes
Cook time: 5 minutes
Servings: 5
Ingredients:
- ⅓ cup almond flour
- 1 tablespoon Erythritol
- ¼ cup heavy cream
- ½ teaspoon vanilla extract
- 3 tablespoons cocoa powder
- 3 tablespoons butter
- 1 ounce dark chocolate

Preparation:
1. Place the almond flour in the springform pan and flatten to make the layer.
2. Then place the springform pan in the pot and lower the crisping lid.
3. Cook the almond flour for 3 minutes at 400 degrees F or until the almond flour gets a golden color.
4. Meanwhile, combine together cocoa powder and heavy cream, whisk the heavy cream until smooth.
5. Add vanilla extract and Erythritol.
6. Remove the almond flour from Ninja Foodi and chill well.
7. Toss butter and dark chocolate in the pot and preheat for 1 minute on Sear/Sauté mode.
8. When the butter is soft – add it in the heavy cream mixture.
9. Then add chocolate and almond flour.
10. Stir the mass until homogenous and serve!
Nutrition Values Per Serving: Calories 159, Fat 14.9, Carbs 9, Protein 2.5

Coconut Pie

Prep time: 6 minutes
Cook time: 10 minutes
Servings: 4
Ingredients:
- 1 tablespoon coconut flour
- 5 ounces coconut, shredded
- ½ teaspoon vanilla extract
- 1 tablespoon Truvia
- 1 teaspoon butter
- 1 egg, whisked
- ¼ cup heavy cream

Preparation:
1. Mix up together the coconut flour, coconut shred, and butter.
2. Stir the mixture until homogenous.
3. Add whisked egg, vanilla extract, Truvia, and heavy cream. Stir well.
4. Transfer the pie mixture into the basket and lower the crisping lid.
5. Set the Bake mode 355 degrees F.
6. Cook the pie for 10 minutes.
7. Check if the pie is cooked with the help of the toothpick and chill it till the room temperature.
8. Serve it!
Nutrition Values Per Serving: Calories 185, Fat 16.9, Carbs 8.2, Protein 3

Sweet Zucchini Crisp

Prep time: 5 minutes
Cook time: 10 minutes
Servings: 4
Ingredients:
- 1 zucchini, chopped
- 1 teaspoon Vanilla extract
- 2 tablespoons Erythritol
- 1 tablespoon coconut flakes
- 2 tablespoons butter
- 1 tablespoon almond flour

Preparation:
1. Preheat Ninja Foodi at Sear/Sauté mode for 5 minutes at 360 degrees F.
2. Toss the butter in the Ninja Foodi basket.
3. Add chopped zucchini and sauté the vegetables for 3 minutes.
4. Add vanilla extract, coconut flakes, Erythritol, and stir well.
5. Cook the zucchini for 4 minutes more.
6. Then add almond flour and stir well.
7. Sauté the dessert for 1 minute.
8. Use the Air Crisp mode for 2 minutes to get a crunchy crust.
9. Serve the cooked dessert immediately!
Nutrition Values Per Serving: Calories 84, Fat 8.5, Carbs 6.1, Protein 0.3

Mint Cake

Prep time: 8 minutes
Cook time: 62 minutes
Servings: 6
Ingredients:
- 1 teaspoon dried mint

- 1 cup coconut flour
- 1 teaspoon baking powder
- ¼ cup Erythritol
- 2 eggs, whisked
- ¼ cup heavy cream
- 1 tablespoon butter
- ½ teaspoon lemon zest, grated

Preparation:
1. In the mixing bowl mix up together all the ingredients.
2. Use the cooking machine to make the soft batter from the mixture.
3. Pour the batter in the Ninja Foodie basket and flatten it well.
4. Close the pressure cooker lid and set Pressure mode. Seal the lid.
5. Cook the cake on Low pressure for 55 minutes.
6. Then lower the crisping lid and set Air Crisp mode.
7. Cook the cake for 7 minutes more at 400 degrees F.
8. Chill the cake well and serve!
Nutrition Values Per Serving: Calories 136, Fat 7.2, Carbs 22, Protein 4.7

Cinnamon Bun

Prep time: 10 minutes
Cook time: 15 minutes
Servings: 8
Ingredients:
- 1 cup almond flour
- ½ teaspoon baking powder
- 3 tablespoons Erythritol
- 2 tablespoons ground cinnamon
- ½ teaspoon vanilla extract
- 1 tablespoon butter
- 1 egg, whisked
- ¾ teaspoon salt
- ¼ cup almond milk

Preparation:
1. Mix up together the almond flour, baking powder, vanilla extract, egg, salt, and almond milk.
2. Knead the soft and non-sticky dough.
3. Roll up the dough with the help of the rolling pin.
4. Sprinkle dough with the butter, cinnamon, and Erythritol.
5. Roll the dough into the log.
6. Cut the roll into 7 pieces.
7. Spray Ninja Foodi basket with the cooking spray.
8. Place the cinnamon buns in the basket and close the lid.
9. Set the Bake mode and cook the buns for 15 minutes at 355 degrees F.
10. Check if the buns are cooked with the help of the toothpick.
11. Chill the buns well and serve!
Nutrition Values Per Serving: Calories 127, Fat 10.5, Carbs 9.2, Protein 4

Pumpkin Pie

Prep time: 10 minutes
Cook time: 25 minutes
Servings: 6
Ingredients:
- 1 tablespoon pumpkin puree
- 1 cup coconut flour
- ½ teaspoon baking powder
- 1 teaspoon apple cider vinegar
- 1 teaspoon Pumpkin spices
- 1 tablespoon butter
- ¼ cup heavy cream
- 2 tablespoon liquid stevia
- 1 egg, whisked

Preparation:
1. Melt the butter and combine it together with the heavy cream, apple cider vinegar, liquid stevia, egg, and baking powder.
2. Add pumpkin puree and coconut flour.
3. After this, add pumpkin spices and stir the batter until smooth.
4. Pour the batter in Ninja Foodi basket and lower the crisping lid.
5. Set the "Bake" mode 360 degrees F.
6. Cook the pie for 25 minutes.
7. When the time is over – let the pie chill till the room temperature. Serve it!
Nutrition Values Per Serving: Calories 127, Fat 6.6, Carbs 14.2, Protein 3.8

Pecan Muffins

Prep time: 10 minutes
Cook time: 12 minutes
Servings: 6
Ingredients:
- 4 tablespoons butter, softened
- 4 tablespoons coconut flour
- 1 egg, whisked
- 4 tablespoons heavy cream
- ½ teaspoon vanilla extract
- 1 tablespoon pecans, crushed
- 2 tablespoons Erythritol

Preparation:
1. In the mixing bowl, combine together the coconut flour, softened butter, whisked egg, heavy cream, vanilla extract, and Erythritol.
2. Use the hand mixer to mix up the mixture until smooth.
3. Pour the smooth batter in the silicone muffin molds.
4. Top every muffin with the pecans and transfer in Ninja Foodi rack.
5. Lower the crisping lid and set Bake mode.
6. Cook the muffins for 12 minutes at 350 degrees F.
7. Check if the muffins are cooked and transfer on the plate. Chill well and serve!
Nutrition Values Per Serving: Calories 170, Fat 15.1, Carbs 11.1, Protein 2.8

Chocolate Cakes

Prep time: 10 minutes
Cook time: 22 minutes

Servings: 3
Ingredients:
- 1 tablespoon cocoa powder
- 4 tablespoons almond flour
- ½ teaspoon vanilla extract
- 1 tablespoon Truvia
- ⅓ cup heavy cream
- ¼ teaspoon baking powder
- Cooking spray

Preparation:
1. Mix up together the cocoa powder, almond flour, vanilla extract, Truvia, heavy cream, and baking powder.
2. Use the mixer to make the smooth batter.
3. Spray the silicone molds with the cooking spray inside.
4. Pour the batter into the silicone molds and transfer then in Ninja Foodi basket.
5. Close the crisping lid and set Bake/Roast mode.
6. Cook the cakes at 255 degrees F for 22 minutes.
7. Serve the dessert chilled!
Nutrition Values Per Serving: Calories 108, Fat 9.6, Carbs 5.2, Protein 2.6

Almond Bites

Prep time: 10 minutes
Cook time: 14 minutes
Servings: 5
Ingredients:
- 1 egg, whisked
- 1 cup almond flour
- ¼ cup almond milk
- 1 tablespoon coconut flakes
- ½ teaspoon vanilla extract
- ½ teaspoon baking powder
- ½ teaspoon apple cider vinegar
- 2 tablespoons butter

Preparation:
1. Mix up together the whisked egg, almond milk, apple cider vinegar, baking powder, vanilla extract, and butter.
2. Stir the mixture and add almond flour and coconut flakes. Knead the dough.
3. If the dough is sticky – add more almond flour.
4. Make the medium balls from the dough and place them on the rack of Ninja Foodi.
5. Press them gently with the hand palm.
6. Lower the crisping lid and cook the dessert for 12 minutes at 360 degrees F.
7. Check if the dessert is cooked – and cook for 2 minutes more for a crunchy crust.
8. Enjoy!
Nutrition Values Per Serving: Calories 118, Fat 11.5, Carbs 2.4, Protein 2.7

Vanilla Custard

Prep time: 5 minutes
Cook time: 10 minutes
Servings: 4
Ingredients:
- 3 egg yolks
- 1 cup almond milk
- 1 teaspoon vanilla extract
- 2 tablespoons Truvia

Preparation:
1. Whisk together egg yolk and Truvia.
2. Add vanilla extract and almond milk.
3. Preheat Ninja Foodi at Sauté/Sear mode at 365 degrees F for 5 minutes.
4. Then pour the almond milk mixture and sauté it for 10 minutes.
5. Stir the liquid all the time.
6. When the liquid start to be thick – transfer it into the serving jars and leave it for 1 hour in the fridge.
7. Serve it!
Nutrition Values Per Serving: Calories 181, Fat 17.7, Carbs 6.2, Protein 3.4

Chocolate Cheesecake

Prep time: 15 minutes
Cook time: 15 minutes
Servings: 6
Ingredients:
- 2 cups cream cheese, softened
- 2 eggs
- 2 tablespoons cocoa powder
- 1 teaspoon pure vanilla extract
- ½ cup Swerve

Preparation:
1. Add eggs, cocoa powder, vanilla extract, swerve, cream cheese in an immersion blender and blend until smooth.
2. Pour the mixture evenly into mason jars.
3. Put the mason jars in the insert of Ninja Foodi and close the lid.
4. Select "Bake/Roast" and bake for 15 minutes at 360 degrees F.
5. Refrigerate for at least 2 hours.
Nutrition Values Per Serving: Calories 244, Fat 24.8 g, Carbs 2.1 g, Protein 4 g

Strawberry-Rhubarb Compote

Prep time: 10 minutes
Cook time: 20 minutes
Servings: 3
Ingredients:
- 2 pounds rhubarb
- ½ cup water
- 1 pound strawberries
- 3 tablespoons date paste
- Fresh mint

Preparation:
1. Peel rhubarb using a paring knife and chop into ½-inch pieces.
2. Add chopped rhubarb to Ninja Foodi, add water.

3. Lock pressure lid and cook on HIGH Pressure for 10 minutes.
4. Stem and quarter strawberries and keep them on the side.
5. Add strawberries and date paste, stir.
6. Lock lid and cook on HIGH Pressure for 20 minutes more.
7. Naturally, release the pressure over 10 minutes.
8. Enjoy!
Nutrition Values Per Serving: Calories: 50, Fat: 2 g, Carbs: 5 g, Protein: 1.4 g

Subtle Potato Gratin

Prep time: 10 minutes
Cook time: 15 minutes
Servings: 3
Ingredients:
- 3 tablespoons olive oil
- 3 cups sliced up parsnips
- 3 cloves garlic, chopped
- 2 cups vegetable broth
- 1 tablespoon black pepper
- 1 tablespoon garlic powder
- 1 cup mayo

Preparation:
1. Set your Ninja Foodi to Sauté mode, add listed ingredients except for mayo.
2. Lock lid and cook on HIGH Pressure for 5 minutes.
3. Release pressure naturally over 10 minutes.
4. Spread mayo on top, set your Ninja Foodi to Sauté mode, Low Heat.
5. Let it warm.
6. Serve and enjoy the gratin!
Nutrition Values Per Serving: Calories: 201, Fat: 10 g, Carbs: 22 g, Protein: 6 g

Nut Porridge

Prep time: 15 minutes
Cook time: 10 minutes
Servings: 4
Ingredients:
- 4 teaspoons coconut oil, melted
- 1 cup pecans, halved
- 2 cups water
- 2 tablespoons stevia
- 1 cup cashew nuts, raw and unsalted

Preparation:
1. Put the cashew nuts and pecans in the precision processor and pulse till they are in chunks.
2. Put this mixture into the pot of Ninja Foodi and stir in water, coconut oil and stevia.
3. Select Sauté on Ninja Foodi and cook for 15 minutes.
4. Serve and enjoy.
Nutrition Values Per Serving: Calories 260, Fat 22.9 g, Carbs 12.7 g, Protein 5.6 g

Poached Pear Dessert

Prep time: 10 minutes
Cook time: 10 minutes
Servings: 3
Ingredients:
- 6 firm pears, peeled
- 1 bottle dry red wine
- 1 bay leaf
- 4 garlic cloves, minced
- 1 stick cinnamon
- 1 fresh ginger, minced
- 1 and ⅓ cups stevia
- Mixed Italian herbs as needed

Preparation:
1. Peel the pears leaving the stems attached.
2. Pour wine into your Ninja Foodi.
3. Add bay leaf, cinnamon, cloves, ginger, stevia, and stir.
4. Add pears to the pot and lock up the lid and cook on HIGH Pressure for 9 minutes.
5. Perform a quick release.
6. Take the pears out using tong and keep them on the side.
7. Set the pot to Sauté mode and allow the mixture to reduce to half.
8. Drizzle the mixture over the pears and enjoy it!
Nutrition Values Per Serving: Calories: 150, Fat: 16 g, Carbs: 2 g, Protein: 0.5 g
1.
Nutrition Values Per Serving: Calories: 170, Fat: 15.1g, Carbs: 31.1g, Protein: 2.8g

Savory Donuts

Prep time: 20 minutes
Cook time: 10 minutes
Servings: 5
Ingredients:
- 1 ½ cups flour
- ½ teaspoon baking soda
- 1 teaspoon vanilla extract
- 1 egg, whisked
- 2 tablespoons sugar
- ½ cup heavy cream

Preparation:
1. Mix the whisked egg, heavy cream, sugar, vanilla extract, and baking soda.
2. When the mixture is homogenous, add flour.
3. Stir well and knead the non-sticky dough.
4. Let the dough rest for 10 minutes.
5. After this, roll the dough with the help of the rolling pin into 1 inch thick.
6. Then make the donuts with the help of the cutter.
7. Select the Ninja Foodi "Bake/Roast" cooking mode and set 360 degrees F.
8. Place the donuts in the basket and cover the Ninja Foodi's lid.
9. Cook the donuts for 5 minutes.
10. Chill the donuts well and serve!
Nutrition Values Per Serving: Calories: 118, Fat: 11.5g, Carbs: 24g, Protein: 2.7g

Glazed Carrots

Prep time: 5 minutes
Cook time: 5 minutes
Servings: 4
Ingredients:
- 2 pounds carrots
- Pepper as needed
- 1 cup water
- 1 tablespoon coconut butter

Preparation:
1. Wash carrots thoroughly and peel then, slice the carrots.
2. Add carrots, water to the Ninja Foodi.
3. Lock pressure lid and cook for 4 minutes on HIGH Pressure.
4. Release pressure naturally.
5. Strain carrots and strain carrots.
6. Mix with coconut butter, enjoy with a bit of pepper.
Nutrition Values Per Serving: Calories: 228, Fat: 8g, Carbs: 36g, Protein: 4g

Delicious Pot-De-Crème

Prep time: 10 minutes
Cook time: 20 minutes
Servings: 3
Ingredients:
- 6 egg yolks
- 2 cups heavy whip cream
- ⅓ cup cocoa powder
- 1 tablespoon pure vanilla extract
- ½ teaspoon liquid stevia
- Whipped coconut cream for garnish
- Shaved dark chocolate for garnish

Preparation:
1. Take a medium-sized bowl and whisk in yolks, heavy cream, sugar, cocoa powder, vanilla.
2. Pour mixture in 1 and ½ quart baking dish, stir.
3. Transfer the mix to Ninja Foodi basket.
4. Add water to about the halfway point of the ramekin.
5. Lock lid and cook on HIGH Pressure for 12 minutes.
6. Quick release pressure, remove the baking dish and let it cool.
7. Let it chill in the fridge.
8. Garnish with coconut cream, add chocolate shavings.
9. Serve and enjoy!
Nutrition Values Per Serving: Calories: 258, Fat: 18 g, Carbs: 3 g, Protein: 5 g

Coconut and Avocado Pudding

Prep time: 10 minutes
Cook time: 5 minutes
Servings: 4
Ingredients:
- 1 pack, 12 ounces frounceen broccoli florets
- 2 tablespoons butter
- salt and pepper as needed
- 8 whole eggs
- 2 tablespoons milk
- ¾ cup white cheddar cheese, shredded
- Crushed red pepper, as needed
- Optional bacon strips

Preparation:
1. Take a bowl and add coconut milk, avocado, vanilla extract, sugar, lime juice, and blend well.
2. Pour the mix into a ramekin.
3. Add water to your pot.
4. Add a cook & crisp basket and place the ramekin in the pot.
5. Close lid and cook on HIGH Pressure for 5 minutes.
6. Release pressure naturally over 10 minutes.
7. Serve cold and enjoy it!
Nutrition Values Per Serving: Calories: 190, Fat: 6 g, Carbs: 6 g, Protein: 4 g

Peanut Butter Cups

Prep time: 15 minutes
Cook time: 30 minutes
Servings: 3
Ingredients:
- 1 cup butter
- ¼ cup heavy cream
- 2 ounces unsweetened chocolate
- ¼ cup peanut butter, separated
- 4 packets stevia

Preparation:
1. Mix well and pour the mixture in a baking mold.
2. Put the baking mold in the Ninja Foodi and press "FUNCTION", turn the dial to "Bake/Roast".
3. Set the timer for 30 minutes at 360 degrees F and dish out to serve.
Nutrition Values Per Serving: Calories 479, Fat 51.5 g, Carbs 7.7 g, Protein 5.2 g

Carrot and Pumpkin Pudding

Prep time: 10 minutes
Cook time: 20 minutes
Servings: 3
Ingredients:
- 1 tablespoon extra-virgin olive oil
- 2 cups carrots, shredded
- 2 cups pureed pumpkin
- ½ sweet onion, finely chopped
- 1 cup heavy whip cream
- ½ cup cream cheese, soft
- 2 whole eggs
- 1 tablespoon brown sugar
- 1 teaspoon ground nutmeg

- ½ teaspoon salt
- ¼ cup pumpkin seeds, garnish
- ¼ cup water

Preparation:
1. Add oil to your Ninja Foodi pot and whisk well.
2. Add carrots, pumpkin, onion, heavy cream cheese, eggs, sugar, salt, and water.
3. Mix well.
4. Lock lid and cook on HIGH Pressure for 10 minutes.
5. Release pressure naturally over 10 minutes.
6. Top with pumpkin seeds and serve.
7. Enjoy!
Nutrition Values Per Serving: Calories: 239, Fat: 19 g, Carbs: 7 g, Protein: 6 g

Vanilla Yogurt

Prep time: 15 minutes
Cook time: 4 hours
Servings: 2
Ingredients:
- ½ cup full-fat milk
- ¼ cup yogurt starter
- 1 cup heavy cream
- ½ tablespoon pure vanilla extract
- 2 scoops stevia

Preparation:
1. Add milk, heavy cream, vanilla extract, and stevia in Ninja Foodi.
2. Let yogurt sit and set the Ninja Foodi to "Slow Cook" and set the timer to 4 hours on "low".
3. Add yogurt starter in 1 cup of milk.
4. Return this mixture to the pot.
5. Close the lid and wrap the Ninja Foodi in small towels.
6. Let yogurt sit for about 9 hours.
7. Dish out, refrigerate and then serve.
Nutrition Values Per Serving: Calories 292, Fat 26.2 g, Carbs 8.2 g, Protein 5.2 g

Ninja Foodi Vanilla Shake

Prep Time: 7 minutes
Cook Time: 2 minutes
Servings: 2
Ingredients:
- 1 cup water
- 1 cup almond milk
- ½ cup vanilla ice cream
- 2 teaspoons sugar

Directions:
1. Add every ingredient in the Ninja Foodi Multi-cooker and select "Pressure".
2. Close the pressure Lid and press the "Start/Stop'" button.
3. Cook for 2 minutes and open the lid.
4. Take out and set aside.
5. Refrigerate overnight, serve and enjoy!
Nutritional Values Per Serving: Calories: 325, Fat: 30.4g, Carbs: 14.7g, Protein: 3.3g

Ninja Foodi Mocha Cake

Prep Time: 2 minutes
Cook Time: 2 minutes
Servings: 4
Ingredients:
- ½ cup water
- 2 tablespoons beaten egg
- 4 teaspoons chocolate chips
- ½ teaspoon baking powder
- 4 teaspoons Splenda
- 4 teaspoons coffee

Directions:
1. Add all the ingredients to a large bowl and mix well.
2. Place the bowl in Ninja Foodi Multi-cooker, press the "Bake" button and close the lid.
3. Press the "Start/Stop" button and bake for 2 minutes.
4. Open the lid and take out.
5. Serve and enjoy!
Nutritional Values Per Serving: Calories: 46, Fat: 1.5g, Carbs: 6.4g, Protein: 0.8g

Amazing Chocolate Brownies

Prep time: 15 minutes
Cook time: 32 minutes
Servings: 4
Ingredients:
- 3 eggs
- ½ cup butter
- ½ cup sugar-free chocolate chips
- 2 scoops stevia
- 1 teaspoon vanilla extract

Preparation:
1. Take a bowl and mix eggs, stevia, and vanilla extract.
2. Pour this mixture in the blender and blend until smooth.
3. Sauté for 2 minutes until the chocolate is melted.
4. Add the melted chocolate into the egg mixture.
5. Set the Ninja Foodi to "Bake/Roast" and set the timer for about 30 minutes at 360 degrees F.
6. Bake for about 30 minutes, cut into pieces and serve.
Nutrition Values Per Serving: Calories 266, Fat 26.9 g, Carbs 2.5 g, Protein 4.5 g

Vanilla Brownie

Prep Time: 10 minutes
Cook time: 32 minutes
Servings: 6
Ingredients:
- 3 tablespoons sugar
- 1 ounce chocolate chips
- 2 eggs, whisked
- ½ teaspoon vanilla extract
- 3 tablespoon butter, melted
- 1 tablespoon flour
Preparation:

1. Whisk the melted butter, flour, vanilla extract, and sugar.
2. Melt the chocolate chips and add them to the butter mixture.
3. Add eggs and stir until smooth.
4. Pour the batter into Ninja Foodi's insert, select "Bake/Roast" cooking mode and cook at 360 degrees F for 32 minutes.
5. Then check if the brownie cooked and chill well.
6. Cut it into the Servings: and serve!
Nutrition Values Per Serving: Calories: 99, Fat: 8.8g, Carbs: 19g, Protein: 2.4g

Ninja Foodi Chia Seed Smoothie

Prep Time: 10 minutes
Cook Time: 2 minutes
Servings: 2
Ingredients:
- 2 cups unsweetened almond milk
- ½ cup chia seeds
- 2 teaspoons sugar
Directions:
1. Add almond milk, chia seeds and sugar in a Ninja Foodi Multi-cooker and select "Pressure".
2. Close the pressure lid and press the "Start/Stop" button.
3. Cook for 2 minutes and open the lid.
4. Take out and refrigerate overnight.
5. Serve and enjoy!
Nutritional Values Per Serving: Calories: 89, Fat: 5.7g, Carbs: 9g, Protein: 2.2g

Cocoa Avocado Mousse

Prep Time: 10 minutes
Cook time: 2 minutes
Servings: 7
Ingredients:
- 2 avocados, peeled, cored
- 1 teaspoon cocoa powder
- ⅓ cup heavy cream
- 1 teaspoon butter
- 3 tablespoons sugar
- 1 teaspoon vanilla extract
Preparation:
1. Preheat your Ninja Foodi cooker at "Sear/Sauté" cooking mode for 5 minutes.
2. Meanwhile, mash the avocado until smooth and mix it with sugar.
3. Place the butter into the Ninja Foodi's pot and melt.
4. Add mashed avocado mixture and stir well.
5. Add cocoa powder and stir until homogenous. Sauté the mixture for 3 minutes.
6. Meanwhile, whisk the heavy cream at high speed for 2 minutes.
7. Transfer the cooked avocado mash to the bowl and chill in ice water.
8. Add whisked heavy cream and vanilla extract. Stir gently to get swirls.
9. Transfer the mousse into small cups and chill for 4 hours in the fridge.
10. Serve!
Nutrition Values Per Serving: Calories: 144, Fat: 13.9g, Carbs: 15g, Protein: 1.3g

Chocolate Chip Cookies

Prep Time: 10 minutes
Cook time: 9 minutes
Servings: 8
Ingredients:
- 1 ounce chocolate chips
- 3 tablespoon butter
- 1 cup flour
- 1 egg, whisked
- 2 tablespoons sugar

Preparation:
1. Mix the flour and whisked the egg.
2. Add butter and sugar, and mix the mixture until homogenous.
3. Add chocolate chips and knead the homogenous dough.
4. Make 8 small balls from the dough and transfer them to the rack of Ninja Foodi.
5. Close the Ninja Foodi's lid and Cook on the "Bake/Roast" cooking mode.
6. Cook the chip cookies for 9 minutes at 360 degrees F.
7. Chill the cookies and serve!
Nutrition Values Per Serving: Calories: 145, Fat: 12.3g, Carbs: 12g, Protein: 3.9g

Pumpkin Pudding

Prep Time: 10 minutes
Cook time: 25 minutes
Servings: 4
Ingredients:
- 3 eggs, whisked
- ½ teaspoon vanilla extract
- 4 tablespoons pumpkin puree
- 1 teaspoon pumpkin pie spices
- 1 cup heavy cream
- 2 tablespoon sugar
- 1 cup water for cooking

Preparation:
1. Whisk the eggs, pumpkin puree, vanilla extract, pumpkin pie spices, cream, and sugar.
2. Pour the liquid into the non-stick cake pan.
3. Pour water into the Ninja Foodi's pot.
4. Place the pudding in a cake pan into the Ninja Foodi's pot on the rack and close the Ninja's lid.
5. Select Steam mode and cook the dessert for 25 minutes.
6. Let the cooked pudding rest for 10 minutes then open the lid.
7. Place it in the fridge for a minimum of 4 hours.
8. Enjoy!
Nutrition Values Per Serving: Calories: 159, Fat: 14.5g, Carbs: 27g, Protein: 5g

Ninja Foodi Fruity Frozen Treat

Prep Time: 5 minutes
Cook Time: 3 minutes
Servings: 3
Ingredients:
- ½ cup frozen pineapple chunks
- 1 cup almond milk
- 4 tablespoons fresh lime juice
- 2 cups banana slices

Directions:
1. Add pineapple slices, almond milk, lime juice and banana slices in a Ninja Foodi Multi-cooker and select "Pressure".
2. Close the pressure Lid and press the "Start/Stop" button.
3. Cook for about 3 minutes and open the lid.
4. Dish out and freeze for about 1 hour.
5. Take out, serve and enjoy!
Nutritional Values Per Serving: Calories: 464, Fat: 31.4g, Carbs: 45.2g, Protein: 5.4g

Ninja Foodi Ricotta Mousse

Prep Time: 10 minutes
Cook Time: 2 minutes
Servings: 2
Ingredients:
- 2½ cups water
- 2 teaspoons stevia powder
- ½ teaspoon vanilla extract
- 1 cup ricotta cheese
- 2 teaspoons cocoa powder

Directions:
1. Add everything to a Ninja Foodi Multi-cooker and select "pressure".
2. Close the pressure Lid and press the "Start/Stop" button.
3. Cook for about 2 minutes and open the lid.
4. Pour the mixture in serving glasses and refrigerate for about 6 hours.
5. Serve and enjoy!
Nutritional Values Per Serving: Calories: 178, Fat: 10.1g, Carbs: 7.5g, Protein: 14.5g

Ninja Foodi Chickpea Fudge

Prep Time: 10 minutes
Cook Time: 1 hour 5 minutes
Servings: 3
Ingredients:
- ½ cup cooked chickpeas
- 2 dates, pitted and chopped
- ½ tablespoon cocoa powder
- 2 tablespoons almond butter
- 2 tablespoons almond milk
- ¼ teaspoon vanilla extract

Directions:
1. Add everything except cocoa powder in the Ninja Foodi Multi-cooker and select "Pressure".
2. Close thepressure Lid and press the "Start/Stop" button.
3. Cook for about 5 minutes and open the lid.
4. Transfer the mixture to a bowl and stir in cocoa powder.
5. Pour the mixture in Ninja Foodi Multi-cooker and press the "Bake" button.
6. Bake for about an hour and take out.
7. Refrigerate, slice and serve.
Nutritional Values Per Serving: Calories: 228, Fat: 10.5g, Carbs: 27.4g, Protein: 9.2g

Ninja Foodi Blackberry Crumble

Prep Time: 10 minutes
Cook Time: 45 minutes
Servings: 6
Ingredients:
Blackberries Filling:
- ¼ cup coconut flour
- 3 tablespoons water
- ¼ cup arrowroot flour
- 2 tablespoons melted butter
- ¼ cup mashed banana
- 1½ cups fresh blackberries
- ¾ teaspoon baking soda
- ½ tablespoon lemon juice

Crumble Topping
- ½ cup old fashioned oats
- ½ cup coconut flour
- ½ cup brown sugar, packed
- ⅛ tsp baking powder
- ⅛ tsp baking soda
- ¼ cup butter, softened

Directions:
1. Add all the ingredients for filling except blackberries in a bowl and mix well.
2. Combine the ingredients for crumble topping in another bowl.
3. Arrange blackberries in the bottom of Ninja Foodi Multi-cooker and pour the filling batter on them.
4. Top with the crumble topping.
5. Press the "Bake" button and close the lid.
6. Press the "Start/Stop" button and bake for 40 minutes at 300 degrees F.
7. Open the lid and take out.
8. Serve and enjoy!
Nutritional Values Per Serving: Calories: 292, Fat: 10.7g, Carbs: 45.7g, Protein: 5.9g

Ninja Foodi Yogurt Cheesecake

Prep Time: 15 minutes
Cook Time: 30 minutes
Servings: 10
Ingredients:
- 6 drops liquid stevia
- 1 teaspoon vanilla extract
- 4 egg whites
- ½ cup cocoa powder
- 3 cups low-fat Greek yogurt
- ¼ cup arrowroot starch
- Pinch of salt

Crust
- ¼ cup white sugar
- 7 graham crackers
- ¼ cup brown sugar
- 1 pinch salt
- 6 tablespoons butter, melted

Directions:
1. Gather all the crust ingredients and dump into the blender.
2. Blend until all the ingredients are well combined and form the sand like consistency.
3. Combine all crust ingredients in a blender and blend until mixture becomes the consistency of damp sand.
4. Shift the crust mixture into a 7-inch springform pan and pat it down with spatula.

5. Add all the ingredients of cheesecake filling in a large bowl and mix well.
6. Pour the mixture in the springform pan over the top of the crust and place it in the pot of Ninja Foodi Multi-cooker.
7. Press the "Bake" button and close the Crisping Lid.
8. Press the "Start/Stop" button and bake for about 30 minutes at 350 degrees F.
9. Open the lid and take out.
10.   Slice and serve.
Nutritional Values Per Serving: Calories: 236, Fat: 9.3g, Carbs: 35.1g, Protein: 5.9g

Ninja Foodi Banana Custard

Prep Time: 10 minutes
Cook Time: 25 minutes
Servings: 4
Ingredients:
- 1 banana, mashed
- 1 cup almond milk
- ¼ teaspoon vanilla extract
- 2 eggs

Directions:
1. Add all the ingredients in a large bowl and mix well.
2. Pour the batter evenly in custard cups and place them in Ninja Foodi Multi-cooker.
3. Press the "Bake" button and close the Crisping Lid.
4. Press the "Start/Stop" button and bake for 25 minutes at 350 degrees F.
5. Open the lid and take out.
6. Serve and enjoy!
Nutritional Values Per Serving: Calories: 196, Fat: 16.6g, Carbs: 10.3g, Protein: 4.5g

Ninja Foodi Chocolate Tofu Mousse

Prep Time: 10 minutes
Cook Time: 1 minute
Servings: 2
Ingredients:
- 1 banana, peeled and sliced
- ¾ cup firm tofu, drained
- 1 teaspoon cocoa powder
- 1 teaspoon chopped almonds

Directions:
1. Add all the ingredients in a Ninja Foodi Multi-cooker and select "Pressure".
2. Close the lid and press the "Start/Stop" button.
3. Cook for 1 minute and open the lid.
4. Pour the mixture in serving glasses and refrigerate for about 3 hours.
5. Take out, serve and enjoy!
Nutritional Values Per Serving: Calories: 264, Fat: 2.7g, Carbs: 51.7g, Protein: 14.2g

Ninja Foodi Raspberry Ice Cream

Prep Time: 20 minutes
Cook Time: 2 minutes
Servings: 4
Ingredients:
- 1 cup fresh raspberries
- ½ banana, sliced
- 2 tablespoons shredded coconut
- ½ cup coconut cream

Directions:
1. Add all the ingredients in a Ninja Foodi Multi-cooker and select "Pressure".
2. Close the lid, press the "Start/Stop" button and cook for about 2 minutes.
3. Open the lid and transfer the mixture to an ice-cream maker.
4. Process according to manufacturer's directions and take out.
5. Pour the mixture into an air-tight container and freeze for about 4 hours. Stir after every half an hour.
6. Take out and serve.
Nutritional Values Per Serving: Calories: 107, Fat: 8.2g, Carbs: 9.1g, Protein: 1.3g

Rocky Road Fudge

Prep Time: 5 Minutes
Cook Time: 5 hours
Servings: 6
Ingredients:
- 8 ounces pretend condensed milk
- 9 ounces chocolate chips
- 1 teaspoon vanilla extract
- ¼ teaspoon sea salt
- ½ cup almonds
- 2 ounces marshmallows

Directions:
1. On Broil, preheat the Ninja Foodi Multi-Cooker for 10 minutes with the Basket inside. Now add almonds to the Basket and Broil it for 3 to 5 minutes. Take out the almonds and let them cool.
2. Line the square pan with parchment paper, add in chocolate chips and sweetened condensed milk, and then cover it again with the foil.
3. Place the pan in Ninja Foodi Multi-Cooker. Add two cups of water in it and cook at Steam setting for 5 minutes.
4. Set the valve to the Vent position while the chocolate mixture is steaming.
5. Meanwhile, crush the almonds coarsely and cut marshmallows if you're using large ones.
6. Remove the pan from Ninja Foodi Multi-Cooker and add vanilla, marshmallows, salt, and chopped almonds. Give it a good mix.
7. Then the fudge will start to thicken up as it cools down. Let it cool down for two to four hours in the refrigerator and cut it into bite-size squares!
Nutritional Values Per Serving: Calories: 328, Fat: 18.7g, Carbs: 38.1g, Protein: 7.1g

Chocolate Brownies

Prep Time: 5 Minutes
Cook Time: 4 hours
Servings: 8
Ingredients:
- ½ cup butter
- 4 ounces dark chocolate chips
- 4 ounces milk chocolate chips
- 1 cup sugar
- 2 tablespoon canola oil
- 3 beaten eggs
- ½ teaspoon vanilla extract
- ¼ cup unsweetened cocoa powder
- ¼ cup all-purpose flour

Directions:
1. Turn the Ninja Foodi Multi-Cooker on and select the Pressure Cook option on High, then add in the butter.
2. Once it's half-melted, add chocolate chips on one side and keep melting the chips until 75% are melted.
3. Turn off the Ninja Foodi Multi-Cooker and continue to cool down the chocolate. When it reaches room temperature, add in oil and sugar and stir it well.
4. Beat eggs lightly in a bowl and add in the eggs slowly in the chocolate batter and keep stirring it, then add vanilla extract. Now add in cocoa powder and stir it to incorporate well.
5. Add in flour gradually. Make sure to add ⅓ portions at a time and then mix it well to avoid any lumps.
6. Now put the Ninja Foodi Multi-Cooker Pressure Lid back on and turn the valve to Vent. And then select the Slow Cook function on Low for 4 hours. Scoop out brownies if you want them gooey. And if you want to achieve that flaky top then for 8 to 20 minutes put the lid.
7. Serve warm with your coffee!
Nutritional Values Per Serving: Calories: 458, Fat: 27.7g, Carbs: 50.5g, Protein: 6.9g

Pineapple Chunks

Prep Time: 3 Minutes
Cook Time: 10-12 Minutes
Servings: 6
Ingredients:
- 1 stick melted butter
- ½ cup brown sugar
- ½ teaspoon cinnamon
- 1 sliced pineapple

Directions:
1. Combine melted butter, cinnamon, and brown sugar in a low-sided dish. Mix it well.
2. Put in your pineapple pieces to allow it to soak in the flavors for a bit.
3. Select the Bake option, and set the temperature to 375° F. Add pineapple pieces and let them Bake for 12 minutes.
4. Flip the pineapple slices gently halfway through.
5. Serve immediately when ready!
Nutritional Values Per Serving: Calories: 455, Fat: 22.4g, Carbs: 39g, Protein: 4.5g

Banana Bread

Prep Time: 10 Minutes
Cook Time: 30 Minutes
Servings: 4

Ingredients

- 2 large ripe bananas
- ¾ cup all-purpose flour
- 1 egg
- 3 teaspoons brown sugar
- 2 teaspoons butter
- ¼ cup sour cream
- ½ teaspoon baking soda
- ½ teaspoon salt

Directions:

1. Preheat the Ninja Foodi Multi-Cooker at Bake Mode at 375° F.
2. Now grease the mini loaf and set it aside.
3. Take all ingredients in a medium bowl and combine them and stir until combined well.
4. Put the batter evenly in a butter paper-lined loaf pan. Dump the pan and Bake it for 25 to 30 minutes.
5. To check the doneness, make sure that when a toothpick is inserted in the center, it comes out clean. Check the banana bread with a toothpick and serve it warm!

Nutritional Values Per Serving: Calories. 271, Fat. 10.4g, Carbs: 40.8g, Protein: 4.8g

4-Week Plan

Week 1

Day-1
Breakfast:
Lunch: Cod Fish
Snack: Ninja Foodi Spiced Almonds
Dinner: St. Patty's Corned Beef Recipe
Dessert: Banana Bread

Day-2
Breakfast: Flaxseeds Granola
Lunch: Chicken Rissoles
Snack: Ninja Foodi Spicy Popcorns
Dinner: Ninja Foodi Ginger Salmon
Dessert: Subtle Potato Gratin

Day-3
Breakfast: Ninja Foodi Eggs with Spinach
Lunch: Tangy Pork Carnitas
Snack: Ninja Foodi Spicy Cashews
Dinner: Cheesy Chicken Fillets
Dessert: Chocolate Brownies

Day-4
Breakfast: Broccoli Quiche
Lunch: Ninja Foodi Mushroom & Beef Stew
Snack: Ninja Foodi Spicy Peanuts
Dinner: Salmon in Dill Sauce
Dessert: Savory Donuts

Day-5
Breakfast: Almond Quinoa Porridge
Lunch: Chicken with Veggies
Snack: Air Crisped Chicken Nuggets
Dinner: Onion Pork Chops
Dessert: Ninja Foodi Raspberry Ice Cream

Day-6
Breakfast: Chorizo Frittatas
Lunch: Hearty Cod Fillets
Snack: Stuffed Egg Whites
Dinner: Salmon with Soy Sauce
Dessert: Glazed Carrots

Day-7
Breakfast: Mason Jar Omelet
Lunch: Cod Parcel
Snack: Buffalo Cualiflower Platter
Dinner: Amazing Duck Pot Pie
Dessert: Ninja Foodi Banana Custard

Week 2

Day-1
Breakfast: Roasted Potatoes
Lunch: Crisp Duck Patties
Snack: Bowl Full of Broccoli Salad
Dinner: Hearty Cod Fillets
Dessert: Ninja Foodi Blackberry Crumble

Day-2
Breakfast: Bacon Eggs
Lunch: Ninja Foodi Beef Chili
Snack: Braised Kale Salad
Dinner: Spicy Pulled Duck
Dessert: Peanut Butter Cups

Day-3
Breakfast: Rise and Shine Casserole
Lunch: Breathtaking Cod Fillets
Snack: Simple Treat of Garlic
Dinner: Beef Pork Chili
Dessert: Ninja Foodi Ricotta Mousse

Day-4
Breakfast: Bacon Egg Scramble
Lunch: Thyme and Carrot Dish with Dill
Snack: Cheesy Chicken Parmesan
Dinner: Chicken Noodle Soup
Dessert: Vanilla Yogurt

Day-5
Breakfast: Sausage Cheese Frittata
Lunch: Sweet Tomato Salsa
Snack: Orange Cauliflower Salad
Dinner: Limed Haddock Fish
Dessert: Ninja Foodi Chia Seed Smoothie

Day-6
Breakfast: Avocado Egg Cups
Lunch: Turmeric Cauliflower Rice
Snack: Nutty Brussels Sprouts
Dinner: Herbed Cornish Hen
Dessert: Delicious Pot-De-Crème

Day-7
Breakfast: Soft Eggs
Lunch: Garlic and Lemon Prawn Delight
Snack: Buttered Up Garlic and Fennel
Dinner: Potatoes, Beefy-Cheesy Way
Dessert: Ninja Foodi Vanilla Shake

Week 3

Day-1
Breakfast: Hash Brown Casserole
Lunch: Creamy Chicken Soup
Snack: Saucy Chicken Thighs
Dinner: Mexican Beef Short Ribs
Dessert: Chocolate Chip Cookies

Day-2
Breakfast: Chicken Breakfast Burrito
Lunch: Hot Turkey Cutlets
Snack: Bacon-Wrapped Drumsticks
Dinner: Adobo Beef Steak
Dessert: Cocoa Avocado Mousse

Day-3
Breakfast: Air Crisp Cheese Casserole
Lunch: Italian Chicken Breasts
Snack: Pork Packed Jalapeno
Dinner: Packets of Lemon and Dill Cod
Dessert: Vanilla Brownie

Day-4
Breakfast: Scrambled Eggs
Lunch: Shredded Up Salsa Chicken
Snack: Cider Dipped Chili
Dinner: Broccoli Pork with Rice
Dessert: Pumpkin Pudding

Day-5
Breakfast: Low Carb Morning Casserole
Lunch: Tomato Dipped Tilapia
Snack: Crispy Zucchini Fries
Dinner: Taiwanese Chicken Delight
Dessert: Amazing Chocolate Brownies

Day-6
Breakfast: Soft-Boiled Eggs
Lunch: Seafood & Tomato Stew
Snack: Creamy Fudge Meal
Dinner: Honey Glazed Ham
Dessert: Ninja Foodi Mocha Cake

Day-7
Breakfast: Zucchini Quiche
Lunch: Chicken Cauliflower Pilaf
Snack: Crispy Beet Chips
Dinner: Ranch Beef Roast
Dessert: Carrot and Pumpkin Pudding

Week 4

Day-1
Breakfast: Milky Tomato Omelet
Lunch: Salmon Pasta
Snack: Cheesy Mushroom Appetizer
Dinner: Saucy Lamb Roast
Dessert: Coconut and Avocado Pudding

Day-2
Breakfast: Creamy Pumpkin Slow Cook
Lunch: Lobster Tail
Snack: Excellent Bacon and Cheddar Frittata
Dinner: Healthy Cranberry BBQ Pork
Dessert: Ninja Foodi Fruity Frozen Treat

Day-3
Breakfast: Breakfast Muffins
Lunch: Creamy Chicken Zoodles
Snack: Mexican Cheese Frittata
Dinner: Sea Bass Curry
Dessert: Nut Porridge

Day-4
Breakfast: Crispy Chicken Sandwiches
Lunch: Herbed Chicken Wings
Snack: Buffalo Wings
Dinner: Salmon Pasta
Dessert: Ninja Foodi Chickpea Fudge

Day-5
Breakfast: Aromatic Keto Coffee
Lunch: Ninja Foodi Ginger Cod
Snack: Ninja Foodi Cod Sticks
Dinner: Lemon Pork Cutlets
Dessert: Poached Pear Dessert

Day-6
Breakfast: Authentic Western Omelet
Lunch: Complete Cauliflower Zoodles
Snack: Veggies Dredged in Cheese
Dinner: Bagel Chicken Tenders
Dessert: Ninja Foodi Yogurt Cheesecake

Day-7
Breakfast: Spicy Bacon Bites
Lunch: Instant Catfish Fillet
Snack: Ninja Foodi Spinach Chips
Dinner: Jalapeno Chicken Nachos
Dessert: Strawberry-Rhubarb Compote

Conclusion

Cook tender to crispy food, easy-to-clean, nine useful cooking functions in one pot. Whether you want to eat crispy, tender, juicy, broiled, dehydrated, baked, sautéed, or roasted food, the Ninja Foodi TENDERCRISP Pressure Cooker is a perfect option for you. You can prepare delicious and healthy food for your family and friends in less time with your favorite cooking options. I added delicious recipes for your appliance. You can choose recipes for the whole day or any occasion. Thank you for reading this book. I hope you will get to know more about your appliance.

Appendix 1 Measurement Conversion Chart

VOLUME EQUIVALENTS(DRY)

US STANDARD	METRIC (APPROXIMATE)
1/8 teaspoon	0.5 mL
1/4 teaspoon	1 mL
1/2 teaspoon	2 mL
3/4 teaspoon	4 mL
1 teaspoon	5 mL
1 tablespoon	15 mL
1/4 cup	59 mL
1/2 cup	118 mL
3/4 cup	177 mL
1 cup	235 mL
2 cups	475 mL
3 cups	700 mL
4 cups	1 L

VOLUME EQUIVALENTS(LIQUID)

US STANDARD	US STANDARD (OUNCES)	METRIC (APPROXIMATE)
2 tablespoons	1 fl.oz.	30 mL
1/4 cup	2 fl.oz.	60 mL
1/2 cup	4 fl.oz.	120 mL
1 cup	8 fl.oz.	240 mL
1 1/2 cup	12 fl.oz.	355 mL
2 cups or 1 pint	16 fl.oz.	475 mL
4 cups or 1 quart	32 fl.oz.	1 L
1 gallon	128 fl.oz.	4 L

TEMPERATURES EQUIVALENTS

FAHRENHEIT(F)	CELSIUS(C) (APPROXIMATE)
225 °F	107 °C
250 °F	120 °C
275 °F	135 °C
300 °F	150 °C
325 °F	160 °C
350 °F	180 °C
375 °F	190 °C
400 °F	205 °C
425 °F	220 °C
450 °F	235 °C
475 °F	245 °C
500 °F	260 °C

WEIGHT EQUIVALENTS

US STANDARD	METRIC (APPROXIMATE)
1 ounce	28 g
2 ounces	57 g
5 ounces	142 g
10 ounces	284 g
15 ounces	425 g
16 ounces (1 pound)	455 g
1.5 pounds	680 g
2 pounds	907 g

Appendix 2 Recipes Index

Printed in Great Britain
by Amazon